The Origins of Anglo-Saxon Towns

DEBATES IN ARCHAEOLOGY

Series editor: Richard Hodges

Against Cultural Property, John Carman
The Anthropology of Hunter-Gatherers, Vicki Cummings
Archaeologies of Conflict, John Carman
Archaeology: The Conceptual Challenge, Timothy Insoll
Archaeology and International Development in Africa, Colin Breen and Daniel Rhodes
Archaeology and State Theory, Bruce Routledge
Archaeology and Text, John Moreland
Archaeology and the Pan-European Romanesque, Tadhg O'Keeffe
Beyond Celts, Germans and Scythians, Peter S. Wells
Bronze Age Textiles, Klavs Randsborg
Building Colonialism, Daniel T. Rhodes
The Byzantine Dark Ages, Michael J. Decker
Changing Natures, Bill Finlayson and Graeme M. Warren
Combat Archaeology, John Schofield
Debating the Archaeological Heritage, Robin Skeates
Early European Castles, Oliver H. Creighton
Early Islamic North Africa: A New Perspective, Corisande Fenwick
Early Islamic Syria, Alan Walmsley
Empowering Communities through Archaeology and Heritage, Peter G. Gould
Ethics and Burial Archaeology, Duncan Sayer
Evidential Reasoning in Archaeology, Robert Chapman and Alison Wylie
Fishing and Shipwreck Heritage, Sean A. Kingsley
Fluid Pasts, Matthew Edgeworth
From Stonehenge to Mycenae: The Challenges of Archaeological Interpretation, John C. Barrett and Michael J. Boyd
Gerasa and the Decapolis, David Kennedy
Heritage, Communities and Archaeology, Laurajane Smith and Emma Waterton

Houses and Society in the Later Roman Empire, Kim Bowes
Image and Response in Early Europe, Peter S. Wells
Indo-Roman Trade, Roberta Tomber
Islamization and Archaeology: Religion, Culture and New Materialism, José C. Carvajal López
Loot, Legitimacy and Ownership, Colin Renfrew
Lost Civilization, James L. Boone
Museums and the Construction of Disciplines, Christopher Whitehead
Negotiating Migrations: The Archaeology and Politics of Mobility, Daniela Hofmann, Catherine J. Frieman, Martin Furholt, Stefan Burmeister and Niels Nørkjær Johannsen
The Origins of the Civilization of Angkor, Charles F. W. Higham
The Origins of the English, Catherine Hills
Pagan and Christian, David Petts
The Remembered Land, Jim Leary
Rethinking Wetland Archaeology, Robert Van de Noort and Aidan O'Sullivan
The Roman Countryside, Stephen L. Dyson
Roman Reflections, Klavs Randsborg
Shaky Ground, Elizabeth Marlowe
Shipwreck Archaeology of the Holy Land, Sean A. Kingsley
Social Evolution, Mark Pluciennik
State Formation in Early China, Li Liu and Xingcan Chen
The State in Ancient Egypt: Power, Challenges and Dynamics, Juan Carlos Moreno Garcia
Towns and Trade in the Age of Charlemagne, Richard Hodges
Tradition and Transformation in Anglo-Saxon England, Susan Oosthuizen
Vessels of Influence, Nicole Coolidge Rousmaniere
Villa to Village, Riccardo Francovich and Richard Hodges

The Origins of Anglo-Saxon Towns

A Viking Gift?

Richard Hodges

BLOOMSBURY ACADEMIC
LONDON • NEW YORK • OXFORD • NEW DELHI • SYDNEY

BLOOMSBURY ACADEMIC

Bloomsbury Publishing Plc, 50 Bedford Square, London, WC1B 3DP, UK
Bloomsbury Publishing Inc, 1359 Broadway, New York, NY 10018, USA
Bloomsbury Publishing Ireland, 29 Earlsfort Terrace, Dublin 2, D02 AY28, Ireland

BLOOMSBURY, BLOOMSBURY ACADEMIC and the Diana logo are trademarks
of Bloomsbury Publishing Plc

First published in Great Britain 2025

Copyright © Richard Hodges, 2025

Richard Hodges has asserted his right under the Copyright, Designs and Patents Act, 1988, to be identified as Author of this work.

For legal purposes the Acknowledgements on p. xiii constitute an extension of this copyright page.

Cover image © Craig Coulthard

All rights reserved. No part of this publication may be: i) reproduced or transmitted in any form, electronic or mechanical, including photocopying, recording or by means of any information storage or retrieval system without prior permission in writing from the publishers; or ii) used or reproduced in any way for the training, development or operation of artificial intelligence (AI) technologies, including generative AI technologies. The rights holders expressly reserve this publication from the text and data mining exception as per Article 4(3) of the Digital Single Market Directive (EU) 2019/790.

Bloomsbury Publishing Plc does not have any control over, or responsibility for, any third-party websites referred to or in this book. All internet addresses given in this book were correct at the time of going to press. The author and publisher regret any inconvenience caused if addresses have changed or sites have ceased to exist, but can accept no responsibility for any such changes.

A catalogue record for this book is available from the British Library.

Library of Congress Cataloging-in-Publication Data
Names: Hodges, Richard, author.
Title: The origins of Anglo-Saxon towns : a Viking gift? / Richard Hodges.
Other titles: Viking gift?
Description: New York, NY : Bloomsbury Academic, 2025. | Series: Debates in archaeology / series editor, Richard Hodges | Includes bibliographical references and index.
Identifiers: LCCN 2024051068 (print) | LCCN 2024051069 (ebook) | ISBN 9781350523180 (pb) | ISBN 9781350523197 (hb) | ISBN 9781350523210 (epdf) | ISBN 9781350523203 (ebook)
Subjects: LCSH: Great Britain--History--Anglo-Saxon period, 449-1066. | Cities and towns, Medieval--England. | London (England)--History. | Ipswich (England)--History. | Southampton (England)--History. | York (England)--History.
Classification: LCC DA152 .H594 2025 (print) | LCC DA152 (ebook)
LC record available at https://lccn.loc.gov/2024051068
LC ebook record available at https://lccn.loc.gov/2024051069

ISBN:	HB:	978-1-3505-2319-7
	PB:	978-1-3505-2318-0
	ePDF:	978-1-3505-2320-3
	eBook:	978-1-3505-2321-0

Series: Debates in Archaeology

Typeset by RefineCatch Ltd, Bungay, Suffolk, UK
Printed and bound in Great Britain

For product safety related questions contact productsafety@bloomsbury.com.

To find out more about our authors and books, visit www.bloomsbury.com and sign up for our newsletters.

*To my teachers: Peter Addyman, David Hinton,
David Peacock & Colin Platt*

Contents

List of Illustrations	x
Preface and Acknowledgements	xiii
1 A Century of Debate	1
2 The 'False Dawn of the Age of Emporia'?	35
3 'Business as Usual'?	77
4 A Gift from the Vikings?	113
5 Re-reading Pirenne (Again)	159
Bibliography	179
Index	205

Illustrations

1.1	A poster for Henri Pirenne's lectures on *Medieval Cities*, 1922 (after Keymeulen and Tollebeek 2011)	2
1.2	Professor Søren Sindbæk points to the deep stratigraphy in the Viking-Age workshop at Posthustorvet, Ribe (photo: author)	20
1.3	Map showing the principal places mentioned in the text	30
2.1	View of the east-facing terraces on Tintagel Head (photo: author)	37
2.2	Map showing the trading zones, Franks versus Frisians	45
2.3	A primary sceatta, series BII, bird and cross type, NMS-732075 (courtesy of the British Museum's Portable Antiquities Scheme)	50
2.4	Map of Gipeswic (Ipswich) in the Middle Saxon period (modified after Keith Wade forthcoming)	54
2.5	Map showing the location of Hamwic, the Saxon Shore fort of Clausentum and the Late Saxon burh of Southampton (modified after Blair 2018: fig. 58)	59
2.6	Interpretative plan of the urban topography of the Six Dials site, Hamwic (modified after Andrews 1997: fig. 91)	62
2.7	View of the Six Dials excavations, Southampton in progress (courtesy of Phil Andrews and Southampton City Museums)	63
2.8	A selection of imported pottery from Hamwic (after G. C. Dunning, *Medieval Archaeology* 3 1959: fig. 23)	64
2.9	Map showing the location of Lundenwic and Lundenburg (after Naismith 2019; Blair 2018; Hadley and Richards 2021: 176)	67

2.10	Map showing the location of the Fishergate excavations and the site of Eoforwic, York (modified after Mainman 2019: fig. 29)	71
3.1	A penny of King Beonna of East Anglia found at Wordwell, Suffolk (SF-298063) (courtesy of the British Museum's Portable Antiquities Scheme)	81
3.2	Map of the excavated Early Saxon secular site and Middle Saxon minster at Lyminge (modified after John Blair 2018: fig. 34)	86
3.3	Representation of different mints within all finds from East Anglia, *c.* 760–865 (after Naismith 2012a: fig. 8.2)	96
3.4	Regional representation of finds of pennies minted at Southampton/Winchester, *c.* 760–865 (after Naismith 2012a: fig. 8.7)	97
3.5	Regression analysis of Hamwic type H sceattas (distributed across Wessex) (after Metcalf 2003: fig. 4.1)	98
3.6	Coin finds from Hamwic (after Blackburn 2003: fig 3.3)	101
3.7	The western ditch at Hamwic from above (courtesy of Phil Andrews and Southampton City Museums)	103
3.8	Selection of Ipswich ware (courtesy of Keith Wade and Suffolk County Council)	106
4.1	A map showing the Viking invasions and the location of Torksey in the later ninth century (after Hadley and Richards 2021: 61)	116
4.2	A selection of metal-detector finds from Torksey (courtesy of Andy Woods and Dawn Hadley)	121
4.3	Anglo-Scandinavian signature antler combs from Gipeswic with crossing diagonal decoration	133
4.4	Plans of periods 3 (late ninth century) and 4 (late tenth century) found in excavations at the Bull Wharf Thames waterfront (modified after Ayre and Wroe-Brown 2015: illustrations 9 and 13)	139

4.5 A map of the Anglo-Saxon burhs and their hypothetical territories (after Baker and Brookes 2013: fig. 74)   145

5.1 Map showing the location of the late ninth- to early tenth-century D-shaped fortress at Ghent (modified after Verhulst 1989: 25, map 4)   166

5.2 Reconstruction of Hedeby (Germany) in the tenth century (courtesy of Flemming Bau)   175

Preface and Acknowledgements

In this book I aim to contribute to a debate that I first engaged with as a doctoral student at Southampton University in 1973–6. There, I studied the imported pottery from the West Saxon emporium of Hamwih, later re-named Hamwic (see Hodges 1981). This led me to examine the origins of early Medieval towns and trade in *Dark Age Economics* (1982), setting out an argument that I revised in a new version thirty years later (Hodges 2012). The archaeological evidence has grown over these decades to make what was a poorly known area of research into one enriched by a range of excavated discoveries, extraordinary metal-detectorist finds, and exceptional scientific appraisals of the objects of the era. The playing field has changed remarkably, as has the nature of the discussions and debates.

This book takes account of the centennial anniversary of Henri Pirenne's canonical study of *Medieval Cities* (2014 [1925]) to use some of this new research to evaluate the origins of Anglo-Saxon towns. Pirenne largely ignored Anglo-Saxon England in his influential book, though his American pupil, Carl Stephenson (1933), was credited with echoing his ideas for pre-Conquest English towns. A century on, and the debates about Europe's urban evolution are taking entirely new directions, yet the echoes of Pirenne's bold thesis still matter (cf. Boone 2012; Lebecq 2020; Sindbæk 2020).

In *Medieval Cities*, Pirenne identified the origins of the first politically independent communities of burghers, which emerged in his native Belgium as a force in world history. With this book, he effectively launched a new narrative for the origins of Europe's economy which was to be set out more fully in his posthumously published, *Mohammed and Charlemagne* (1939). Now we possess increasingly refined new tools for interrogating Pirenne's thesis.

Modern archaeology, in particular, has provided us with the means to analyse the chronology, geography and social implications of his thesis. Much of Pirenne's model may no longer hold, but nonetheless the essential thinking behind his histories remains compelling. The opportunity to explore a new narrative is now possible thanks to extraordinarily well-dated archaeological evidence. It is this evidence which informs the argument explored in this book. Thanks to some remarkable new archaeological discoveries, emphasis is given to the Viking contribution to this English and post-Carolingian continental story.

The Viking sea-kings as agents of disruption have long dominated the documented sources of western Europe. Much of this story, as the historian Dame Janet Nelson scathingly disparaged, belongs to a history of 'harmless cultural props, like horned helmets worn by Scandinavian football fans or IKEA publicity girls. Yes . . . as fit subjects for historians, especially if the histories are comparative. But ready-made, hand-me-down Others, totemic props to chauvinism, we can do without. In that sense, the twenty-first century should see the last of the Vikings' (Nelson 2003: 28). Now, thanks, to a golden age of Viking-period archaeology, much of it being eagerly surveyed by historians, the history of these totemic Others is being reappraised. We belong to a generation that has come to recognize not only the vastness of the northern arc from which the Vikings came – the distance from the northern tip of Norway to the southern border of Denmark is more than half the total length of Europe (Jesch 2015: 19) – but also the complex mental template of these peoples. As Neil Price writes in *Children of Ash and Elm* (2020: 25): 'if abstract concepts can describe their impact upon and interactions with the world around them, then one should look to curiosity, creativity, the complexity and sophistication of their mental landscapes, and, yes, their openness to new experiences and ideas'. One key aspect of this template according to Price is *hamingja*, 'a remarkable being that is the personification of a person's luck' (2020: 61). Important though luck was to the success of the hydrarchs, it was an essential ingredient in the making of the Viking diaspora at places that stretched from Dublin to Kyiv. Through these places flowed the commerce and industry which powered the managed Scandinavian landscape and its sheep farmers. From richly excavated Viking sites – and from the economic and social models drawn from them – craftsmen and merchants emerge alongside sea-kings as equally influential change-makers, masterful in experimentation based upon the premise of procurement of materials from faraway sources. The presence of such craftsmen (and presumably traders) with the Great Danish Army in England and subsequently in new Anglo-Scandinavian towns was, I shall argue, to be a gift that was to significantly change England after the 870s, and contribute to what Pirenne described by the twelfth century as Medieval (European) civilization.

This book grew out of an essay for a festschrift (Hodges 2025), and a lecture based upon it when I was visiting professor at UrbNet, Aarhus University in 2022, thanks to Søren Sindbæk. I would like to re-double my thanks to Søren, not least for the opportunity to participate in the Ribe Reflections workshop in 2023. He also drew my attention to the need to confront Pirenne's views on the centenary of the publication of *Medieval Cities*. I should also like to thank Phil Andrews, Brian Ayers, Kim Bowes, Mark Brisbane, Peter Brown, Pieterjan Deckers, Matt Garner, Wolfram Giertz, Dawn Hadley, Thomas Kind, Ailsa Mainman John Mitchell, John Moreland, Julian Richards, Ian Riddler, Frans Theuws and Dries Tys. A special thanks to Keith Wade for allowing me to read *Gipeswic: the Anglo-Saxon Town of Ipswich* in advance of its publication as a monograph in the East Anglian Archaeology series, and to Dries Tys for guidance on the archaeology of Ghent. My lasting debt is to those who shaped my thinking in the 1970s, especially Philip Grierson, John Hurst and Klavs Randsborg.

Ian Riddler kindly read the manuscript and made many helpful suggestions, guiding me through the maze of contemporary publications following both research and rescue excavations. To him I am immensely indebted.

I am grateful to Sarah Leppard for preparing the illustrations. A special thanks to Phil Andrews (and Southampton City Museum) for photographs of Hamwic's western ditch and the excavations at Six Dials, Southampton; to Dawn Hadley and Andy Woods for the illustration of metal-detector finds from Torksey; to Sam Moorhead and John Naylor (as well as the British Museum's Portable Antiquities Scheme) for the images of a primary sceatta and a King Beonna penny; and to Keith Wade for an illustration of Ipswich ware. Thanks, too, to Flemming Bau for his reconstruction drawing of tenth-century Hedeby.

Looking back, I recognize how especially fortunate I have been. As an undergraduate I excavated at Hamwih, as it was then known, with David Hill. I also supervised excavations of the Mercian burh at Gloucester, thanks to Henry Hurst; these were my first real steps into the world of Anglo-Saxon archaeology. Then, thanks to David Peacock and Colin Renfrew, I was awarded a research scholarship by Southampton Archaeological Research Committee (SARC) to study the Hamwih pottery, 1973–6. My research was mentored by exceptionally kind and learned scholars: Jean Chapelot, Gerald Dunning, David Hinton, John Hurst, David Peacock and Wim van Es. In 1974 I also had the good fortune to collaborate with David Hinton in excavating an area within the Anglo-Saxon burh at Wareham (Dorset). All of these experiences added to my academic formation where I was privileged to have had such original and committed thinkers as teachers. It is to them, Peter Addyman, David Hinton, David Peacock and Colin Platt, that I dedicate this book about a debate which is certain to take many other forms in the next half century.

1

A Century of Debate

This little volume ... is an attempt to expound, in a general way, the economic awakening and the birth of urban civilization in Western Europe during the Middle Ages.

Pirenne 2014 [1925]: 1

A century ago, Henri Pirenne published his short book, *Medieval Cities: Their Origins and the Revival of Trade* (2014 [1925]). Acclaimed as a classic from the start, it is still read in university classrooms throughout the English-speaking world. As such it has remained a cornerstone of Medieval studies, marking the beginnings of a historical debate about the origins and form of Medieval towns in Europe. Over the decades, this has informed analyses of town-making across the globe. Pirenne's book, however, did more than propose how towns took shape in the post-Roman period. He argued that urbanism spawned a middle-class culture – of burghers – who led the way in creating social privileges, civic consciousness and new forms of economic organizations. This middle class – as opposed to aristocrats and peasants – he reasoned, shaped the making of Europe's Medieval civilization and the bedrock of European society.

Pirenne's book was derived from lectures he delivered in American universities on a tour in 1922. There was a purpose to his argument. Pirenne was appealing to his New World audiences to understand the genesis of European civilization at a time, following the dystopian circumstances of the First World War, when there was a sense of despair. In particular, he was pleading for the non-classical roots of Europe. He was also making a clear distinction that Medieval civilization was not the fruit of the Germanic peasants who had swept away Roman institutions, but an invention of a class of town-dwellers, principally from his homeland, Belgium, and especially Flanders (where he was professor in Ghent). In making this distinction, Pirenne was defining a Medieval civilization and its ultimate importance to his New World audiences of erstwhile immigrants as a product of those who had fought against the Germans in the First World War. He was also promoting a progressive European past and its exceptional place in world history (cf. Lyon 1974; Keymeulen and Tollebeek 2011; Boone 2012; Effros 2017; Sindbæk 2020).

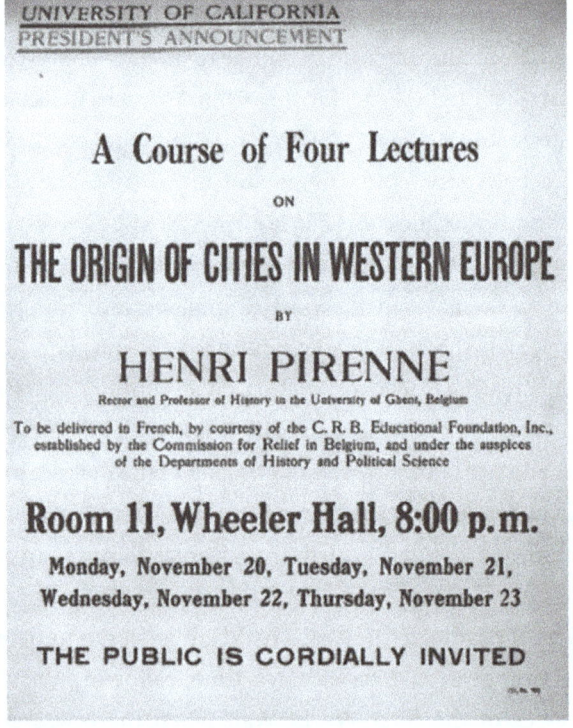

Figure 1.1 A poster for Henri Pirenne's lectures on *Medieval Cities*, 1922 (after Keymeulen and Tollebeek 2011).

Medieval Cities was the first of a pair of books which comprise the so-called Pirenne thesis. Its unfinished counterpart, *Mohammed and Charlemagne* (1939 [1937]), enlarges on the earlier lectures and focused principally on the fifth- to ninth-century circumstances that created the conditions for town-building in the tenth century. *Mohammed and Charlemagne* has been challenged vigorously over the past decades. Pirenne's argument that the Roman empire lasted until its defeat by the Arab conquest of North Africa is no longer tenable. Archaeological evidence, as well as textual analysis, trace a very different history. Nonetheless, the great divergence between Mediterranean Europe and North-West Europe, advanced by Pirenne, remains debated, championed by some scholars (eg. Hodges and Whitehouse 1983; McCormick 2001) and challenged by others (eg. Wickham 2005). Pirenne's views on the revival of Medieval Europe, however, has attracted less criticism. He identified the importance of the Carolingian revolution led by Charlemagne at the end of the eighth century, leading to the invention of feudalism, and from this, in the midst of Viking raids and internecine struggles between local lords, the need for fortified settlements. These settlements, in Pirenne's telling in *Medieval Cities*, became the seeds of towns and ultimately civic society. This part of Pirenne's narrative merits citing because its shadow has been long and influential over the past century.

Pirenne observed:

> It is therefore a safe conclusion that the period which opened with the Carolingian era knew cities neither in the social sense, nor in the economic sense, nor in the legal sense of that word. The towns and the burgs were merely fortified places and headquarters of administration. Their inhabitants enjoyed neither special laws nor institutions of their own, and their manner of living did not distinguish them in any way from the rest of society. Commercial and industrial activity were completely foreign to them. In no respect were they out of key with the agricultural civilization of their

times. The groups they formed were, after all, of trifling importance. It is not possible, in the lack of reliable information, to give an exact figure, but everything indicates that the population of the burgs never consisted of more than a few hundred men and that that of the towns probably did not pass the figure of two to three thousand souls. The towns and the burgs played, however, an essential role in the history of cities. They were, so to speak, the stepping-stones thereto. Round about their walls cities were to take shape after the economic renaissance, whose first symptoms appeared in the course of the tenth century, had made itself manifest.

2014: 47–8

In an important passage, Pirenne attributes the origins of this urban post-Roman revival to traders and engagement in international commerce:

This revival received its impetus from two centers of activity, one located in the south and the other in the north: Venice on one side and the Flemish coast on the other. And this is merely another way of saying that it was the result of an external stimulus. The contact with foreign trade, maintained at these two points, first caused it to appear and spread. Quite likely it could have come about in some other way. Commercial activity might have been revived by virtue of the trend of general economic life. The fact is, however, that this was not the case. Just as the trade of the west disappeared [in the seventh century] with the shutting off of its foreign markets, just so it was renewed when these markets were reopened.

2014: 52

(It is not difficult to envisage that by identifying international trade in luxuries – and the role of the merchants involved – Pirenne was intentionally appealing to his audiences in the United States in 1922 by illustrating a progressive European past based upon an internally evolving economic prosperity that justified the European status of his country, Belgium (cf. Keymeulen and Tollebeek 2011; Boone 2012).)

This new urban life appeared, as Pirenne saw it, in the course of the tenth century, when once more an external stimulus – in this case, the revival of trade – provoked the rise of new urban settlements (*suburbia*) outside the walls of many old clerical *civitates* and close to new fortifications (*castra*). These fortifications had been built against the Viking attacks and invasions along the coastline of Belgium and northern France. Pirenne considered the duality – *suburbium/civitas* or *suburbium/castrum* – to be a pivotal feature of Medieval towns arising out of military rather than economic needs. Protection was the primary driver behind these places. The tenth-century revival of trade, his *deus ex machina* to explain the renaissance of urban life, was attributed to subsequent external causes. Principally this occurred, in his opinion, thanks to the restoration of connections with Scandinavia (and by way of the Baltic Sea and Russia to the Abbasid Caliphate), as the Vikings prioritized commerce over aggression (Pirenne 2014: 60–2).

Pursuing this line of argument, Pirenne proposed:

> perhaps it would be possible to say that the city of the Middle Ages, as it existed in the twelfth century, was a commercial and industrial commune living in the shelter of a fortified enclosure and enjoying a law, an administration and a jurisprudence of exception which made of it a collective, privileged personality.
>
> 2014: 137

> The birth of cities marked the beginning of a new era in the internal history of Western Europe. Until then, society had recognized only two active orders: the clergy and the nobility. In taking its place beside them, the middle class rounded the social order out or, rather, gave the finishing touch thereto. Thenceforth its composition was not to change; it had all its constituent elements, and the modifications which it was to undergo in the course of centuries were, strictly speaking, nothing more than different combinations in the alloy.
>
> 2014: 138

Not all historians, of course, have subscribed to Pirenne's provocative synthesis. His fellow Belgian historian, Jan Dhondt, some thirty years later observed that Pirenne's thesis was a 'scientific disaster', an idea 'conceived when access to sources was still limited, and worked out during a phase of his life in which he was already so closed off to facts that were inconsistent with it that the thesis had become an axiom to him' (Dhondt 1966: 65; Keymeulen and Tollebeek 2011: 90; Boone 2012: 333). Shortly afterwards, the Italian historian, Cinzio Violante also condemned Pirenne's thesis, concluding that he was discomforted by the extra-scientific motivation, specifically the revenge on Germany and German historiography with its intentional minimization of the role of the Germanic migrations and Germanization itself. Violante believed Pirenne sought evidence in the sources only as an afterthought (Keymeulen and Tollebeek 2011: 90; Boone 2012: 335). More recently, the British historian, Chris Wickham has been equally dismissive for other reasons. He charged Pirenne and his advocates with championing a metanarrative that attempts to explain the 'secular economic triumph of north-west Europe' (Wickham 2005: 822).

Turning to specifics, Pirenne's reading of the beginnings of Flemish towns like Ghent has been challenged by generations of historians (for concise overviews, see Verhulst 1999; Boone 2012). Notably, Pirenne's fellow Belgian (who was familiar with the later twentieth-century archaeological evidence), Adriaan Verhulst has advocated a different evolutionary sequence for the Flemish towns that, as I shall explain, has important implications: '...in the eleventh century, international trade was grafted onto these tenth-century, regional market functions. International trade became possible just as soon as these cities began to produce luxury products suitable for export (cloth, metal) on an industrial scale. So it is incorrect to say that the large cities with long-distance trade were the result of a "revival of trade", as Pirenne believed. In fact, the reverse was true. The industrialization process in the cities was complete towards the end of the eleventh century. It had come about partly because of the transfer of the age-old artisanal activities from the rural manors to the city following the disintegration of the manorial system and because of the new techniques in the city. Trade and industry were in the hands of the bourgeoisie, largely indigenous in origin, whose wealth enabled them to acquire great autonomy in Flanders' (1999: 152; see now Vannieuwenhuyze and Rutte 2024 for an overview of Verhulst's thesis). Verhulst's critique of Pirenne has been well received by Belgian archaeologists, as we shall see in Chapter 5 (cf. Vannieuwenhuyze and Rutte 2023). Note, however, that Wickham, on the other hand, broadly pursues Pirenne's thesis about the origins of towns – and Flemish towns in particular – as he traces the beginnings of urbanism and the Medieval North Italian communes in the tenth and eleventh century (2023: 671).

The debate about the rise of cities in the Low Countries is complicated by the limited apparent absence of archaeological evidence for townlife in the earlier Carolingian realms, other than in the so-called emporia (see below). As the Belgian archaeologist, Frans Verhaeghe observed:

> we still know too little about [Carolingian] royal perceptions of, and attitude towards, towns. Indirect intervention seems clear – notably by influencing the economy with measures related to coinage, tolls and markets – but that is about as far as we can go at present. [...] In fact, it is also quite possible that the Carolingians had only a limited or perhaps even parasitic interest in the urban phenomenon, given their predilection for the rural world that was the basis of their power and income, and where they chose to build their palaces.
>
> 2005: 284

The first major excavations in Belgium at Antwerp, however, superficially lent support to Pirenne's thesis. In excavations near the city's waterfront made in 1961, rich tenth-century archaeological remains were found by Adelbert Van de Walle (1961). The Mattenstraat excavations brought to light a sequence of sub-divided wooden buildings bordering a wooden trackway. More recent excavations in other Flemish towns, however, have made it possible to trace their urban story in a detail that is still uncommon in many regions of Ottonian Europe (Tys 2010; Tys, Deckers and Wouters 2016; Verhulst 1999).

Anglo-Saxon England has largely been treated as peripheral to Pirenne's narrative, as indeed has Scandinavia. Pirenne, to be fair, was influenced by the legal arguments made by his British contemporary, F. W. Maitland, regarding the civic apparatus of new towns which were appraised by the Belgian historian's American pupil, Carl Stephenson (Pirenne 2014: 48; Stephenson 1933). But beyond this Pirenne and most subsequent historians have not ventured far. Likewise, Pirenne cast the Scandinavians – essentially the Viking raiders and their traders – as outsiders, whose impact could not be ignored, but had a limited part to play in the organizational developments in Medieval townlife.

The thesis of this book is that archaeology reveals how important the Scandinavian and English connections are to the emergence not just of fortified urban centres in late Carolingian Europe, but also how models from these two regions contributed to the Flemish urban culture that Pirenne defined as the foundations of Medieval civilization.

The genesis of Anglo-Saxon and Viking urbanism

Henri Pirenne, of course, did not omit London from *Medieval Cities*. For example, he observes that: 'At the end of the tenth century the port of London was. regularly frequented by merchants from Cologne, Huy, Dinant, Flanders and Rouen' (2014: 78). He also observes that: 'In 991–1002 the list of market tolls at London makes mention of the Flemings as if they were the most important group of foreigners carrying on business in that city' (2014: 62). But London and other Anglo-Saxon towns do not figure in his enduring perorations about

Medieval institutions and Medieval civilization. As much as Pirenne admired British academic life, his gaze was set, as a historian of Belgium, in promoting the signal importance to Europe of places like Antwerp, Bruges and Ghent as well as towns in the Meuse valley.

Pirenne's views of the Vikings and the role of Scandinavia in his histories were advanced for a scholar writing in the 1920s. Of course, he laid emphasis upon the disruption caused by the Vikings and the violence that led to the creation of fortified centres in Carolingian Europe (2014: 44). But he also recognized the Vikings as traders who were reaching deep into Russia and the Abbasid Caliphate (2014: 29–34). In his observations on this farflung commerce involving 'Norsemen' as he called them, he writes tellingly: 'Russia was living by trade at an era when the Carolingian Empire knew only the demenial regime, and she in turn inaugurated this form of government at the very moment when Western Europe, having found new markets, broke away from it' (2014: 34). To the Vikings he was to attribute a civilization that mattered, principally because Pirenne admired traders as agents of change (Pirenne 1939: 239–40). This excursus into the world of the Vikings was almost certainly prompted by his groundbreaking appreciation that trade between Quentovic and Dorestad (or Duurstede as he refers to it) and points in Frisia and further north played an important part in shaping the later (tenth-century) rise of trading communities in Flanders (Pirenne 2014: 20–1).

Pirenne was almost certainly familiar with the archaeological salvage excavations made at Dorestad (Duurstede) by J. H. Holwerda (1929), while he noted that the site of Quentovic in the Canche valley, near Boulogne-sur-Mer was lost. He may also have been aware of the site of the Viking town of Hedeby (Haithabu) on the Schlei, opposite modern Schleswig that was mentioned in the *Frankish Annals*. (Research excavations at Hedeby (Haithabu) began in 1930 under the direction of the German archaeologist, Herbert Jankuhn (cf. Hilberg 2022: 42–4).) This has led Søren Sindbæk to conjecture that Pirenne may have had some knowledge of these places as fortified trading places with wharfs – places that, citing the written sources, Pirenne described as a *portus* (now generally known as an emporium) (Sindbæk 2020: 134).

Pirenne's thesis, in other words, was based on texts with incidental references to numismatic studies. The archaeological record for urban sites in Anglo-Saxon England, Carolingian Europe and Scandinavia was at a very preliminary stage when he was writing *Medieval Cities*, and indeed, even in 1935, when he passed away before completing *Mohammed and Charlemagne*. As a result, he was not familiar with Jankuhn's first monograph on Haithabu (Hedeby) published in 1937 that was to prompt many similar archaeological projects after the Second World War (Jankuhn 1937).

Historians of Anglo-Saxon England were familiar with the impact of the Danish conquest of eastern England in the 870s that led to the founding of new boroughs. As Pirenne was in lecturing in the United States on Medieval cities, Allen Mawer was writing about 'the redemption' of the five Danish boroughs (1923). Pirenne's erstwhile student, the American historian, Carl Stephenson, pursued his teacher's thesis in contending that urbanism played a marginal role in pre-Norman England (1933). Stephenson, plainly echoing Pirenne, made the case based upon legal sources for a largely rural Anglo-Saxon economy until the Norman Conquest. In a critique of Stephenson's book, *Borough and Town: A Study of Urban Origins in England* (1933), the British historian James Tait opined: 'the under-estimate of the trading aspect of the Anglo-Saxon boroughs of the eleventh century is closely connected with a clear exaggeration of its agricultural aspect, resulting partly from failure always to distinguish between what Domesday reports for 1066 and what for 1086, and partly from a tendency to interpret ambiguous evidence in the light of a theory' (1933: 644). Taking an altogether different view, Tait contended that: 'In England, on the contrary, the beginnings of urban life were worked out within the walls of its burhs, not without' (1933: 646). In all fairness, Stephenson recognized that one problem with his deployment of the Pirenne model for Anglo-Saxon England was a lack of archaeological evidence (1933: 186–214). Nevertheless, James Tait followed up his brief critique with a book substantiating his argument, *The Medieval English Borough* (1936). Thereafter, English historians fell into line, awaiting archaeologists to confirm Tait's interpretation. In doing so, Henry Loyn, explained forty years later as a burst of major urban archaeological excavations was underway, 'we are all Taitians now' (1971: 116).

Before the 1950s, excavations in English towns, however, were rare. London was the exception, largely because of interest in finding its Roman origins. The young Mortimer Wheeler, as Director of the London Museum between 1926 and 1933, placed weight on Bede's description of London as a great mart in the early eighth century, but was puzzled by the absence of archaeological proof. He interpreted London as 'an urban anachronism standing strong against the devolution of culture and town life in the post-Roman centuries' (Wheeler 1934: 290; 1935; Naismith 2019: 76). Wheeler's students investigated building sites for possible signs of Anglo-Saxon remains and made what was to be known as 'watching briefs'. This was to become a standard procedure in the aftermath of the Second World War. Small urban archaeological surveys were made of bomb-sites in Oxford, Norwich and Southampton, for example, as early as the late 1940s. Within a few years, systematic trenching occurred in bombed areas of Oxford, Norwich, Canterbury, and Ipswich as well as London and Southampton. In Canterbury, for example, Sheppard Frere discovered the last phases of Romano-British occupation of the city, as well as sherds belonging to Middle Saxon times. In Ipswich, Stanley West identified Middle Saxon kilns producing distinctive coil-made Ipswich ware. In Norwich, John Hurst traced the evolution of parts of the Medieval town, and found good evidence of its extensive Late Saxon phase. In London, W. F. Grimes found major Roman remains but little of Anglo-Saxon date, and believed that Wheeler's projected city was exaggerated (Gerrard 2003; Naismith 2019: 76). In Southampton, Dudley Waterman identified the extensive evidence of the Middle Saxon town in the district of St Mary's which, then, was known as Hamwih (cf. Brisbane and Hodges 2018).

The archaeology of English towns took a giant leap forward in the 1960s. It began when Martin Biddle created the Winchester Research Unit and embarked on more than a decade of careful stratigraphic investigations of large areas within the West Saxon capital. Biddle introduced open-area excavation to British urban archaeology, placing great emphasis upon identifying palimpsests of structures within large areas as opposed to disruptive trenching. These excavations brought to light the sub-Roman town in astonishing detail, as well as the revival of the town in the tenth century. Excavations of the Old Minster founded in the late seventh century revealed its small size until the tenth-century reform-period basilica was erected emulating Ottonian grandeur. Biddle with David H. Hill deployed these findings in a landmark essay to illustrate the planned towns of the early tenth-century Burghal Hidage, a remarkable collection of documents in Old English that sets out the legal obligations for defending a network of West Saxon refuges (Hill 1969; Biddle and Hill 1971). Meanwhile, urban archaeology imitating Winchester was taking root in numerous English cities to take advantage of a boom in redevelopment. One of these projects stood out, even at the time. Close to Winchester, Peter Addyman and David Hill made the first open-area excavations at Hamwih (Addyman and Hill 1968; 1969 see also Addyman 1973) (later re-named as Hamwic), and, more importantly, published their Middle Saxon discoveries. These first publications showed what an extraordinary array of distinctive finds characterized this largely unknown but large eighth- and ninth-century port. Addyman then founded the York Archaeological Trust in 1972 and pursued major excavations there as Biddle had in Winchester. The largest of these, 16–22 Coppergate, would soon become the site of the celebrated and much-visited Jorvik

Centre (Hall et al. 2014). Many other towns were now the object of major open-area excavations. Durham, Gloucester, Exeter, Lincoln and Norwich were just a few of the many places, including almost every site recorded in the Burghal Hidage, to come under the spotlight in this boom in extraordinary archaeological activity.

This pioneering phase of urban archaeology committed archaeologists to joining historians as 'Taitians'. In a magisterial essay, Martin Biddle (1976) summarized the arguments and reviewed the growing urban evidence for this approach to Anglo-Saxon England. He concluded this essay using archaeology to essentially echo James Tait's thesis made some forty years earlier: 'by the end of the Anglo-Saxon period there were more than a hundred places with some claim to be regarded as towns ... it has been calculated that some 10 per cent of the population lived in towns by the eve of the Conquest' (1976: 141).

By 1980 English urban archaeology had not only come of age but had also identified three key features. First, continuity between townlife in the Romano-British and Late Saxon periods was disproved. Many archaeologists had previously been attracted to showing how Winchester or York, for example, had somehow existed through the 'Dark Ages' because texts incidentally mentioned these places. The evidence, however, was missing. Second, the rich archaeology of later seventh- to ninth-century Ipswich and Hamwih, renamed as Hamwic in this period, was unmistakably special in a period when towns were mostly missing. Both were large urban centres, and both boasted a combination of distinctive local pottery and an array of imported Late Merovingian/Carolingian wares as well as numerous coins. The mystery remained as to why such clear evidence had not been found in London. Third, the Late Saxon phases of all the towns excavated in the 1960s and 1970s were astonishingly rich in evidence for craft production, as well as framing the introduction of urban topography. The explosion of town-building was especially apparent at Thetford in Norfolk, where the creation of new town for 'overspill populations from London' allowed for a massive area of the tenth- to eleventh-century town to be excavated. Rich though these Late Saxon levels were in these many towns, they curiously lacked imported items of the kinds found in Hamwic and Ipswich.

This was the context for my book, *Dark Age Economics* (1982). Greatly influenced by the positivism of the (American) New Archaeology, it placed emphasis upon long-distance trade in the process of culture change. Anthropological models were employed to make the case for the economic evolution of post-Roman North-West Europe. I gave special emphasis to Karl Polanyi's (substantivist) interpretation of embedded pre-market economies in which reciprocity and redistribution as opposed to markets were the principal forms of exchange (Polanyi 1957; 1963). Like many, I was perhaps guilty of subscribing to Polanyi's division between a fractured modern world and a past that had ostensibly been more coherent and humane. In particular, I treated emporia such as Hamwic and Ipswich, along with Dorestad and Hedeby, for example, as a category of urban site created by a pre-state élite to control, and to marshal imported luxury goods as a way of facilitating gift-exchange economies. The emporia, following this argument, grew out of periodic landing-places and dendritic distribution systems. Then, following this approach, these monopolistic centres paved the way for a ranked hierarchy of regional (Late Saxon) towns with their emphasis upon creating local production and distribution ('the first [English] industrial revolution' (cf. Hodges 1989; Hadley and Richards 2021: 251; 279, n.4)) that was taxed to support the administrative apparatus of the embryonic state. By using archaeology to re-examine a historical issue, as opposed to illustrating and effectively ground-truthing the textual sources, led to *Dark Age Economics* being widely criticized! As this present book aims to make clear, with the benefit of new data, much of the central argument of *Dark Age Economics* is no longer sustainable. As a source, the archaeological evidence is now much richer than it was in 1980. Archaeological critiques of England's early urban history increased by three initiatives: in large part as the material evidence was transformed in the 1980s and 1990s with ubiquitous urban excavations (eg. Astill 2000; 2011; Hill and Cowie 2001; Samson 1997; Saunders 1991; 2001; Theuws 2004), the adoption of the Portable Antiquities Scheme (instituted by the UK government's Treasure Act of 1996) in 1997 to track metal-detector evidence (see, for example, Pestell and Ulmschneider 2003) and the invention of the so-called Third Science Revolution which ramped up the characterization and provenancing of objects as well as improved dating techniques (Kristiansen 2014).

All this new information showed that I had placed too much emphasis in *Dark Age Economics* upon the monopolistic role of the emporia and then the burhs – on an evolutionary urban (and economic) process – in shaping the Anglo-Saxon economy. What became clear was that these urban centres – the emporia and the burhs – had to be evaluated in terms of the rural archaeology and its insights into local production and peripheral markets. Pursuing this approach, John Moreland argued that it no longer made sense to understand the emporia as 'active cores' surrounded by 'conservative, autarkic peripheries' (2000b: 69). Instead, in Moreland's opinion, the function of the emporia was more varied and complicated (and interesting) than had previously been envisaged. He contended that a model, focused exclusively on royal (top-down) control of international trade, and also involving a gift-exchange phase followed by a production phase, are both idealized, whereas in reality 'gifts and commodities are not mutually exclusive' (2000a: 31). Moreland, followed by Ben Palmer and Grenville Astill, pointed the way towards an English economy in the eighth century in which commodification and the beginnings of markets as loci of non-kin exchange were being shaped while gift-exchange spheres continued to operate. The evolutionary model in *Dark Age Economics* was an over-simplification. It belonged to what Blanton and Feinman (2024) have described as a Polanyian anti-market mentality that was very common in anthropology in the 1970s. This mitigated against identifying bottom-up social change and consensus. Blanton and Feinman proceed to conclude as follows:

> because paragovernance preceded centralized polities and often operated outside any polity's scope of direct control, its strategic egalitarianism constitutes an alternate pathway to the evolution of authoritative governance, one that was never addressed by substantivists following Polanyi, nor has it been addressed in depth by neoevolutionist theorists who have focused attention on the exercise of political dominance as the central causal force of sociocultural evolution.
>
> 2024: 11

It is an issue to which I shall return below as this reworking of Polanyi's economic model has been pursued by both Dutch and Scandinavian archaeologists.

The introduction of regionally-distributed markets to Anglo-Saxon England may have been slow and at first, largely ephemeral as local producers, for example, exchanged foodstuffs. Some measure of this early Anglo-Saxon economic history can be found in Mahir Saul's' study of nineteenth-century (pre-colonial) markets in West Africa, where money and commerce existed in the interstices of a society consisting mostly of self-provisioning farming communities. The larger economy was not integrated by market-made prices, nor by other, alternative social mechanisms. It was, on the contrary, disjointed. Reciprocity and redistribution had only a limited part to play outside narrow kinship networks and local areas. These social flows did not shape the general features of resource allocations (Saul 2018: 148). Nevertheless, the Anglo-Saxon market, even in its incipient form in the eighth and earlier ninth centuries, followed some essential guiding principles. These principles, according to the economist, Roger Guesnerie (1996; Hahn 2018: 7), can be summarized as follows: a market is an instrument for the coordination of diverse actors who (a) pursue their own interests, (b) have different interests and (c) solve conflicts by fixing prices. In this definition, a market is primarily an interface where opposing sellers and buyers appear and repeatedly use specific conflict-solving strategies. These strangers engage in negotiating prices because they are concerned with the achievement of a relation of equivalence. The only condition for market participation is a readiness to calculate. No less importantly, the market is scalable. Regardless of whether it is a large or a small market, the basic principles stay the same. Guesnerie's model of the market as an interface between various groups of actors necessarily adopts a kind of temporary dis-embedding of exchange. The end product of the readiness to calculate, commodification, then, is the process through which personal goods become anonymous tradeable goods.

Developing this point, John Moreland laid emphasis upon the major expansion of production of commodities in seventh-century England just as the emporia were being founded, and proposed that 'patterns of production [in England] had dramatically altered long before the production phase of the emporia' (2000b: 76). In essence, emporia like Hamwic and Ipswich had larger trading elements than other settlements and were larger in size, but an additional role in craft production has been first understated and then in some cases overstated. The English emporia were clearly focal points for international trade, but also had a role in regional commerce. Reviewing the eighth-century economy in Anglo-Saxon England, Moreland advocated greater regional integration based upon a four-tier settlement rural hierarchy (Moreland 2000b: 96–7). Ben Palmer broadly echoed Moreland's model. Making use of metal-detector evidence he identified a similar structure amongst sites with traded goods, featuring the 'richest', many of which were ecclesiastical sites, followed by rural sites with strong evidence of production, then rural sites with 'neither an ecclesiastical connection nor specialized production but which appear to have been involved in trade in some way, simply as a result of their location on major trade routes' (Palmer 2003: 54–5). As we shall see in Chapter 3, the Thames-side trading site found in large rescue excavations at Dorney would seem to be an illustration of exactly what Palmer had in mind (see p.116).

In retrospect, *Dark Age Economics* advanced a critical use of the urban evidence for historical purposes. It focused scholars to enquire as to who founded the emporia and for what purposes. It led to a debate about whether the emporia as such amounted to a genuine category. It may also have indirectly helped to prompt an eureka moment, the discovery of Lundenwic in London's West End in 1983-4 (cf. Naismith 2019: 76). Similarly, it was no coincidence that the discovery of the later Merovingian and Carolingian emporium of Quentovic in northern France was made at this time by one of the (vocal, if friendly) critics of *Dark Age Economics* (David H. Hill and his team) (Hill, Barrett, Maude, Warburton and Worthington 1990).

In sum, a vast amount of information is now available for Anglo-Saxon urban origins and development, and it shows that Carl Stephenson by following Pirenne was mistaken in understating the role of towns in pre-Conquest England. The urban narrative has now been complemented by four major research projects devoted to characterizing the Anglo-Saxon countryside. Each, from a different viewpoint, revisits W. G. Hoskins' *The Making of the English Landscape* (1954) – a canonical interpretation of England's topographical (and landscape) history. First, the Britannia Fields project (Rippon, Smart and Pears 2015) charted the landscape history across the first millennium. It drew attention to the revival of rotation and investment as early as the seventh century. Second, the *Beneath the Tribal Hidage Project* mapped the archaeological and ecological background to the making of the early Saxon polities in England (Harrington and Welch 2014). Third, John Blair (2018) took a different approach, mapping the constructed history (and planning) of the Anglo-Saxon age through the prism of measured building and settlement plans. Blair explains: 'I have tried to show how the....fugitive ...traces of buildings and settlements are bringing to light a harnessing and a re-planning of the natural environment that was often complex, and sometimes achieved with a artifice and skill comparable to the small-scale works of art' (2018: 419). Then, fourthly, through the 'FeedSax Project', Mark McKerracher and Helena Hamerow (2022) with collaborators have introduced a new narrative for agricultural production in this period based upon crop and livestock studies as well as an analysis of the instruction of technical innovations, principally the mouldboard plough package probably imported into England in the later seventh century.

To this impressive body of new research can be added a vast assemblage of mapped metal-detector finds from rural sites that complements the archaeology found in towns. These finds include large numbers of coins which, with the Third Science Revolution, have been systematically subjected to isotopic analyses of their metal contents, but also analysed spatially and in terms of their quantification (cf. Blackburn 2003; Metcalf 2003; 2009; 2014; Naismith 2012a; Kershaw et al. 2024). The result is a body of data that transforms the numismatic narrative of this age.

Re-thinking urban origins and urban communities

In re-thinking urban origins and their communities in Anglo-Saxon England, we need to take our bearings from a golden age of Viking-Age studies of towns and their economies (Kalmring 2024). Harnessed to fine excavation techniques and digital mapping of finds, there has been exceptional analyses of materials. The results provide a level of detail exceeding anything from the archaeology of Anglo-Saxon towns (although see the Torksey discoveries (Hadley and Richards 2016; 2020; 2023), described in Chapter 4). Especially pertinent are research excavations and forensic scientific analyses of the dating and of objects initiated by Dagfinn Skre in his study of the Norwegian emporium of Kaupang (2008), and emulated and exceeded by the

Figure 1.2 Professor Søren Sindbæk points to the deep stratigraphy in the Viking-Age workshop at Posthustorvet, Ribe (photo: author).

'high definition' investigations made at the Danish emporium of Ribe (Sindbæk 2022; 2023) (see below). Both projects with their exceptional recording invite many questions – about urban evolution on the eve of the Middle Ages, historical chronologies, the foundation and management of towns, and, importantly, the signal importance of craft production and supply chains in the culture of these places. These studies, as I aim to show, are pertinent to the origins of Anglo-Saxon towns as the body of information from later ninth-century Danish colonial towns in England has been refined and published.

Notably, these twenty-first-century projects have opened up new perspectives about the definition of emporia as a category. The positivist interpretation in *Dark Age Economics* (1982) of how emporia were founded and managed is clearly over-simplistic. Its central argument put a good deal of emphasis upon the scale and investment in the emporia as evidence that these trading places were founded by rulers. This *'reges ex machina'* explanation has been supported by some English archaeologists (cf. Scull 1997; Astill 2000) and challenged by others. Ben Palmer, for instance, opined that: 'the "Hodgean" model of development has survived as long as it has partly because of the prevalence of the "kings and bishops" school of Anglo-Saxon history, and partly because it was believed that the archaeological evidence for rural sites of the Middle Saxon period was insignificant' (2003: 50; see also, Samson 1999). Much more excavated evidence is now available to clarify the evolution of such places, their origins and, importantly, their cultural and historical contexts (cf. McCormick 2007: 42–3). A study by Christopher Loveluck and Dries Tys (2006) essentially argued that the emporia were part of a spectrum of places where long-distance trade was located. Within a less centralized set of social relationships, beach sites or landing-places (type A emporia in *Dark Age Economics*) – principally periodic places of exchange – were not necessarily precursors of permanent towns. Loveluck and Tys proposed that the periodic and permanent points of exchange reflected different mercantile functions, echoing in a sense Moreland's critique of the emporia (2000a; 2000b). This argument has carried weight insofar as the emporia now appear to have operated as importantly as places of regional production and distribution, as much as places engaged in the transshipment of imported luxuries.

Closer analysis of the procurement and redistribution strategies of the emporia, thanks to the intervention of Johan Callmer, has raised the essential question of the emporia as a category (2002; 2007; 2020). Some emporia were apparently places of transshipment, while others were in receipt of imports and managed regional production. But, as Callmer has argued, lumping the emporia into a category obfuscates the economic motives for their foundation. With some justification he has challenged my previous interpretations: 'Hodges has repeatedly tried to include Scandinavian early medieval developments in a discussion on the north-west European emporia (Hodges 1982; 2012).

the craft production' (Callmer 2020: 46).

Approaching the issue from another angle, Frans Theuws (2004) has proposed that the emporium of Dorestad – one of the largest places in ninth-century Europe, with some estimates pointing to an emporium at its zenith covering up to 100 hectares along the Rhine and Lek riverbanks – was founded and maintained by merchants until changes in exchange controls in the late eighth century. Deliberating on this, Dries Tys proposes that the emporium began as an assembling place for the polyfocal communities ranged around these rivers close to the North Sea (Tys 2017: 40). One such community may have been the sixth- to early eighth-century riverside village of Oegstgeest, described in Chapter 2 (de Bruin, Bakels and Theuws 2021). Theuws is far from convinced by the top-down model in early Medieval Europe advanced in *Dark Age Economics*. Instead, he contends that cooperation, consensus and persuasion were elemental behaviorial aspects of early Medieval societies as opposed to top-down élite rule (Theuws 2008: 220; cf. Blanton and Feinman 2024). The importance of cooperation has also been advanced by Stuart Brookes: 'A general consensus amongst historians is that early medieval kingship was predicated to a great degree on politics of consensus – power resided in and drew from, the group over which it was exercised. In small-scale societies, rule is embedded in local social structures, personal relationships, and community dynamics, so that authority resides in the consensus that forms and legitimizes the existence of a political centre' (2020: 288–9; Escalona, Vésteinsson and Brookes 2019: 17–18 for a review of the concept). Persuasion and finding consensus as well as trust (in Max Weber's sense) mattered, as I shall argue, although this is not easily traced in the textual or archaeological record (Weber 1978: 212–16; cf. Wickham 1991: 191).

Callmer's model is also in many respects a Weberian approach to a subject often seen through the lens of Marxist traditions. It has received strong support from other Scandinavian archaeologists. Together they have concluded that it was craftsmen by necessity working together who trusted that they might operate outside kin-based circumstances that founded the emporia as nodal markets. Launching this theme, Callmer focused on how skilled individuals brokered established social customs. Through their economic agency, an urban class emerged that played a major social part in the Viking Age. Mutual solidarity, fuelled by a common economic interest and perhaps marginalization from mainstream rural society, may have led to the emergence of these dedicated trading places. This class, according to Søren Sindbæk, can be characterized by means of the sociologist Mark Granovetter's concept of 'weak ties' (1973). As defined by Granovetter, these are context-dependent, often professional or function-dependent relationships of friendship or trusted partnership established between people who are not initially related. They can be strongly involved and may be invested with considerable emotional significance. 'Such characteristics would have been indispensable for many of the practices associated with early towns and activities such as taking part in boat crews, forming trade partnerships, or even hosting or bartering' (Sindbæk 2023: 423). No less importantly, the mobility of craftsmen and merchants was perhaps the reason for the symbiotic relationship between these two classes of non-farmers. Callmer sums this up as follows: 'the Scandinavian or north European system with its characteristic craft production is, in my opinion, a singular phenomenon alien to the continent and the insular world. It more or less collapsed c. AD 1000. Some rather weak links to the later development of urbanism in Scandinavia cannot be denied, but what comes later is in many ways something new and more compatible with the continental and insular development of urbanism, trade and craft production' (Callmer 2020: 46; cf. Skre 2015).

Callmer's thesis has been strongly affirmed by Charlotte Hedenstierna-Jonson who, on the bases of her analyses of burial practices at the Swedish island-emporium of Birka, argued that

> the structural power still lay with the king and chieftains in the region, but they were unable to exercise direct power on the extensive network Birka belonged to. Instead, the real power shifted towards trading families. They owned resources and contacts abroad. They were also flexible and could provide themselves with the required military power to guard the commercial traffic. In the tenth century, Birka appears to have become increasingly self-governed.
>
> 215 (translated by Kalmring 2024: 156)

A century earlier, in the first decade of the ninth century, the status and well-being of the traders at *Reric* led to a high-profile conflict between Charlemagne and the Danish king, Godfred. Both leaders were evidently strongly committed to long-distance trade extending to Sweden and probably the emporium at Birka. *Reric* lay beyond the eastern border of Denmark at Groß Strömkendorf, on the eastern (Baltic Sea) shore of Wismar bay. The Danish king appropriated its merchants, and transplanted them on the very limits of his territory at a probable landing-place, Hedeby on the Schlei (see Kalmring 2010: 458 on the Hedeby chronology supported now by dendrochronology). This act angered Charlemagne to the extent that he marched with an army to confront the Danes. Godfred was eliminated by his peers and a treaty with Charlemagne was concluded. Significantly, though, the merchants whose plight attracted this extraordinary attention, settled at Hedeby. Their status was apparently safeguarded by both parties, and they operated as before as intermediaries with mercantile partnerships in Sweden. The importance of the conflict is perhaps best illustrated by the investment in the timber jetties at Hedeby in c. AD 815 to facilitate what was to be the first step in the making of a major Baltic Sea commercial hub.

Dagfinn Skre has advanced these points about traders and craftsmen still further. He contended that:

> the social sanctions on economic agency were reduced already in the nodal markets of the eighth century. However, the development of silver as currency and a generally accepted measure of value and means of saving in the ninth and tenth centuries demonstrated that the economic life of the towns was far more expansive and dynamic. The transformative significance of the early towns regarding the economies of the Scandinavian societies was not, however, primarily a matter of currencies and measures of value. Rather, it lay in the opportunity that the loose social networks and high frequency of transactions in the towns, created by long-distance trade and the urban way of life, provided for the growth of economic agency.
>
> 2015: 168

These issues of operating outside social sanctions, coupled with opportunities, have been formidably developed by Søren Sindbæk as a result of the (Danish Research Council's) Northern Emporium Project with its 'high-definition' excavations (and subsequent finds' studies) made at Posthustorvet, Ribe (Denmark) during 2016–22.

Sindbæk describes high-definition archaeology as part of the Third Science Revolution, as Kristiansen (2014) called it. This revolution involves the use of techniques for investigating materials at the level of isotopic and biomolecular composition. As we have seen, Third Science techniques have made a great impact in characterizing and provenancing materials and artefacts. As a result, materials like bone fragments and metalworking residues, which once had limited value for research, are now invaluable for identifying processes and interactions between craftsmen. Equally important, has been the improvement in dating archaeological contexts. The introduction of Bayesian statistical methods to refine the precision of radiocarbon dates, and the adoption of high-resolution calibration curves, have made it possible to bring archaeological levels into historical generations (Sindbæk 2022: 17). Isotopic analysis, proteomics and aDNA have been refined to shed new light on all aspects of the archaeological record. As a result, archaeology has moved beyond establishing relative sequences of major constructional events, to deploy elemental and biomolecular analysis of remains as a means to interpret micro-deposits in well-stratified sequences. Improvements in spatial recoding using flexible GIS platforms with laser scanned data have been as important. In sum, 'the archaeology of the emporia has thus developed in a hermeneutic dialogue between assumptions about historical dynamics and the design of excavations that were established to investigate them. For a generation at least, the most determined efforts have been directed towards revealing social organization and political embedment, reflecting a view of urbanism and exchange as a corollary of political evolution' (Sindbæk 2022: 18). Using detailed data, as I shall now show, Sindbæk and his collaborators have thrown new light on the very nature of an emporium community at Ribe.

The western Jutish emporium of Ribe at its zenith comprised at most 200 households, an estimated settled population of fewer than 1,000 people. Its cemeteries reveal a community of men, women and children, associated with material culture reflected by the emporium's crafts. They lived in timber dwellings with a heated main room, which could have accommodated an elementary family or a similar sized group such as a traveling party. 'That many of the excavated buildings stood for one or several decades and that artefact finds often reflect a similar pattern of craft activities throughout the course of the building's use-life imply that some of the inhabitants were long-term residents' (Sindbæk 2023: 443).

Ribe's population was largely displaced from their social networks. Rather than a community of family and kinsfolk, according to Sindbæk, this was 'a society of guests and neighbours' (2023: 416). They would have needed to work to construct the networks of mutual support and trust which were essential to an individual's survival and well-being. As Sindbæk (2023: 417) colourfully puts it, the emporium thus put socializing strategies on trial. To meet the socializing challenges the inhabitants had to devise tactics. One was clearly to rationalize obligations. The many finds of means of exchange, in particular (Wodan) sceatta coins minted in Ribe, suggest a situation in which coin circulation was used to resolve minor agreements and to define relations with foreign traders. 'Another option would be to reinforce bonds through the language of kinship. Runic texts from the late Viking Age abound in people related as *félagi* (fellows, partners), *gildar* (guild brothers), or styling each other as 'brothers' in circumstances where we may suspect that they were not related by birth' (Sindbæk 2023: 416). It is not known when exactly these terms and institutions evolved, yet a similar appeal to professed kinship or oath-sworn bonds may have been conceived and practised in the eighth- or ninth-century emporium. Yet another way for the inhabitants to forge links was by marriage.

What the finds from the excavations provide is an astonishing assemblage of artefacts relating to craft and household activities. These include equipment for drinking, gaming pieces, and a striking number of hair combs. Managing one's hair and combing were social activities. Like the tonsured hair of ninth-century monks, visual communication of social status in the town as well as the opportunity to expend time and resources on the appearance mattered (Ashby 2014). Tuning pegs and a fragment of a lyre show that music and other entertainment were also part of these socializing strategies.

The emporium, then, following Callmer's model, was a laboratory for professional or function-dependent relationships of friendship or partnerships established between strangers who were not kin-related. These relationships may have been formed by taking part in boat crews, forming trade partnerships, or even hosting or bartering. The bedrock of craft relations in Ribe was the opportunity to work collectively

(Ashby, Coutu and Sindbæk 2015; Ashby and Sindbæk 2020). There were practical benefits facilitated from a gathering of networks, what economists call agglomeration effects. These relationships are especially visible in craft production. Many processes in craftsmanship required more than one pair of hands. At the same time, learning the skills of a craft was a long process. Maintaining a refined craft like those discovered in the Posthustorvet excavations presupposes that craftsmen and their apprentices had the opportunity to work together over long periods, not just at a summer market. At the same time, the archaeology indicates that many craftsmen were associated with Ribe over decades. 'It may be precisely the concentration of work, not incessant round trips, which lies behind the uniformity of the Viking-age art culture: urban craftsman could mass-produce standardized goods made for a market, rather than something that was processed to order for an individual buyer' (Sindbæk 2023: 424). Access to other artisans was the hallmark of the town. Craftsmen had opportunities to develop their skills that were impossible when working in isolation. Maintaining craftsmanship was not an individual occupation, but a practice made possible by craft collectives. Craft procurement chains, it is now known, extended over large distances, involving other specialists became fundamental to maintain output and standards (Ashby, Coutu and Sindbæk 2015; Ashby and Sindbæk, 2020). Unlike the flat structure of networks, supply chains were by nature polar structures which convey connections and, as often as not, tensions brought about by distance (Hahn 2018: 10).

The crafts in the towns of the Viking Age were thus not just an occupation for individuals – a bead-maker, a blacksmith, a carpenter, a comb-maker, a jeweler, or a leather worker. Much of what was made in Ribe required a combination of different materials and techniques, and invariably called for the collaboration of several craftsmen. As a result, these artisans were rooted in Ribe as a community to an even greater degree than visiting merchants, or rulers who patronized the place and its trade. Without these specialists' access to materials, to far-reaching supply chains just as King Alfred's Norwegian visitor, Ohthere described in the 890s (see below, p.154), to customers, and to skills' training, a large part of the refined material culture would not have been possible (Croix, Neiss and Sindbæk 2019; Sindbæk 2023: 425). All of this brings to mind the anthropologist Mary Helms' observations on how craftsmen stood outside social sanctions (1993; 52): 'Skilled artisans are generally judged to be "different". Artisans are 'distinct from ordinary people pursuing the mundane, pragmatic affairs associated with the immediate needs of daily life.' Helms adds: 'Their separation from their home setting may be temporary or permanent, voluntary or involuntary, characteristic of a particular stage in their careers or characteristic of their calling in general. Their reasons may be immediately pragmatic or may reflect more esoteric political-ideological ends. Whatever the reasons for or whatever the degree of their involvement with spatial distance, skilled artisans nonetheless are frequently associated with the geographically outside realm, a world which also generally carries supernatural associations of some sort' (Helms 1993: 32; see also Helms 2004).

Craftsmen like merchants, as Callmer, Hedenstierna-Jonson, Skre and now Sindbæk and his collaborators have shown, may have been detached from the established rules of a kin-based society, yet through networking these specialists possessed a status (and an opportunity to experiment) that was every bit as much of the hallmark of the Viking Age by the ninth century as the infamous sea-kings.

As I shall show, these Scandinavian models help to reframe the new evidence for the history of the English emporia, their productive territories, and the beginnings of regional towns. This evidence is now complimented by new archaeological discoveries arising from the activities of metal-detectorists, pre-eminent of which are the remains of the overwintering camp at Torksey made by the Danish Great Army of AD 872–3 (Hadley and Richards 2020). Here, as I shall explain in Chapter 4, a large Viking army was accompanied by craftsmen as well as ample means of exchange, who before very long were actively involved in the creation of new urban colonies – diasporas. In sum, as the Vikings conquered territories, the 'gift' (Price 2020: 399) that they gave to these places was a comprehension of the opportunities inherent in exchange and industrial production – as well as of a distinctive (Scandinavian) urban culture and its socializing strategies.

This book: the debate

This book aims to pursue the (ongoing) debates about the genesis of Anglo-Saxon towns, addressing the Scandinavian models using new ('high-definition') data. It explores the question of when and how English early Medieval settlements gained a distinctive urban identity as centres of production as well as distribution. To do this, it considers the historical contexts of the four known English emporia and their relationship to

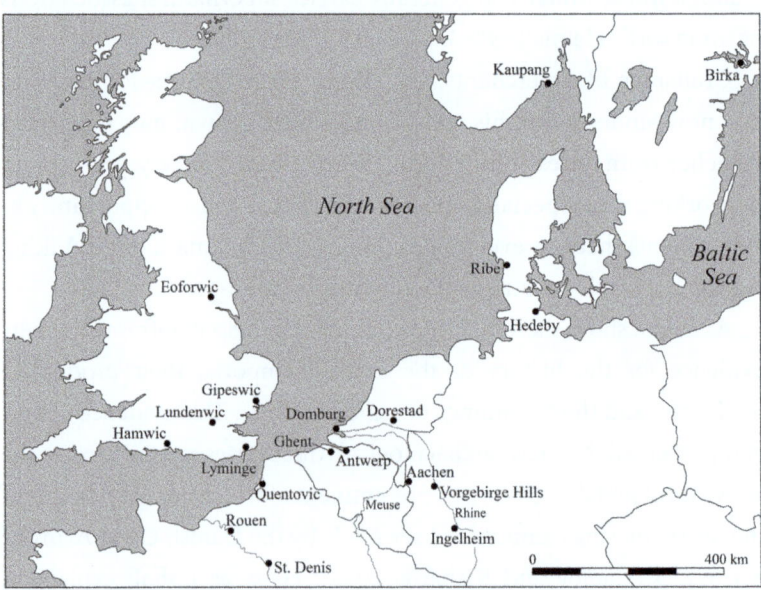

Figure 1.3 Map showing the principal places mentioned in the text.

earlier landing-places. It then assesses their individual histories, showing that the continuity of each of these places into the mid-ninth century has been largely assumed and now merits reassessing. (The absence of 'high-definition' archaeological methods employed in Ribe, for example, has restricted the development of finer chronological interpretations of these English places.) This reassessment shows the growing prominence of Anglo-Saxon regional production and exchange for political purposes similar in some respects to the process of rural development in Francia. It also emphasizes the importance of changing relations of political power (with the demotion of the church), based upon tribute to support military forces. This political development on the path to state formation was embedded in the kingdoms and landscapes of England when the Great Danish Army invaded in AD 865, and over the following decade conquered East Anglia, Mercia and Northumbria. Looking closely at the archaeological and numismatic evidence, Wessex – which under King Alfred's leadership, eventually resisted and defeated the Danes – emerges as arguably the least developed region at this time. West Saxon history, promoted in the *Anglo-Saxon Chronicle*, stands to be re-read in the light of the archaeological and numismatic evidence. What swiftly followed was an urban revolution in the later 880s and 890s (articulated by a silver bullion then a monetary economy (cf. Skre 2011; 2017)), led initially by the Danes who brought craftsmen and moneyers with them to settle the newly conquered territories. New towns were established in the Danelaw territory, and in Ipswich's case, the East Anglian emporium was revived as one of several major centres in the region.

The diaspora's urban revolution prompted two reactions from the West Saxons. A fortified London was re-founded in about AD 886 within the old Roman walls of Londinium as Lundenburh. From the outset it appears to have been envisaged as a large emporium. At the same time, a new capital was created at Winchester. A decade later at most, a civil defence system of refuges was established across the kingdom, recorded in a text known as the Burghal Hidage. This system, created in the 890s and early 900s, was to evolve only slowly over the course of the later tenth century to evolve into a network of regional market towns mirroring the Anglo-Scandinavian towns. By 1066 and the Norman Conquest, England boasted as many as 100 towns with about 10 per cent of the population living in these places. The debate about the origins of Anglo-Saxon towns – about who founded them and who managed them and how – hinges on detailed chronological evidence, analysed archaeological materials including metal-detector finds (especially coins), and an interpretation of an established urban culture within the ninth-century Viking world.

As Pirenne pointed out in *Medieval Cities*, the system of West Saxon refuges has been often compared to the fortified ports and towns of the County of Flanders (2014: 46–7). These were some of the earliest towns within the late Carolingian and post-Carolingian realms. Based in established coastal assembly and periodic trading places, these embryonic ports were to prosper and create a distinctive merchant culture by the eleventh century. As such, their origins, as I have pointed out, were signally important to Pirenne's narrative. It is appropriate, then, to make an excursus to examine if there was an English contribution to Flanders and its towns.

This debate needs now to examine why the Danish towns in their newly conquered territories prospered so quickly, and why this impacted one late Carolingian region in particular. Was it, for example, Danes – erstwhile sea-kings – who introduced an urban ethos that a century ago intrigued Henri Pirenne (2014 [1925]) and Max Weber (1966 [1921]), and during the tenth century set in motion a process that ultimately was to underpin Europe's Medieval civilization? In this context, agent-oriented socioeconomics are often overlooked yet are emerging as an increasingly important factor in interpreting the economic strategies of this transformative period (cf. Ögren, Hedenstierna-Jonson, Ljungkvist, Raffield and Price 2022). This foregrounds the importance of mobile tax structures and (oral) jurisdiction practices – issues beyond the scope of the archaeological record itself – that evolved through connections between the Viking diaspora and the mercantile groups each interacted with. It also highlights the importance of bullion and coinage to increasingly centralized kingship as methods of expressing status as well as controlling exchange. By asking questions about the political intentions and strategies of the seventh to tenth centuries, archaeology is shedding new light on key chapters in the canonical history of not just English urbanism but also the making of the European economy.

2

The 'False Dawn of the Age of Emporia'?

given the scarce indications from the sources…., an enquiry into possible sub-periods is nevertheless a step towards a more nuanced approach of the period as a whole

Verhulst 2002: 133

Roman Britain was a province with a highly intensive agricultural regime and manufacturing largely managed in the countryside. Townlife was significant but not central to the economy. With the abandonment of the province by the army and its bureaucracy in the early fifth century, this economy collapsed and with it, towns. Britannia was quite clearly failing for a generation before the Roman administration quit the island. The archaeology of fourth-century Britain before the withdrawal reveals a steady political fissioning as well as a sharp economic deterioration – a 'great disentanglement', as the historian, Robin Fleming has called it (Fleming 2021). Almost certainly Britannia was a victim of fourth-century inflation and the collapse of fiduciary instruments like credit that had been for several centuries a cornerstone of the Roman economy (Jones 1953; cf. Bagnall and Bransbourg 2019). Some sub-Roman statelets attempted to resist the political fragmentation. Connections across the English Channel to Gaul may have sustained pockets of continuity, but these should not be exaggerated. Major later Roman towns such as St Albans and Wroxeter, for example, appear to have become nodal centres of sub-Roman resilience. Other centres surely existed supporting reduced intra-regional redistribution of limited agricultural goods. At the erstwhile regional capital of Wroxeter, for example, excavations show that large timber buildings for a generation or two filled the area of the open space that was once the old Roman forum (Crabtree 2018: 32–6; 47–9). Large though these many buildings were, the accompanying material culture was minimal. Commodities that had been manufactured and consumed in massive quantities, no longer existed. Specialized production had collapsed. As it happens, Wroxeter is a fifth-century illustration of a ruralisation that was to occur in many Roman towns a century or two later in the Mediterranean regions.

The absence of manufactured goods almost certainly contributed to the reception of Continental traders bringing prestige goods in exchange for British products. Three (Merovingian-period) trade routes reaching to the British Isles, beginning in the later fifth century, have been identified. The first of these was an Atlantic Ocean trade route; the second reached across from northern France to southern England between the Solent and Kent; the third connected the mouths of the rivers Scheldt and Rhine to areas in eastern England, ranging from Kent to Lincolnshire.

The Atlantic Ocean trade route had two distinct phases. The earliest, in the period, *c.* AD 480–550, brought Late Roman amphorae, tableware and glassware as well as perhaps perishables by way of Vigo in north-west Spain to Tintagel Head, and other small landing places in western Britain. This was the only direct trade between the Mediterranean and the British Isles at the time, and the only Late Roman route to deliver transport amphorae to north-west Europe. Tintagel Head on the north Cornish coast – Pen Du, in Cornish – is a place long associated with King Arthur. For the period between AD 400–650, it was the largest and in material terms arguably the richest settlement in the British Isles. Recent excavations show that it possessed rectangular buildings set upon south-facing terraces not unlike the timber halls found at Wroxeter. Associated with the settlement were middens in which the debris of the imported goods have been discovered (Nowakowski 2018). The diagnostic potsherds are predominantly Bi (LRA 2) and Bii (LRA 1) amphorae, primarily from the Cypro-Syrian region and the Aegean coast of western Asia Minor respectively, and polished ceramic tablewares – principally Phocaean Red Slip wares from Asia Minor. Accompanying these are also sherds of southern French (Provençal) grey decorated tablewares and fine glassware (Duggan 2018). The most striking features of this commerce are the signal concentration of imports at Tintagel, and a lesser redistribution of the vessels throughout greater Dumnonia that is remarkable by later Medieval distribution standards. These Mediterranean imports have also been found in small quantities at minor royal sites in Wales and Ireland. Some imported amphorae also had an afterlife. These were reused, we now know from a recent analysis, almost certainly to store mead (Moffett 2017). The household middens suggest that Tintagel's inhabitants were imitating Roman dining culture. Whether the oils and wine were also employed in a Christian liturgy, of course, is a matter of speculation. We may suppose, nevertheless, that these imports in an otherwise materially

Figure 2.1 View of the east-facing terraces on Tintagel Head (photo: author).

underdeveloped world spoke eloquently through visuality and touch of coming from afar.

Tintagel appears as though it was a redistributive nodal centre in the Irish Sea provinces and Dumnonia, a greater Cornwall encompassing territory as far as Selwood Forest in eastern Somerset – an imagined Atlantic Sea community – bringing Iberian and Aquitanian knowledge to a peripheral region of the former Roman Britain.

A second but separate wave of imports into the Irish sea province, almost certainly emanating from Aquitaine, occurred in the mid-sixth to later seventh centuries. Distinctive E-ware pitchers and tablewares as well as glass vessels occur in Cornwall, and in larger numbers in Ireland, Wales and South-West Scotland (Campbell 2007; Doyle 2021). This trade coincided in the mid-sixth century with the emergence of the Irish church as a major force in Ireland, and an apparent spike in fortified settlements associated with the intensification of agriculture.

The rise of 'Tintagel' as a redistributive centre cannot have gone unnoticed by the Anglo-Saxon polities in southern and eastern England. The polities were coalescing and by the end of the sixth century were formed around 'ostentatious' leaders occupying post-built timber palaces not so dissimilar in size from the Wroxeter halls of the preceding century (cf. Blair 2018: 115–25; see also McBride 2020). These almost certainly formed parts of new polyfocal districts in which a combination of social and economic operations occurred. Certainly, by the later seventh century, this polyfocality became very apparent. Driving it were mortuary practices accompanying the political evolution amongst the many tribal communities. These led to a demand for imported luxuries as gifts to the gods, as well as increasing production in village settings of mortuary vessels. As noted above, the imported luxuries arrived by way of two different routes, the northern French route and those stemming from the Low Countries. Unlike the Atlantic Ocean routes, luxuries were brought by way of western Europe's riverine networks to these two staging points for transshipment to southern and eastern England. One route followed the Rhône valley from Marseilles, leading to the Seine valley or north to the Meuse valley. The other was a transalpine route that brought Mediterranean goods and exotica by way of upper Adriatic Sea ports up the Rhine.

By the mid-to later sixth century, Frankish mariners were trading from the Canche valley, where the emporium of Quentovic was to be created by about AD 600; from the Seine mouth, and from points along the Normandy coast. Together, these traders formed the southern zones of what the historian, Ian Wood described as the Merovingian North Sea (see Wood 1983; for a counter argument, see Clarke-Neish 2021). There appears to have been little or no overlap of exchange involving the Aquitanian traders and their partners operating in the Irish Sea provinces.

Traders operating to the north set out from what was to become known as Frisia. These sixth-century mariners were the celebrated Frisian traders, who later traveled from the port of Dorestad and its neighbour, Domburg to eastern England, northern Frisia and the western Baltic Sea regions. A remarkable archaeological insight into the character of these early traders has come to light in the sixth-century riverine village at Oegstgeest, less than 3 kilometres from open water, on the banks of the River Rhine. We cannot be sure that Oegstgeest organized and participated in this international trade from the mid-sixth to the early eighth centuries, but the archaeology is revealing (de Bruin, Bakels and Theuws 2021). The extensive excavations now fully published illustrate the heady rise of this village engaged in Rhine-riverine transshipment, and its abandonment soon after Dorestad was founded about AD 680. It is not too farfetched to envisage these villagers were some of the stakeholders in creating the emporium.

It is unclear whether the village at Oegstgeest was built on the bank of the main river channel or a channel parallel to the main channel. The inhabited site was not an uninterrupted dry strip of land as it was dissected by gullies, little streams and depressions. The timber houses were built on raised platforms. The villagers combatted the water by building dams, but these measures were only partly successful against flooding. Twenty-nine excavated buildings were identified as houses. Another seven possible houses were noted. The settlement existed between c. AD 550 ± 15 and 725 ±15. The excavators estimated six houses existing contemporaneously with approximately ten persons per house, making an average settlement population of sixty.

Each farm lay within a fenced, wickerwork compound. Within the compound were multiple timber outhouses, pits and wells, as well as one or more timber houses. Many of the dwellings were partitioned internally, to accommodate livestock. Animal husbandry was important; every farmhouse had a stable to keep ten to fifteen cows. Even short houses may have incorporated a stable for keeping cows. These numbers are likely to be minimum numbers. The stables may have been used for special animals such as milking cows. Cattle that needed less attention were kept on the flood plains. Although it is difficult to identify amenities for keeping sheep in the compounds, the faunal remains suggest the villagers kept sheep too. Pigs, too, were probably raised in the farmyards. Grain production was modest in view of the limitations of the landscape surrounding the settlement and the available space to plough. Oegstgeest's inhabitants were probably involved in fishing both on the river and in coastal waters. The archaeological evidence shows the inhabitants practised crafts such as iron smelting, copper alloy working and working with imported amber. Other non-agricultural activities such as textile production, bone-working and wood-working may have been normal practice in each farmstead. What is surprising is how much Oegstgeest's inhabitants depended on the provisioning of utensils, base materials and food from outside sources, some of them as far away as the middle Rhine valley, the Mediterranean, the Baltic Sea region and England.

Oegstgeest's inhabitants belonged to the last generations of Merovingians to be interred with rich grave goods. Consequently, the range of their connections is particularly clear. Apart from the graves, the ditches, pits, wells and gulleys in the compounds also produced an extraordinary wealth of objects. Pride of place goes to a silver hanging bowl with garnet inlaid escutcheons decorated with figures picked out in gold leaf. Found discarded in a gulley, this magnificent seventh-century object was probably made in an Austrasian workshop. Eight gold tremisses from Frankish mints and twenty-five (later seventh- to early eighth-century) silver sceattas were discovered, showing paradoxically an evolved use of currency. From the graves come gold, silver and copper alloy jewellery, glasses and bead, some of which originated from Near Eastern or Indian Ocean sources (Langbroek in de Bruin, Bakels and Theuws 2021: 278–93). Perhaps the most remarkable finds are prosaic discoveries: these include leather turnshoes, grape pips and remains of a fig (de Bruin, Bakels and Theuws 2021: 443).

The key to the rationale and economy of this riverside settlement and its exotic wealth, vulnerable as it was to Rhine floods, is almost certainly the wooden barrels reused as wells by the inhabitants. These arrived here as wine containers, although they may have contained grain too. Sixteen barrels have been found at Oegstgeest. Two types of barrels were found. The smaller barrels were on average 133 centimetres high and 74 centimetres wide and had a capacity to contain some 480 litres of wine. The larger barrels stood more than 2 metres high, resembling those from the later emporium of Dorestad, were on average 300 centimetres high and 70–80 centimetres wide with a capacity of 1,500 litres (de Bruin, Bakels and Theuws 2021: 455). The Oegstgeest barrels show that the wine trade, so important to Dorestad, existed generations before the town existed.

Consumption at Oegstgeest took two contrasting forms. Agrarian consumption resembles the many Frisian mound settlements excavated over the past century. It is unexceptional. The moveable material culture, on the other hand, strongly resembles the emergence of ostentatious wealth in eastern England around AD 600, as well as that found in the central Swedish Vendel-era tombs. Mediterranean and middle Rhine goods were being consumed in life and death. On this coastal edge, however, while subscribing to an apparent display of wealth, the dwellings, unlike the ostentatious timber halls of England or southern Scandinavia at this time, broadly conformed to contemporary farming norms.

Theuws (in de Bruin, Bakels and Theuws 2021) proposes that the inhabitants of Oegstgeest and similar riverine communities were sometimes known as *Ribuarii*, 'dwellers of river banks'. These were different from coastal dwellers and inland inhabitants. Near the coast, this distinction might blur because some of the people in the estuaries such as the Rhine might also be interpreted as coastal dwellers. In an important assessment of these liminal communities, Christopher Loveluck and Dries Tys (2006) suggested that the trade of the mariners lay beyond the control of (Merovingian) domanial lords, which is one of the reasons for their freedom to specialize and exchange goods. Later written sources, their argument goes, have seduced us to search for aristocrats and control of (agrarian) production and exchange. The world of the riverine inhabitants must be interpreted differently. The excavated evidence from Oegstgeest shows how dependent its inhabitants were for their provisioning on the riverine exchange network. The role of these riverine people in what unfolded in north-west Europe, as the Mediterranean economy steadily collapsed in the sixth and seventh centuries, reveals a world that lay not only beyond the landed producers but no less importantly, outside the grasp of the church. This makes the entrepreneurial outcomes of their trading activities, as Pirenne long ago anticipated, all the more fascinating. Viewed alongside their later Merovingian contemporaries, the importance of the Oegstgeest traders is inescapable. We need to note that their Frankish peers in Aquitaine, trading to the Irish Sea communities, delivering E wares, glass vessels and surely much more besides to an economically expansive Celtic world, failed to stimulate the creation of permanent emporia or any enduring reputation (Campbell 2007). By contrast, these Rhine-mouth entrepreneurs secured Mediterranean and Frankish exotica through dendritic networks not only from the Rhineland, but in time also by way of the Rhône (from Marseilles) and through Neustria to the Meuse valley. No less remarkable were the consumption and apparent display of moveable goods by these Rhine-mouth farmer-traders. They appear to have lived like kings without palaces.

It was probably mariners from places like Oegstgeest that arrived at beach sites around the south and east coast of England, neutral places where luxuries could be exchanged for English products including staples like woolen goods. The impact of these traders and their luxuries for exchange – as in Dumnonia and the Irish sea provinces at this time – is hard to gauge but cannot be understated. A century later with the creation of the English emporia (about AD 680), international commerce came to define a stage in the political economies of England. These neutral, landing places were sites that I described as type A emporia in *Dark Age Economics*, periodic places of intra-regional exchange that articulated gift-giving within the emerging English polities, and especially fueled mortuary rites where the dead were accompanied with grave goods. Coastal erosion has removed many of these landing-places. An important site, however, is believed to have existed near Burnham Overy on the north Norfolk coast, where an associated cemetery is rich in imported jewellery and objects (Rogerson 2003; I. Hodges 2025). Might the associated village have been an Anglo-Saxon version of Oegstgeest that transshipped imports to points along the East Anglian, Lincolnshire and Yorkshire coasts? The vestigial remains of a beach site, of a later date – probably eighth to ninth century – was excavated in south-east Kent at Sandtun (Gardiner et al. 2001). Otherwise, as along the perforated Pas-de-Calais, Flemish, Frisian and Danish coastlines, these ephemeral places are generally known – in the absence of discovering versions of Oegstgeest – from unprovenanced finds, especially after the later seventh century by concentrations of coins (see, for example, Loveluck and Tys 2006; Tys 2010; 2018; and Søvsø 2020: 127). These landing places, though, were not permanent nodal hubs any more than Oegstgeest or Tintagel were, and not urban in any institutional sense but almost certainly formed part of polyfocal settlements (cf. Skre 2008). They were, however, experiments in building trust with strangers. This led to new laws on hosting that paved the way for the creation of larger communities of strangers. The Laws of Hlothhere and Eadric, for instance, issued in Kent between AD 673 and AD 685, make it clear that hosting strangers was a common practice that fashioned social obligations: '[i]f anyone harbours a stranger, a trader or any other man who has come across the frontier, for three nights in his own home, and then supplies him with food ... the man is to bring the other to justice or to discharge the obligations for him' (Whitelock 1955: 361). Trade was ushering in changes in social relations as was the pioneering church.

Nonetheless, hosting strangers was confined to liminal places. It should be noted that the colonization of ruined Roman towns such as Canterbury, Winchester and York by the church after AD 600 did not lead to the institution of production and trading activities in these places with their ancient histories. For the next century or more, these were places of élite settlement with limited or no engagement in manufacturing or obvious material redistribution.

Of the four known Anglo-Saxon emporia – Eoforwic (York), Gipeswic (Ipswich), Hamwic (Southampton) and Lundenwic (London) – all probably began as places of periodic exchange by the early to mid-seventh century before each was eventually re-envisioned as a permanent town. This evolution from a seasonal or periodic point of exchange to a permanent emporium – from my type A to type B emporia, as I called them in *Dark Age Economics* – has been proposed for Domburg (Deckers 2022); Dorestad (Theuws 2004); and further north, at Ribe (cf. Søvsø 2020: 127), and later, in the earlier ninth century, at Hedeby (Søvsø 2020), and Kaupang (Skre 2008). The conditions for re-envisioning each of these places, however, can no longer be assumed to be the same. Each place, as we shall now see, was a keystone in the economic transformation of a kingdom.

The English emporia

The English almost certainly did not invent the early Medieval emporium. The concept owes its origins to the third quarter of the seventh century. Century-old trading zones had been established by this time, essentially separating Frisians from Frankish traders. Whether Anglo-Saxon traders were also active in cross-Channel exchange is largely a matter of speculation, though the case has been

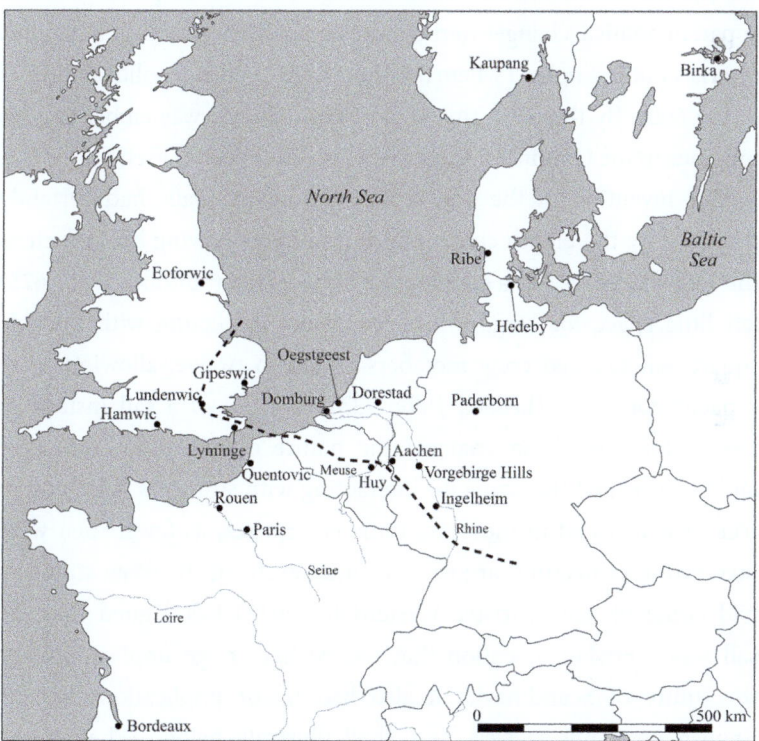

Figure 2.2 Map showing the trading zones, Franks versus Frisians.

made for an Anglo-Saxon diaspora in the Pas-de-Calais (Lebecq, Bethouart and Verslype 2010; Soulat 2010). Anglo-Saxon traders were apparently present at the St Denis fair by the eighth century, although how prominent they were in international trade remains largely enigmatic. Like Frankish traders, those from England were overshadowed in the written sources by the Frisians (Lebecq 2000: 143). With good reason, the historian, Stéphane Lebecq has questioned whether these textual references to these traders may have been a catch-all for merchants from the Frankish coastline (Lebecq 2020).

What prompted this sudden spike in cross-Channel trade in the 660s and 670s that led to the foundation of the first emporia? A conjunction of two new technical developments certainly occurred at this time, the sail and the sceatta, the new silver coinage. More to the point, the most apparent political changes were occurring not in the Frankish kingdoms or Frisia but in England where the church emerged as a political force as of the 660s. By the 680s, the Anglo-Saxon church was embarking on missions to the Continent, such was its bullish belief in itself.

The invention of the sail, replacing rowing boats, had certainly occurred by the eighth century in Frisia. Large rowing boats such as the ship that served as a cenotoph at Sutton Hoo (Suffolk) (*c.* AD 625) left little space for cargoes. Improvements in rigging with a single square sail reduced crew members to ten to twelve, allowing more capacity for cargo (Lebecq 1999: 233). The use of a sail instead of rowers for propulsion changed the nature of maritime commerce and transformed the scope for interacting with strangers. Much more trust was invested in these maritime enterprises, as fewer men were involved in protecting cargoes. Brokering exchange between strangers had come of age. Christer Westerdahl (2015) has argued that the sail was a Frisian invention that was to have huge implications for the future of Scandinavia. It also had major implications for the English economy as well, as I shall illustrate below. Whether the sail was an adaptation of local traditions in Frisia, or of a Byzantine maritime concept remains to be resolved. Certainly, Byzantine sailing ships were still plying the Mediterranean at this time and might have served as models that were adapted in Frisia. The Frisian vessels were presumably the predecessors of the *cog-* and *hulc*-type ships that formed the basis of later boat-building traditions in the North Sea region (Ellmers 1972: 59–64; Crumlin-Pedersen 2010: 75). The most complete example of an early Medieval Frankish ship is the Port Berteau II wreck, a 14.6-metre-long sailing ship constructed c. AD 600 (Rieth, Carrierre-Desbois and Serna 2001). The boat was found in the river Charente in western France, but would certainly have been able to navigate coastal waters, with a capacity of about 6–7 tons of cargo. Sails, for example, appear to be implied in the biography of St Boniface. According to the *Vita*, composed shortly after his death in AD 754, Boniface first travelled to Frisia in AD 716. First, he journeyed to 'a market for the buying and selling of merchandise... called Lundenwic'. From this port 'after a few days, when the sailors were about to embark on their return home, Boniface asked permission of the shipmaster to go on board, and after paying his fare he set sail and came with favourable winds to Dorestad' (Talbot 1954: Chapter 4). Such sailing ships – as opposed to large rowing boats – facilitated open-sea navigation as well as an increase in cargo sizes. The corollary, of course, was that production of sails called for significantly increased wool production. Looking far ahead, textile archaeologists have pointed out that by the early eleventh century the total sailcloth requirements for the Danish and Norwegian fleet would have amounted to about one million square metres – the annual production of two million sheep (Price 2020: 386–93). Of course, in the seventh century the amount of sailcloth required was far less. A sea-going craft at this time would have required about 0.3–0.75 kilograms of wool per square metre, a single sheep producing about 1–2.5 kilograms. A sail of 80 square metres, in other words, needed approximately 40 kilograms of wool. 'It would have taken two-person years of ten hours days to make just one main sail weighing around fifty kilos, and nobody would have put to sea without reserve sailcloth that might save lives' (Price 2020: 388). Did Frisia have enough sheep to support the new requirements of its seventh-century mercantile fleet, or was wool for this purpose being imported from England to the Continent as it was a century later, when Charlemagne mentioned woolen cloaks in correspondence with Offa? I shall return to this question in Chapter 3, but there can be little doubt that the invention of the sail, with larger cargoes, also inaugurated the need to employ acceptable means to broker trade between strangers.

A second invention of these decades in the North Sea region, on a par with the sail, was the introduction of silver coinage in the 670s. This has to be contextualized. It may be no coincidence that the new coinage occurred as the English church was developing new political management methods. Pre-eminently, writing now redefined socio-religious authority: it became a matter of following the correct performance or enactment of the script (Goody 1987: 161). Indeed, the very presence of writing and written records introduced new dynamics: 'producing the sense of breach between then and now, or here and there. Such ruptures can cause conflict, contradiction, a spirit of critical scrutiny of received knowledge, and the incentive to try and overcome historical time' (Bell 1997: 202). The earliest laws issued by Kentish kings, then the West Saxon king, Ina, date to the mid- to later seventh century, accompanied by regulations for charging customs and tolls that Middleton has likened to contemporary Byzantine models (2005). Small denomination coinage now made far more sense to facilitate exchange between strangers than Merovingian gold tremisses (Theuws 2019). However, unlike the sail, this may have been an English rather than a Frisian invention. On the basis of the iconography of the earliest coinage, Frans Theuws has argued that the English church issued the initial, so-called primary sceattas (2019). Millions of these small silver coins would be minted over the following seventy-five years. Tellingly, sceattas occur, not just in trading sites but also in purses in the final phase of interring grave goods with the dead (cf. Brownlee 2021; Scull and Naylor 2016). In this transition period in the decades after c. AD 660, as new mortuary rites were introduced, Christopher Scull and John Naylor conclude that:

> the deposition of silver pennies was the burial of portable wealth in its unequivocal monetary form, and the dead buried with purses or bags of money were being provided with items that symbolized worth in a form divested of symbolic charge linked to other aspects of social identity. It is therefore tempting to see in this very specific and very late feature of furnished burial some indication of an understanding and acceptance of the monetisation implied by the promulgation of the silver coinages.
>
> 2016: 230; cf. Woods 2021: 15, Table 1

As Italy, for example, was becoming a coinless society at this time (Rovelli 2009), early Christian England was being monetized and remained so throughout the following centuries.

The primary series of sceattas dating to c. 665/80–700/10 marked an uptick in the Merovingian North Sea trade, coinciding with the first emporia. Their aim, in Theuws' view, was to control an exchange of silver for Frankish wine and other commodities. Spectrographic analyses throw light on this as well as the role of the Anglo-Saxon church in developing cross-Channel commerce (Kershaw et al. 2024). The analyses show that Byzantine silver plate, of the kind interred in the Sutton Hoo ship burial in c. AD 625, was the principal metal source for these new coins. The acquisition of this plate must surely have been principally in the hands of the churchmen who, already by the 660s, were criss-crossing Europe to seek support and guidance from the Pope in Rome. In sum, building up extant trading relationships stemming back to the later sixth century, these two new technical concepts – the sail and the use of a distinctive silver coinage for brokering exchange – were probably promoted by the church to further advance their political status. This incremental increase in the volume of trade almost certainly instigated the creation of places dedicated to its control, the emporia.

The earliest emporium engaged in cross-Channel commerce, judging from the sceattas, was located at Domburg on the island of Walcharen beyond the Scheldt estuary. It appears to date to *c.* AD 660/70 but it may owe its origins to the pioneering traders who crossed to England from this island as early as the late sixth century (Deckers 2022). Walcharen had been a Roman temple site before it became a large permanent embarkation point for voyages to England and points northward. Who created this place is not known, but with more than a thousand sceatta finds from the present sand dunes, it was undoubtedly very active. To the north, the emporium of Dorestad – later described as the *vicus famosus* by the missionary, Liudger – was

Figure 2.3 A primary sceatta, series BII, bird and cross type, NMS-732075 (courtesy of the British Museum's Portable Antiquities Scheme).

founded about AD 670/80, judging from the dendrochronological dates of its earliest jetties and Rhenish wine barrels, as well as its coins (van Es and Verwers 1980; Theuws 2004; Willemsen and Kik 2010; 2015). In all likelihood some small trading place had existed here associated with the gold tremisses minted by Madelinus as early as AD 650. Some uncertainty remains as to whether it was a permanent urban centre from the 680s. Its excavators now believe that construction only began at a modest scale and on a small number of plots (van Es and Verwers 2015: 381). Initially, the need for landing facilities was slight, possibly because it was only used on a seasonal basis until the 720s (van Es and Verwers 2015: 383).

Who exactly founded this emporium is also a subject of debate. Dorestad may have begun life as a trading hub for a collective of local magnates before it became a place of political contention in the 690s between the Frisian leader, King Radbod and the Austrasian Mayor of the Palace, Pippin II (who controlled the source of the wine traded to England) (Fritze, 1971; Fouracre 2000: 53; Wood 2001: 57). Later Anglo-Saxon written sources link both leaders to Utrecht and its surroundings where the English missionary, Willibrord was to consolidate an important bishopric. In recounting this entangled story, Radbod is described by later biographers of the missionary as a king, possibly using petty Anglo-Saxon kings as a model. By contrast, the Frankish authors refer to him as a *dux*, an aristocrat comparable with other high-ranking aristocrats, such as Pippin II, his principal adversary. The uncertainty about Radbod's status may well confirm the ethnically separate and pivotal circumstances of the loosely associated people he claimed to represent (cf. Lebecq 2020). As we shall see, in the ninth century, the separateness of Dorestad and its territory, despite its established commercial reputation, was recognized when this was given by the Carolingian Emperor to the Danish leader, Rorik (Cooijmans 2020: 174–7).

The third known emporium along this perforated Continental coast that may have prompted the creation of the English emporia was

Quentovic. This had been the site of a Merovingian mint since the beginning of the seventh century, and almost certainly was made into a permanent settlement at the same time as Dorestad. It lay some 15 kilometres inland in the Canche valley, south of Boulogne-sur-Mer at a place now known as Vismarest, close to road connections leading across the kingdom of Neustria. Excavations have yet to determine its foundation date, although a late seventh-century origin is consistent with the ceramic chronology discovered in limited investigations (Lebecq, Bethouart and Verslype 2010; Cense-Bacquet 2021). Whether there were other emporia serving these trading zones remains a matter of conjecture. Rouen certainly emerged as an emporium, but probably not before the later ninth century (Mayo 2003).

These three sites – Domburg, Dorestad and Quentovic – were notable at this time for their liminality. All three lay in coastal territory that was then occupied by marginal ethnic groups: the Frisians at Domburg and Dorestad (cf. Lebecq 2020), and possibly Anglo-Saxon settlers in the coastal strip of the Pas-de-Calais (Soulat 2010). In effect, as many historians have pointed out, these were essentially neutral places – brokerage points – that came to have associations with political élites and churches, but were principally hubs of redistribution of outward flows of Frankish goods and inward flows of English and northern Frisian produce (cf. Theuws 2019). As such, these were non-places, not necessarily at this time engaged in craft production, exploiting commercial opportunities (cf. Augé 1995). Plainly, judging from the distribution of the earliest, so-called primary sceattas, England was the principal target of these traders, as the different kingdoms after the mid-seventh century – in concert with the church – invested in intensifying agricultural production (Blair 2018; Rippon, Smart and Pears 2015; McKerracher and Hamerow 2022).

Gipeswic was the first English emporium to be identified confidently, following excavations by Stanley West in Ipswich in the 1950s and 1960s (Hurst and West 1957; West 1958). It is, however, almost certainly the latest of the four sites to have been made into an emporium, according to Keith Wade (forthcoming; though see Riddler, Trzaska-Nartowski and Hatton 2023: 383–4). Hamwic, once known as Hamwih, was identified in rescue excavations in the 1940s and 1950s, but no substantial publication of the place occurred until Addyman and Hill began their investigations in 1969 (1969; 1970). Their work prompted more than fifty years of excavations that are still ongoing in the Itchen-side district of Southampton known (after its Middle Saxon minster) as St Mary's. Lundenwic, as I noted in Chapter 1, was not identified until the early 1980s, when concurrently Martin Biddle (1984) and Alan Vince (1984) pinpointed its location in the area of the Strand, immediately west of the Roman city. Eoforwic was discovered by chance at York, to the south-east of the walled Roman town, beside the River Ouse in the later 1980s during salvage excavations (Mainman 2019).

Whether other emporia existed, for example in Kent (at Dover or Sandwich, for instance), or close to the Lincolnshire coast remains a matter of speculation.

Let us now look at each of these English emporia:

Gipeswic – Ipswich

The first post Roman activity at Ipswich was in the seventh century, when it appears to have functioned as a landing place for visitors by sea principally for the exchange of goods. This period of occupation is defined by handmade wares associated with later Merovingian imported pots. Apart from the dense activity found on the St Peter's Street site, there is little evidence for the extent of settlement at this period. Handmade pottery has been found in small quantities on most of the sites in the southern half of the town 680as well as south of the river at Stoke Quay (Brown, Teague, Loe, Sudds and Popescu 2020; see however, Riddler, Trzaska-Nartowski and Hatton 2023: 383–4). The

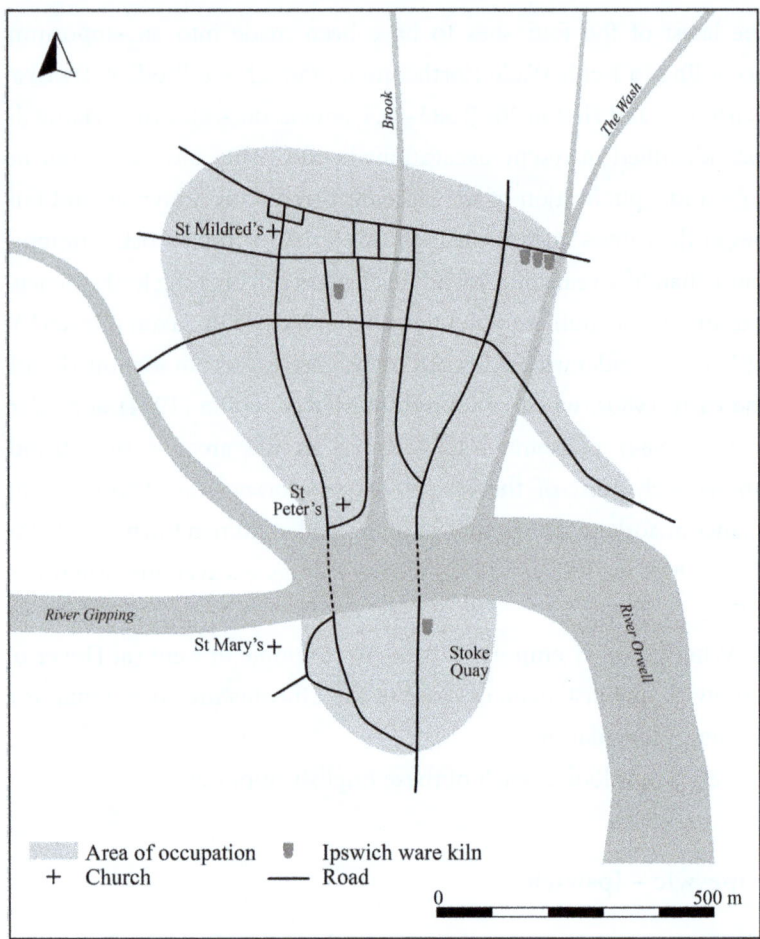

Figure 2.4 Map of Gipeswic (Ipswich) in the Middle Saxon period (modified after Keith Wade forthcoming).

distribution of these wares suggests that the occupation did not exceed 10 hectares in area. Cemetery evidence indicates two zones of burial: one along the northern fringe of occupation at St Stephen's Lane/ Buttermarket and the other south of the river at Stoke Quay, with other isolated burials. Radiocarbon dating of the St Stephen's Lane/ Buttermarket graves indicated burial from *c.* AD 610/635 to AD 665/680

(Scull 2009). The scanty evidence for buildings implies that the visitors camped in the summer months. The traders, judging from their ceramics, were principally from the Rhine region, although Northern French and Meuse valley pots suggest the presence of merchants from the Scheldt and Pas-de-Calais regions. This landing place may have replaced an earlier, sixth to early seventh-century site based upstream where access along the River Gipping was controlled by those buried in the Hadleigh Road cemetery (cf. Scull 2009; 2019). The visitors may have been travelling to inland estate centres, such as the royal palace discovered in excavations at nearby Rendlesham – the centre of a seventh-century polyfocal arrangement (located close to the Sutton Hoo royal burial mounds) (Minter 2023; Wade forthcoming). Scull has argued for a series of 'watershed' territories in east Suffolk based in the valleys of the Rivers Gipping, Deben, Alde and Blyth, each with its own magnates subordinate to the king, each of which could have been served by a landing place (Scull 2019).

This interpretation based upon Keith Wade's overview has been challenged by Riddler, Trzaska-Nartowski and Hatton (2023: 383–4) who contend that the landing-place at Ipswich, especially at Stoke, was of a more permanent nature as early as the mid-seventh century. If this is the case, it would pre-suppose that the East Anglians were actively engaging with Merovingian traders before the English church, deploying Primary sceattas, became a serious protagonist in cross-Channel exchange.

In the early eighth century – about AD 715 when, judging from the excavated materials, the major Rendlesham palace was deserted – a large permanent settlement was established at Ipswich with an economy based on international trade and craft production. The eighth-century emporium occupied higher ground about 400 metres north of the Gipping waterfront.

Here a grid-iron plan of gravelled streets was laid out. Gipeswic covered about 50 hectares in the Middle Saxon period, and did not expand greatly until the post Medieval period. It was not enclosed by defences in the Middle Saxon period; the first town defences, date to the late ninth or early tenth centuries (see Chapter 4). The majority of large rescue excavations between 1974–90 took place away from the waterfront, which remains largely unexplored.

Pottery manufacture was clearly the most important craft activity in the town throughout the Anglo-Saxon and subsequent, Norman period (Hurst and West 1957; Wade forthcoming). In the Middle Saxon period, Ipswich ware was produced on an industrial scale and distributed throughout East Anglia and beyond. The Carr Street area was the centre of this industry, although an early pottery kiln was found south of the river, on the Stoke Quay site. In the later ninth century, production of the Ipswich ware industry ceased and was replaced by the Thetford ware industry. Eight Thetford ware kilns have now been recorded in the town. The earliest (from the Danish period) is the single kiln found at Turret Lane. The other seven kilns, probably tenth- and eleventh-century in date, all came from the north-east corner of the town along a 150-metre stretch of Carr Street and into St Helen's Street.

Metalworking was also important to the Anglo-Saxon economy. In the Middle Saxon period, no *in situ* metalworking hearths were discovered, but the rubbish pits at all the major excavation sites contained metal slag. In the Danish period, there were metal-smiths making iron and copper alloy objects (and probably silver) at the St Stephen's Lane site. The associated rubbish layers were full of metalworking debris, including moulds, crucibles, scrap bronze and iron slag. Significant iron working was also found on the Wolsey Street site in the Danish period. Nearly 180kg of slag was recovered with evidence for both smelting and smithing. At least one certain and one possible furnace base was discovered, and a hearth had large amounts of hammer scale indicating iron smithing. A pit also produced an antler mould for casting base metal (tin and lead) disc brooches.

In the later tenth century, there was a short period of open-air iron smithing on hearths to the immediate rear of the town bank at School Street.

Cloth production, indicated by the presence of loom weights, spindle whorls and pin beaters, is present on most Ipswich sites in the seventh- to ninth-century contexts. However, it is likely that most cloth production was carried out in rural estate centres, such as the monastic site of Brandon (Suffolk). The evidence for cloth making from all the emporia suggests a household-by-household support industry rather than designed specifically for the export trade (Walton Rogers 2018: 111; 2020). To some extent Gipeswic must have been self-sufficient in food. The evidence for occupation on the fringes of the town (at Foundation Street) indicates an agricultural element, which included the keeping of chickens and pigs. This was supplemented by livestock procured from rural estates in its hinterland (Crabtree 2021).

A large number of coins from the excavations indicates the presence of a mint from the inception of the emporium, and certainly from the second half of the eighth century (cf. Metcalf 2000; Naismith 2012a). No less important is the assemblage of imported pottery (Coutts 1991). The imported ceramics appear principally to have been discarded by Continental traders as opposed to being transport vessels. Although not as common as the imported wares in Hamwic, they still represent about 5 per cent of the ceramic assemblage. Vessels from Rhenish sources predominate, but almost as many vessels derive from the regions between the Meuse and Seine valleys, possibly transshipped through the emporium at Quentovic.

The two main imported goods, judging from the archaeological evidence, were wine and Niedermendig lava quernstones from the Eifel mountains, both of which were presumably destined for rural estates in the East Anglia. Thirteen wooden barrels reused to line wells have been found in the excavations, five of which showed a good correlation with tree-ring chronologies from mid-south Germany, suggesting that they were Rhenish wine casks (like those found in great numbers in Dorestad). Strikingly, apart from many silver sceattas and early pennies, there is an absence of high-quality personal possessions. No jewellery in precious metals has been found apart from occasional silver dress pins.

Who founded Ipswich and managed it remains a matter of debate? The principal excavator of the town, Keith Wade contends that, with the abandonment of the royal palace at nearby Rendlesham in *c.* AD 715, it was constructed and maintained by the East Anglian royal family (Wade forthcoming). As I shall explain, Gipeswic had a different history to the other three emporia, described below, where the Anglo-Saxon church may have been involved in their creation and maintenance. In the case of Gipeswic, the church was not a prominent presence. The historian Norman Scarfe proposed that St Peter's Church was the likely early minster church in the town, based on its extensive landholding at Domesday (Scarfe 1972: 122). However, the churchyard is not large, and does not appear to have shrunk as excavation just outside its north and east graveyard walls has failed to find burials, and it is bounded by roads on its west and south sides. The presence of a second church, dedicated to St Mary and set on the same alignment as St Peter's, may belong to this period (Blair 2018: 167, n. 100; Riddler, Trzaska-Nartowski and Hatton 2023: 385).

Hamwic

A landing place for cross-Channel trade has been postulated at Hamwic beside the River Itchen, opposite the ruined Romano-British fort of Clausentum (Riddler and Trzaska-Nartowski 2025). It is proposed that this might at least date back to the earlier seventh

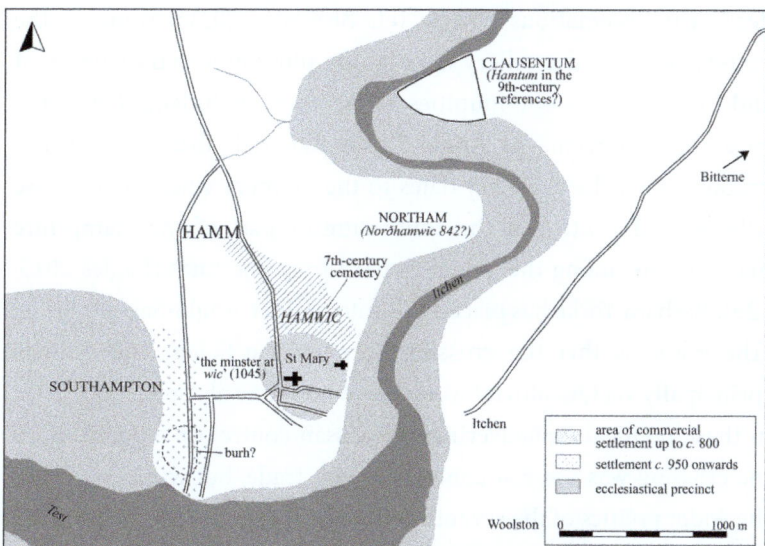

Figure 2.5 Map showing the location of Hamwic, the Saxon Shore fort of Clausentum and the Late Saxon burh of Southampton (modified after Blair 2018: fig. 58).

century. Piecing together a range of information (pottery, small finds and stratigraphic relationships), Riddler and Trzaska-Nartowski (2025) project that the earliest settlement lay in what became the southern and eastern sectors of the later town of Hamwic. A site to the south of Chapel Road and west of Albert Road North revealed a sunken-featured building and provided an early assemblage of organic-tempered local ceramics (whilst the remainder of the site can be assigned to later Middle Saxon phases). Here there is a conjunction of early ceramics and a form of structure that belongs essentially to the early Anglo-Saxon period and not to the Middle Saxon period. Almost certainly associated with this was a small cemetery discovered in excavations close to Southampton F.C.'s stadium, St Mary's (Birbeck 2004). The small cemetery is revealing. Grave goods associated with the cremations and inhumations date from the early to middle decades of the seventh century, the last flourish of accompanying the dead with ostentatious objects (cf. Brownlee 2021). Some of the pottery vessels and jewellery show strong affinities with the Continent and in some cases communities as far north as Jutland. Given the absence of previous of Anglo-Saxon material, Bruce Eagles has proposed that the cemetery dates to the moment when the Gewisse tribe gained control of the southernmost part of the Hampshire mainland including the Solent estuary from the Jutes (Eagles 2015: 129). Barbara Yorke has placed this into a wider Anglo-Saxon setting: 'The point…is that the crossing between the Solent and Francia (principally via Quentovic) would have been one of some importance in these political maneuverings. Gewissan control or supervision of the crossing was not just concerned with trade, but was also part of the wider politics of the seventh century' (Yorke 2018: 41). One grave stands out as special. It contains a copper-alloy scabbard stud with distinctive seventh-century (North Sea) Style II ornamentation. According to David Hinton, the studs apparently were deployed to decorate scabbards for a single-edged long seax, 'not a practical weapon, but one that was probably used for hunting and was therefore redolent of aristocratic practice' (Hinton 2005: 75–7). This type of distinctive mid-seventh-century weaponry, however, is not confined to Hamwic. Examples have also been found at Ipswich and Lundenwic. This being the case, Hinton proposed that the seax belonged to a king's reeve (*wicgerefa*) – a pre-eminent royal administrator – and the associated other burials belonged to his family. Reeves feature in later Anglo-Saxon sources as the aristocratic courtiers that controlled customs and trade (cf. Middleton 2005).

A generation or less later, by the later seventh century, almost certainly after the West Saxon Caedwalla conquered the Isle of Wight in AD 686, this was to become the emporium of Hamwic (Bavuso 2017: 246; Clarke-Neish 2021: 208). King Ina of Wessex, Caedwalla's successor, has been identified as the likely founder of the fifty-hectare town, of which about 1.5 hectares or 3 per cent has been excavated and mostly published in detail. John Blair (2018: 171) has interpreted the town as comprising two distinct halves. The northern half was an artisanal and commercial sector, while the southern half was composed of a precinct around St Mary's Church, which a charter of AD 1045 describes as the 'minster at *wic*' (cf. Morton 1999: 56). I shall return to Blair's interpretation and its significance below, but as yet there is very little evidence of the precinct. By contrast, the northern sector is now well understood from many excavations, notably at the site of Six Dials.

The new emporium was defined by a ditch on its western side and possessed a grid arrangement of gravelled streets. A wide north–south central street, rather like a *decumanus maximus* in a Roman town or fort, was flanked by narrower streets to the east and west. Of the many excavations at Hamwic, the large open-area uncovered at Six Dials offers a sense of the urban topography and its lifeways. This was packed with dwellings, their long-sides parallel to the streets, with mostly unfenced back yards filled with deep rubbish pits. The house plots here were constructed within a staked-out grid (Andrews 1997: 36; 39) that existed from the foundation of the town, unlike those, for example at Dorestad, formalized over time (van Es and Verwers 2015: 378–9). However, in form the plots are quite different to the narrow tenemental spaces created contemporaneously, for example, at Ribe (cf. Sindbæk 2022). Hamwic's cookie-cutter arrangement of structures, most of which were engaged in manufacturing, has suggested the hand of a controlling administrator(s). Small associated cemeteries of inhumations lacking grave goods are dotted across the area of the town (Garner 2025). Any trace of the founding fathers, if that is what the earlier cemetery at the St Mary's Stadium connotes, were soon interred beneath a grid of streets and the plethora of timber dwellings that inhabited new urban quarters.

The industrial production in the dwellings found across Hamwic point to metal and textile production, as at Gipeswic. Middle Saxon pottery principally used in the town was almost certainly made here

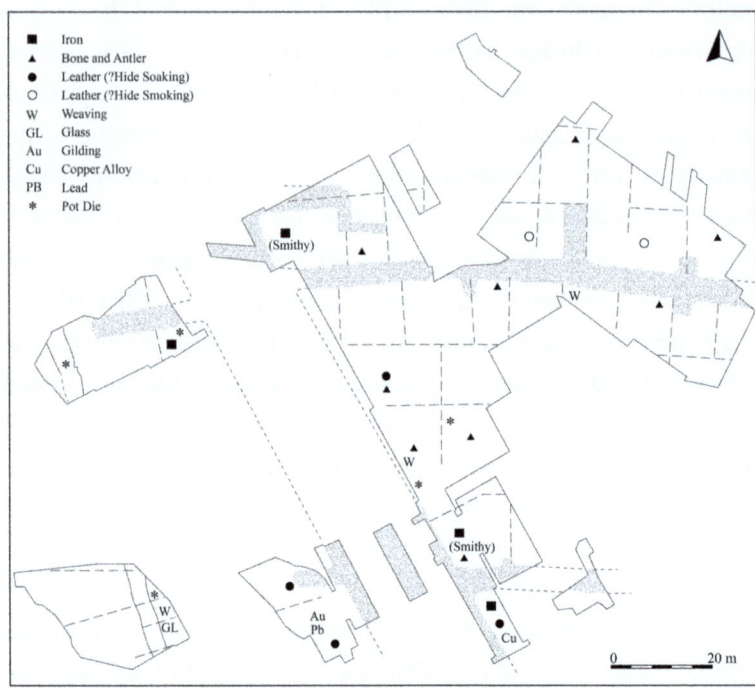

Figure 2.6 Interpretative plan of the urban topography of the Six Dials site, Hamwic (modified after Andrews 1997: fig. 91).

too. A distinctive silver (secondary) sceatta type H was minted here, and is commonly found within the emporium as well as distributed almost exclusively around Wessex (Metcalf in Andrews 1988). A significant number of imported pots of Late Merovingian and Carolingian date again suggest the presence of Continental traders. Almost all the imports originate from sources between the Meuse and Seine valleys, and were and probably channelled through Quentovic and to a lesser extent Seine valley ports such as Rouen. The diversity of vessels and fabrics remains the most striking aspect of the imported assemblage. This led to the conclusion that most imported vessels belonged to Frankish traders and their crews who used them while in the port and then discarded them. Eighty-six per cent of the imports

Figure 2.7 View of the Six Dials excavations, Southampton in progress (courtesy of Phil Andrews and Southampton City Museums).

from the nine SARC sites excavated in the 1970s were either pitchers or cooking pots; 12 per cent were storage vessels (Hodges 1981: fig. 4.3). Only class 14 black ware pitchers and Tating ware occur outside Hamwic in Wessex (cf. Hodges 1981: fig. 7.3). The use of specific imported cooking pots appears to have been localized within the settlement. This may be indicative of immigrant members of Hamwic's civic population, a traders' enclave perhaps, maintaining their identity through their Frankish cooking practices. Even so, most of Hamwic's households made use of imported serving vessels (Jervis 2011).

The scale of trade was matched if not exceeded by the procurement issues involved in maintaining the emporium. Hamwic is estimated to have had a population of between 2,000–3,000 people (Cowie and Blackmore 2012: 203; Hamerow 2007). Feeding this urban community

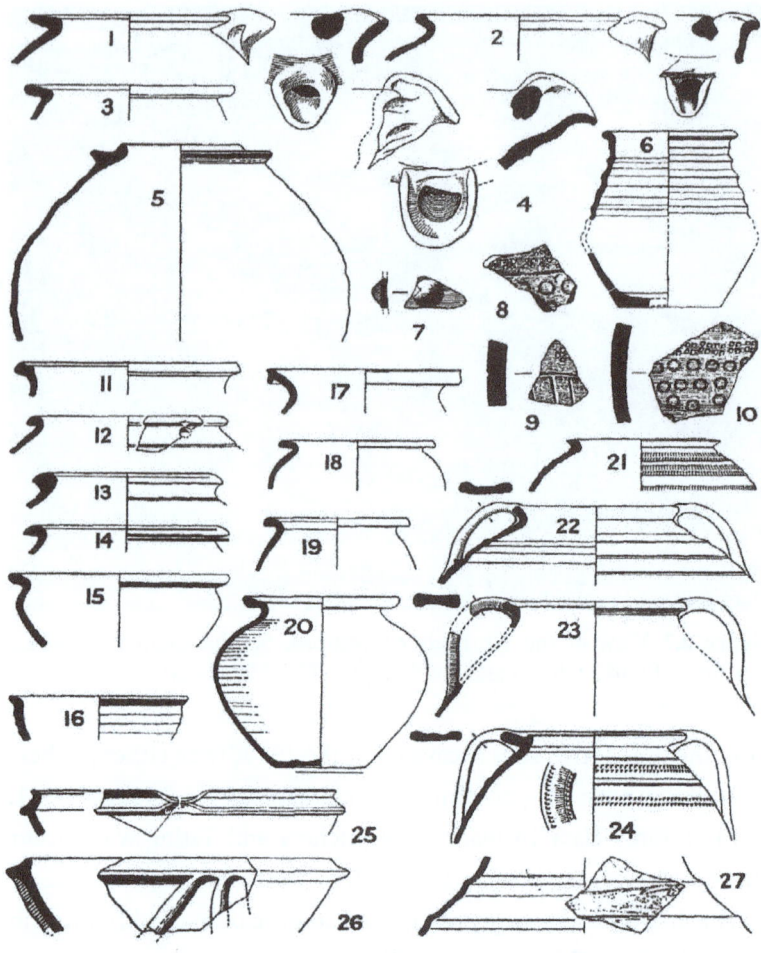

Figure 2.8 A selection of imported pottery from Hamwic (after G. C. Dunning, *Medieval Archaeology* 3 1959: fig. 23).

was a major procurement operation. The botanical record is not sufficient to illustrate the range of cereals and plants consumed. By contrast, the animal bone remains from the rubbish pits are illuminating. Beef was the pre-eminent meat consumed. It represented 75 per cent of the meat consumed at Hamwic; mutton and pork were surprisingly minor constituents of the diet. Most of the cattle and sheep were aged. Pigs were fewer while the increase in sheep is marked by older animals that had already supplied their wool to meet the export demand. At Hamwic, all the major body parts of animals were present, indicating that the beasts arrived at the town on the hoof (Hamerow 2007: 219–21; Crabtree 2018: 112–14). The faunal remains suggest a homogeneous diet across the settlement. Changes, however, occurred in the later phases (late eighth/early ninth-centuries), when the animals were generally smaller and older (Bourdillon, 1980; 1988; Hamilton-Dyer 2005). Procurement strategies were apparently changing by the ninth century. An analysis of cooking practices in the emporium shows that in the earlier eighth century, when the settlement was at its peak, people cooked in similar ways. Households appear to have had strikingly similar proportions of cooking, storage and preparation vessels. Later, in the late eighth to early ninth centuries, these cooking practices persisted, but notably more storage vessels were present (Jervis 2011).

In an analysis of Hamwic's origins, Blair – having defined the town as comprising two halves (see above) – concluded:

> I shall, however, suggest a new way of addressing the curious blankness of these places, the homogeneity of their layout, their lack of major churches or grand public buildings, their elusiveness in the written record. This is that they do not make sense as self-contained entities, but only as components of structured groups; it is to the complementary components, not to the emporia themselves, that we should look for the hierarchical and ceremonial elements. … Instead of Hamwic as a self-contained 'town', we should envisage a polyfocal 'Hamm complex' of which it was one component. ….. At Hamwic, the topography now suggests a serious possibility that the commercial and industrial settlement first developed as a northern adjunct to the minster complex. The emporia were not hierarchical or ceremonial centres themselves, but formed parts of polyfocal complexes – grouped around such centres – whose components interacted with

each other and with the wider world. Nor did they stand aloof from the mainstream rural economy: they were provisioned from the countrysides of their own areas, where farmers generated regular surpluses to feed both the emporia and other places.

2018: 171

Blair's interpretation is now supported by Matt Garner's observation that the evidence from the small excavations 'projects in and around the present churchyard [of St Mary's] indicates that an early Middle Saxon cemetery existed in this area, and that the Saxon and later cemetery was larger than the present churchyard' (Garner 2025). Garner's observations support Blair's interpretation of Hamwic as belonged to an emerging command economy, co-created by the West Saxon church under the umbrella of a pact with the royal household who maintained a palace close by. He interprets Hamwic, in other words, as the trading and industrial zone of a polyfocal settlement arrangement that consisted of a monastery, a palace and this sprawling new town that had begun life as a landing-place for Frankish traders. Taking this polyfocality a step further, in form this corner of Hampshire had come to resemble the Scandinavian central-places of the sixth century, notably the trading site of Lundeborg and the associated sacred and chiefly hub at Gudme on the island of Funen (cf. Randsborg 1990; Skre 2007). It also resembled the arrangements at and near the (early ninth-century) emporium of Kaupang (Norway) where, in Dagfinn Skre's opinion, it was a way to design social relations (2008: 339). Unlike the situation in market sites that served local or regional populations, which could be placed at, or in close to, a ruler's residence, Skre proposed that emporia, with their far-flung traffic and visiting strangers, were deliberately placed at a distance from the real centre of settlements. In this way, the port's inhabitants were within reach, meaning that agreements could be easily checked upon or reinforced by force if necessary, and security might be provided for them. Simultaneously, this arrangement kept strangers at arm's length, and distanced from the royal precinct. In combination, polyfocal sites embraced a wider set of social functions: for example, political assemblies and religious ceremonies, imbuing the locality with a sense of its history and community connections. Structurally it was very different to the classical city.

Lundenwic

Lundenwic was the largest of the known English emporia. The name occurs in the laws of two Kentish kings produced around AD 680, and remains in use until a charter dating to AD 857 (Naismith 2019: 77). The archaeological evidence supports a foundation at about this time

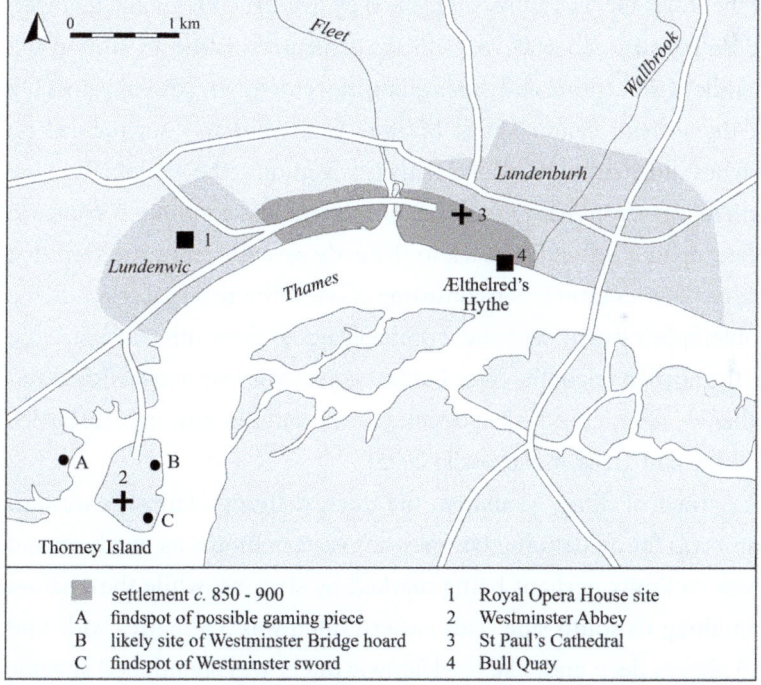

Figure 2.9 Map showing the location of Lundenwic and Lundenburg (after Naismith 2019; Blair 2018; Hadley and Richards 2021: 176).

or a little earlier. Bede famously described it as the 'emporium of many nations' (Naismith 2019: 88). The emporium was discovered in 1984 immediately west and notably outside the ancient Roman of Londinium (as Hamwic was placed close to Clausentum and Eoforwic lay outside Roman York). Its archaeology has been published admirably by Robert Cowie and Lyn Blackmore (2012).

The emporium grew to cover about 60 hectares north of current road known still as The Strand (Cowie and Blackmore 2012: 203). In numerous large and small excavations, the earliest phase appears to be associated with a ring of cemeteries dating to the last period of ostentatious burials similar to those found at the cemetery under St Mary's Stadium in Southampton, at Hadleigh Road at Ipswich and around Eoforwic (see below) (cf. Naismith 2019: 84–5). A small, dispersed cemetery was found at the Royal Opera House, supplanted by five structures and a roadway, all dating to *c.* AD 600–75, with the structures dating to around the middle of the century and superseding the cemetery. A structure possibly of the seventh century at St Martin's Courtyard was surrounded by ditches and quarry pits, whilst a small excavation at the Adelphi Building on the waterfront has provided an important and continuous sequence of occupation extending back to the early seventh century. Given that the cemeteries form a ring consisting of one or more burial grounds, the contemporary early settlement probably lies to the south and east, close to the north bank of the river, but this is yet to be firmly established and other locations are equally possible (Cowie and Blackmore 2012: fig. 99; Riddler and Trzaska-Nartowski 2025).

A tract of ditch, similar to the ditch defining Hamwic's western limit was found defining Lundenwic's eastern limits; its northern and western limits perhaps being marked by streams, while the Thames ran along its south side. This eastern ditch was 3.5 metres wide and 1.5 metres deep and, like the Hamwic ditch, was abandoned at some point in second or third quarters of the eighth century (Cowie and Blackmore 2012: 114–15; 119).

Within the settlement, a grid of streets was laid out, each gravelled and regularly maintained. Excavations at the Royal Opera House in the 1990s provided important topographical detail. As we have seen, initially used for burials, the settlement expanded here in the late seventh century, as at Hamwic, with little reverence for the earlier graves. Buildings were then constructed alongside a substantial gravel road, albeit with no particular alignment (Malcolm and Bowsher 2003: 27–9). The road itself was initially laid out to a width of *c.* 5 metres and constructed with gullies dug along both sides. As at Hamwic, the gravel road surface was regularly maintained (Malcolm and Bowsher 2003: 27–9). Between *c.* AD 730–70, these buildings were replaced by houses aligned towards the street, eventually forming an increasingly regular line of plots (Malcolm and Bowsher 2003: 101).

The core of the town, then, was similar to Hamwic in topography, but around its edges evidence has been found of either open fields or gardens, providing foodstuffs for a community that may have peaked at around 6,000–7,000 (Cowie and Blackmore 2012: 203; Naismith 2019: 81). The settlement appears to have been founded about AD 680, and may be the earliest English emporium. Coins and imported ceramics as well as carbon-14-dated levels indicate that it was at its largest during the next half-century. As in the other English emporia, the town was defined by prodigious waste from craft activities, as well as imported pottery from the Scheldt-Northern France regions as well as less commonly, the Rhineland. Increasingly, imported Ipswich ware from East Anglia occurs in the port, showing strong connections with regions to the north. Some hiatus or decline in long-distance trade and craft activity occurred in the central decades of the eighth century, and then, although there may have been some revitalization of trade at the end of the century, especially with East Anglia, the emporium was plainly waning by about AD 820 (see Chapter 3). There appears to be no overlap between the emporium and the nearby Late Saxon town of Lundenburh founded by King Alfred within the walls of Londinium in AD 886 (see Chapter 4). John Blair, however, has proposed that there was a regrouping on Lundenwic's eastern periphery, in the area of Fleet Street, Blackfriars and Temple. Here, there were high-status enclaves, one of which was owned by the Bishop of Worcester, according to a Mercian charter of AD 857 (Blair 2018: 270). Whether these enclaves maintained craftsmen and traders is a matter of speculation, but on the bases of Carolingian items from salvage excavations on the Thames waterfront between Blackfriars Bridge and Southwark Bridge, Blair posits the presence of international traders (see, however, Ziegler 2019 who employs correspondence analysis of the material from nearly two hundred excavations in London to contest this interpretation).

London is the best documented of the English emporia. It was mentioned in Kentish laws and charters and occurs in several Mercian sources and boasted an active mint throughout this period. Apart from a bishop associated with St Paul's within the old ruined Roman town, several charters attest to ecclesiastical holdings either in the emporium or close to it as in the immediate environs of Hamwic and Eoforwic (Naismith 2019: 95–7). Naismith has characterized its origins, like those of the Continental emporia, as a hub at the intersection of many political spheres of interest. In *c*. 680, in other words, it lay at the intersection between the kingdoms of Kent, the East Saxons and Mercia. Increasingly, it was controlled by the Mercians. Indeed, in *c*. AD 805–10, King Coenwulf of the Mercians issued a gold coin, a *mancus*, which on its reverse was an inscription DE VICO LVNDONIAE ('from the wic/ vicus of London' (Naismith 2019: 100; fig. 4.7).

Eoforwic

Eoforwic was the Anglian name for York. In the late eighth century, Charlemagne's Northumbrian advisor, Alcuin, recalls Frisian traders in the port about AD 766. The foreigners got into a fight and were

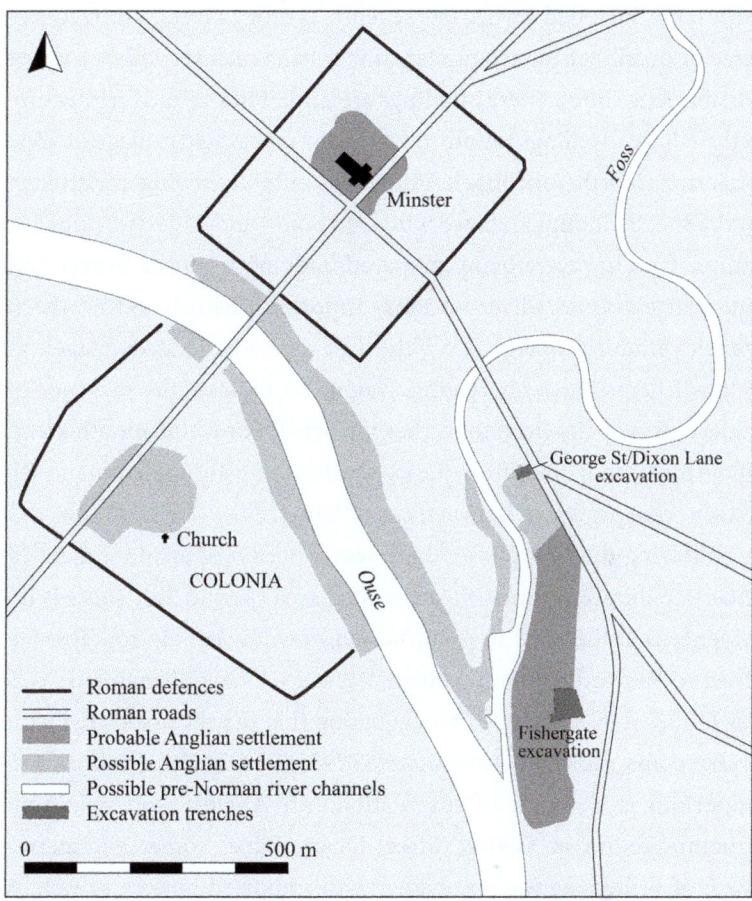

Figure 2.10 Map showing the location of the Fishergate excavations and the site of Eoforwic, York (modified after Mainman 2019: fig. 29).

expelled. The port itself was discovered in 1985 at 46–54 Fishergate, on the north-east bank of the River Foss (close to the confluence with the River Ouse), downstream from the old Roman walled town (Mainman 2019: 79–92). In a limited excavation area, three phases of the settlement were found. The first (period 3a/3z) was the most extensive. A ditch running north–south parallel to the river defined the east side, that was re-cut on several occasions. Finds from the earliest fills included a worn late seventh-century silver coin. Traces of three or possibly five rectangular timber halls each set within rows of possibly fence lines. These buildings are similar in size and architecture to the village dwellings found at the nearby (excavated) village of West Heslerton (North Yorkshire). A range of crafts were being undertaken on the site, including metalworking and bone- and antler-working for combs. Furs too were being prepared, judging from the beaver and pine marten bones. Silver sceattas, imported Rhenish and northern French ceramics (making up a third of the ceramic assemblage), as well as Rhenish lava quernstone fragments indicate the presence of traders, principally from the either the Scheldt or Rhine mouth areas. Of the thirty-four coins from the excavations (mostly unprovenanced), sixteen were produced between *c.* AD 700–37.

Following the first phase, there was a period of abandonment of uncertain duration across the excavated area (period 3b). There is no evidence that the halls were burnt, cut down or left- to rot. The site director, Richard Kemp, postulated that each was dismantled. This was followed by a period of reoccupation that may be associated with twelve coins minted between AD 837–55. The initial extent of the emporium is a matter of speculation. An Anglo-Saxon post-built structure found at George Street/Dixon Lane, some 300 metres north of Fishergate was associated with imported pottery as well as North Lincolnshire ceramics, and debris from industrial activities. This site perhaps suggests there was ribbon development covering a large area alongside the east bank of the Foss. Overall, however, Eoforwic is thought to have occupied about half the area of Gipeswic or Hamwic.

In her description of Eoforwic, Ailsa Mainman draws attention to its possible founder as Aldfrith (AD 685–705), a Northumbrian king much admired by Bede (Mainman 2019: 84). However, this '*reges ex machine*' explanation (cf. McCormick 2007) in this Northumbrian context might come to be re-evaluated. York (and Northumbria), after all, boasted a strong ecclesiastical tradition throughout this period, and has always been associated with its most celebrated eighth-century son, Alcuin, one of Charlemagne's most distinguished courtiers. The salvage archaeology, piecemeal though it has been, has also brought to light several small, richly furnished cemeteries within the halo of low ground around the Fishergate site, not dissimilar to those around Ipswich before the permanent settlement was made in c. AD 715. In this instance, the later seventh-century cemeteries and graves may equate to several stakeholders in the making of the emporium (cf. Mainman 2019: 54–71).

Conclusion

An immense amount of archaeological data has been published for these four emporia. Some aspects of their histories are agreed; some remain a subject of debate. All four emporia appear to be associated with earlier, periodic settlements and a ring of cemeteries with inhumations belonging to the final phase of Early Anglo-Saxon ostentatious burial (cf. Brownlee 2021) as well as documented estates belonging to the early (seventh-century) church. All four are characterized by planned streets and prodigious amounts of disposed artisanal waste as well as a notable presence of imported pottery from kiln sites between the Rhine and Seine. Cemeteries occur in Gipeswic, Hamwic and Lundenwic, but the presence of the church itself has proved elusive. Instead, the emporia appear to be characterized by small inhumation cemeteries that may or may not have been associated with timber chapels (cf. Garner 2025). The chronology of the English emporia suggest Lundenwic was the first by perhaps a few years; Hamwic and Eoforwic were then built in the later 680s, with Gipeswic (following Wade's interpretation which Riddler, Trzaska-Nartowski and Hatton 2023 contest, see above) dating to the second decade of the eighth century. Hamwic and Lundenwic, as I shall argue in Chapter 3, prospered until the second to third decades of the eighth century, as did Eoforwic, but after this their individual histories varied. Gipeswic, the late starter, appears to have been sustained throughout the eighth and ninth centuries.

A debate will remain about the architects of these visionary places. Two apparent facts stand out: Gipeswic, Hamwic and Lundenwic had a grid arrangement of streets, apparent imitations of ancient towns; and each, given their size, is largely ignored by contemporary historians. They were, in short, non-places that mark a moment of social transformation as new social strategies were invoked to interact with people who fell outside close and long-term social ties (Augé 1995). These non-places belong to a pioneering age of sailing ships and a new connectivity. Besides the great changes in extending trust to strangers, emerging secular leadership and the church now managed extra-regional trade to control access to products such as wine, oil, and objects of personal display which in turn reinforced incipient hierarchies at gatherings and assemblies. Whether they were inventions of kings, or of a compact between secular leaders and the church that, the historian, Ian Wood (2022) has likened to a temple society,[1] or a collective of mobile artisan and merchants, as Johan Callmer (2002; 2007; 2020), for example, has argued in the case of the Scandinavian emporia, will remain a subject of debate. Presently, each is interpreted as a calculated response to later Merovingian commercial

---

[1] Wood has likened early Medieval Latin Christendom to temple societies such as Pharaonic Egypt, the Classic Maya, the Chola and Vijayanagara states of India and the Buddhist civilization of Cambodia. Temple societies are those in which religious institutions play a key role in the redistribution of wealth. Normally they are defined by tributary modes of production. In early Medieval Christendom, Wood is referring to an age in which the market is non-existent and pre-market exchange formulae were embedded in social relations. Wood identifies the primary role of the church in advocating salvation in the afterlife as an ethic which framed the economy. Through this strategy the church was gifted vast tracts of land in the seventh and eighth centuries. In this respect, building upon studies by the historian, Peter Brown (for example, 2012), Wood's thesis is that the imaginary or sacred 'places men in the presence of the forces that command the invisible order of the world' (Godelier 2002: 32; cf. Hodges 2022: 89–91).

overtures. The English, in this narrative, were responding to their Frisian and Frankish visitors by sending missionaries to the Continent at exactly the moment the emporia took off as hubs (Palmer 2009). It is a binary relationship that merits further scrutiny.

What is also emerging from the ever-changing archaeological evidence are urban chronologies that no longer determine these places as the evolutionary predecessors of later Saxon towns, but rather as episodic investments – experiments, as Frans Theuws has suggested (2004; 2019) – in political economies that gathered pace with the increasing connectivity around the English Channel and North Sea. In this respect there is growing consensus in support of Joachim Henning's once provocative assertion that this was 'the false dawn of the age of the emporia' (2007: 31). It is the later history and afterlives of these emporia that now invite examination as the origins of England's towns took an unlikely turn.

3

'Business as Usual'?

the decline of the coinage did not herald general economic collapse. On the contrary, careful examination of other artefacts, and scrutiny of sites such as London, Southampton, Ipswich and Dorestad, shows that it was business as usual in the middle of the eighth century.

Naismith 2012b: 331

Such is the rich archaeology of the four emporia that the economic history of the eighth and earlier ninth centuries has been increasingly viewed through the prism of these places. Yet as Frans Theuws pointed out, the histories of the emporia need to be interpreted with care.

> It is clear that important changes occurred in the central places around the year 700. These changes seem to be related to the organization of production in the first place, but what impact do they have on the structural aspects of exchange? Some scholars like Hodges correlate the two and accept changes in the organization of production as indicative of structural changes in the system of exchange. I have already stated that I would like to interpret this period after A.D. 700 provisionally as an experimental phase that ended at the beginning of the ninth century.
>
> Theuws 2004: 133

Theuws' perceptive caution, certainly in the case of the English emporia, now needs to be weighed against two other forms of archaeological evidence – the coins and investment in the English landscape – as well as the meagre textual sources.

Theuws argument was advanced (in an English context) by Grenville Astill (2011: 254). He proposed that the prominence of long-distance trade in the later seventh and eighth centuries could be explained by the importance that élites attached to prestige items as a means of reinforcing their status. A century or so later – by about AD 800 – the entrenchment of the élites as significant property holders who depended for their wealth on agricultural surplus not only meant that their role in society had altered, but also that by necessity they needed local trading networks in order to convert such surpluses into non-perishable assets. Astill echoes Chris Wickham's conclusion (2005: 694–707; 805–13) that the slow growth of state power was a joint project in England, with kings and aristocrats linked in the search for mutual advantage (2006; 2011: 233). What Wickham omits to add is that the great authority of the English Church in the later seventh century had been reduced in this period and was thereafter to remain circumscribed by secular leaders, unlike Francia (cf. Wood 2022).

Astill's contribution to the debate about the emporia and exchange, as I aim to show, has proved to be prescient. The numismatic and rural archaeology as well as the place-name evidence call into question the issue of continuity at the emporia, and indeed the significance of urbanism and long-distance trade in ninth-century England when the Vikings were to raid, then invade, the island.

Recession?

Thousands of silver sceattas as well as early English pennies are now known principally thanks to metal-detectorists and in particular the UK's national Portable Antiquities Scheme (PAS) instituted by law in 1997. Numismatists have eagerly analysed this wealth of information about coins and their find-spots, setting out their own framework for the eighth century. Several features now emerge from this.

First, the primary sceattas, minted between *c.* AD 670/80 and AD 700/10, were followed by many more series that were minted between

c. AD 700/10 and approximately AD 750 at the latest. Millions of sceattas were probably minted, and depending on the series type, were no longer found only in the emporia, but occur to have been regionally distributed in considerable numbers. Twenty years ago, the numismatist Michael Metcalf plotted the location of different issues and employed regression analysis to identify the patterning of finds across regions (2003). The results in some cases suggest the importance of, for example, the sceatta type H attributed to Hamwic in the development of a coin-using economy in Wessex (Metcalf in Andrews 1988; Metcalf 2003: 41; fig. 4.1). Findspots of sceatta type H, according to Metcalf, illustrate an earlier eighth-century diffusion north and westwards as opposed to eastwards, to Sussex, Kent and London. Similarly, sceattas associated with Gipeswic (Ipswich) are associated with a distribution encompassing East Anglia but rarely outside the region (Metcalf 2000). Metcalf's meticulous work invites questions about the nature of this silver coinage in the earlier half of the eighth century, not just as expressions of the impact of the emporia but also as indices of the changing local economy between c. AD 680 and AD 750.

Second, Metcalf pointed to two remarkable trends in the earlier eighth-century numismatic history. First, the silver content which had been high in the primary sceattas was steadily devalued in the secondary sceatta series. Many of the sceattas attributed to the second quarter of the eighth century possessed low amounts of silver. This devaluation led Metcalf to hypothesize that the amount of silver in circulation significantly declined in this period (Metcalf 2009).

Third, Metcalf identified a hiatus or near break in the minting of silver coinage in approximately the third to early fourth quarters of the eighth century. He interpreted this break as an economic crisis which he summed this up as follows:

> The third quarter of the eighth century witnessed a severe recession in the volume of minting and also of monetary exchanges; and, even more severe, in the net inflows of coinage from the Continent. Money

from the Low Countries, which had in the first half of the century been a major component of the English currency, disappeared dramatically. Merovingian silver had never entered England in quantity. The date of the downturn is difficult to specify, but the minting of sceattas appears to have declined as early as the 730s and to have dwindled in the 740s. It is not obvious how this might relate to political or military events in Frisia or the Rhine mouths area.

The recovery in monetary circulation was certainly delayed and gradual.

> Metcalf 2009: 30; see also Grierson and Blackburn 1986: 184–9, esp. tables 13 & 14

I shall return below to examine Metcalf's interpretation of circumstances in late Merovingian and early Carolingian Francia, and especially its emporia. His terminology, it needs to be noted, uncomfortably follows formalist economics (Astill 2011: 254). This said, the so-called insular crisis was accompanied by a new chapter in the production of English coins. Rare, though they are, coins minted after *c.* AD 750 shed light on the changing political circumstances in England, that in turn, as I shall show, have a bearing on this so-called crisis.

This new numismatic chapter involved coins minted in a new form with an entirely different iconography. The abstract motifs minted onto pellets were replaced by Roman or Byzantium style versions – pennies minted on flat flans depicting an issuing king and often the location of the mint. This was a signal step away from the anonymity of the sceattas towards a new baseline of royal recognition and, with it, oversight. The first innovative coinage to do this was issued in the 740s by the Northumbrian king, Eadberht. Eadberht's new coinage seems to have been based upon a general recoinage of older currency (Naismith 2012a: 97; fig. 4.3a). The otherwise enigmatic Beonna, king of the East Angles (749–*c.* 760), followed this Northumbrian model, with an improved silver alloy. 'One local practice which Beonna's coinage inherited was the use of the moneyer's name as a reverse design. This had emerged during the last stages of the East Anglian Series R sceattas, presumably as a measure to help foster the acceptance of an increasingly debased coinage' (Naismith 2012a: 97). The numismatist Rory Naismith argues that this English initiative to make a more reliable weight and metal standard during a crisis brought on by a shortage of bullion led to the Franks also adopting this new version of coins. At some point in the early 750s, the new Carolingian dynasty led by Pippin III minted a Frankish royal issue that, while broader, thinner and finer than the reformed Eadberht and Beonna types, essentially followed their formula. Naismith notes, however, that Pippin was influenced by a weight standard from northern Gaul, while elements of the epigraphy may have been modelled upon Visigothic, Lombard and possibly Islamic precedents (2012a: 97–8). In Francia, the decline in the silver content of late Merovingian coinage was never so steep as in England, and varied region by region (Naismith 2012a: 161). The interconnected

Figure 3.1 A penny of King Beonna of East Anglia found at Wordwell, Suffolk (SF-298063) (courtesy of the British Museum's Portable Antiquities Scheme).

world of the Anglo-Saxon and Carolingian courts, including their moneyers, is immediately apparent in the next episode in this numismatic history. In the 760s, King Offa of Mercia and King Heaberht of Kent followed Pippin's new model coinage. However, each placed the moneyer's name on the reverse, like Beonna's coinage, as opposed to the mint-name on Pippin's *denarii* (Naismith 2012a: 99).

Offa's (light) coins were issued in significant numbers, although in some diversity. His coinage had an unprecedented distribution. Following this his heavy coinage was issued in the last three or four years of his reign after AD 792/93, and a new weight standard of c. 1.45 grams. This set a benchmark for ninth-century Anglo-Saxon minting. After his death, the design and weights were maintained by King Coenwulf at London, King Eadberht II of Kent at Canterbury, and King Eadwald at Ipswich (Gipeswic). (By AD 800, Kent and East Anglia were subsumed to Mercian hegemony.) For the next two decades under Coenwulf, a rigid and universal standardization characterized all mints. A weight fineness was rigorously adhered to, while the English customs appear to have effectively excluded the importation of Carolingian coinage during Charlemagne's reign. The reason for this is that the Carolingian reform to create a comparable heavy coin, similar to Offa's heavy penny, occurred a year later, in AD 793/94 (at the Council of Frankfurt). The heavy denier was targeting a weight of about 1.70 grams, approximately 25 grams of silver more than the Mercian coin. It has been proposed that ten Carolingian *denarii* were worth twelve Offan pennies (Naismith 2012a: 175–6; see also Kershaw et al. 2024 on the mining of Carolingian silver from Melle, Aquitaine).

The sum of this richly detailed numismatic information raises two separate issues. Was there a bullion crisis (and recession) in England, as Metcalf and Naismith have proposed, which somehow was resolved by the 790s with imported Carolingian silver from the Melle mines when Offa issued his heavy penny? Offan pennies, we should remind ourselves, were issued in large numbers with high silver content. Such an economic crisis is not immediately apparent in Francia and, as I shall describe below, certainly did not impact Rhenish trade in the sheltered Wadden-Sea sailing zone, which stretched from Dorestad to Ribe, in western Jutland. Secondly, the numismatic evidence shows *not* how English kings responded to increasing standardization and control of coinage by the early Carolingian authorities after the 740s as this so-called crisis occurred, but the *reverse*. Instead, the earliest English pennies appear to have been a model for Pippin III's reform of his coinage in the 750s. Again, Offa's heavy pennies minted in AD 792/93 appear to have preceded Charlemagne's coin reforms to introduce a heavy denier shortly afterwards. It is well documented that the Frankish court was eclectic in the international models it adopted so not too much weight should be given to these two sequences. What, however, is significant is the better studied motives in Francia for these reforms, as the court sought to control exchange and taxation through ordering and standardization practices, and as it ramped up regional agricultural production (Devroey 2003; 2020). I shall return to both these issues later in this chapter.

Investing in the landscape

Just as urban archaeology was transformed by salvage excavations in inner cities, the archaeology of the English landscape has been transformed by large-area excavations of development sites. In the first edition of the journal *Medieval Archaeology*, an essay by a distinguished archaeologist debated whether Anglo-Saxon villagers lived in pit-houses (Radford 1957). At that time the lives of English farmers were essentially a mystery. Less than seventy years later, no tract of European landscape is better documented than England's (see, for example, Rippon, Smart and Pears 2015; Blair 2018; McKerracher and Hamerow 2022). This was not the densely settled landscape of the Roman period with its highly specialized agricultural production principally destined for the armed forces. The English numbered about 1.7 million people at Domesday, AD 1086; one recent calculation is that it numbered 70 to 80 per cent less in the fifth to ninth centuries (Hamerow 2022: 3). Yet as of the later seventh century, it was managed around new villages, many created in the so-called Middle Saxon shuffle as optimal ecological niches were selected in place of an earlier, Early Anglo-Saxon emphasis upon subsistence (cf. Crabtree 2018: 90–6). Tom Williamson has argued that the natural environment had an important structuring effect on the formation of these new (Middle Saxon) territories (2013: 82–106). These territories, Williamson shows, conform to river valleys with boundaries following the watershed. An emphasis was now placed upon selecting free-draining soils, such as gravel terraces, while valley sides were designated for arable agriculture. Intervening uplands, often comprising less fertile, thinner and exposed lands, were better suited to woodland management and livestock husbandry. These drainage zones lent themselves to particular forms of agriculture and settlement. As a result, communities developed within drainage provinces principally because of interactions determined by agriculture and livestock farming. The lordships that commanded these communities were correspondingly extensive, drawing on services and renders that spanned these ecological zones (Faith 1997: 1–14; Brookes 2020: 288–92). From these new zones emerged consensual organizational farming arrangements (cf. Oosthuizen 2016).

Agricultural intensification clearly occurred through the eighth century following the settlement and land-use changes (Moreland 2000a; Astill 2011: 265). In this era, it is now thought, the concept of open fields and common grazing rights were formed, setting a baseline for the expansion of agricultural production that was to be pursued into the later Middle Ages. This amounted to what in the Neolithic period Andrew Sherratt described as a Secondary Products Revolution: animals were no longer just exploited for meat but for their bones (to make tools), milk, wool, traction and transport (Sherratt 1981). As in the Neolithic, this was a significant shift away from the domestic mode of production which had existed since the end of the Roman colony. The 'revolutionary' emphasis upon managed intensification was prompted almost certainly by a compact between two forces: the secular élite and the church with its knowledge of farming practices in Francia and perhaps Frisia. Their collaboration in creating and sustaining the four English emporia was simply the tip of an economic iceberg now dedicated to regional production and exchange.

Unfortunately, we know too little about the productive capacity of the royal households, although King Ina's laws (686–726) show a clear commitment to taxing (West Saxon) farming regimes. By contrast, the archaeology of the minsters founded at this time and their agrarian strategies is beginning to be documented in detail. In particular, the research project at Lyminge has shone a spotlight on the economic take-off of one relatively modest Kentish minster. Lyminge occupied a strategic position at the head of the valley of the River Nailbourne, which formed a key communication artery between the south coast and the Kentish 'capital' of Canterbury. Large-scale excavations covering almost a hectare in total have shed light on how a site distinguished by two rich sixth-century cemeteries was redesignated as a palace in the seventh century. Here, an Anglo-Saxon family exercised power by controlling a place potent with ancestral and cosmological meanings. Then in the closing decades of the seventh century, the character of this central place changed decisively. The historical sources attest that Lyminge became a royal double monastery. With this new ownership there was a small scale but significant re-siting of the settlement. Its established ancestral focus was forsaken in favour of an elevated location sanctified by the construction of the little minster church of St Mary and St Ethelburga and adjacent buildings (Thomas 2023). The basilica, 6.9 metres long x 4.2 metres wide, was modest by comparison with, for example, the great Northumbrian monastic churches such as

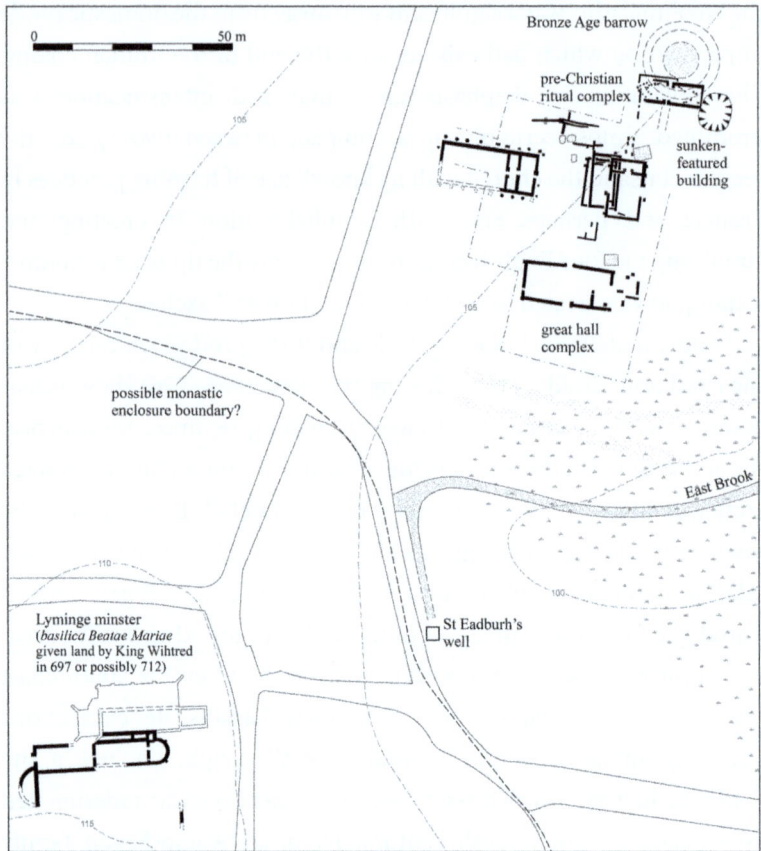

Figure 3.2 Map of the excavated Early Saxon secular site and Middle Saxon minster at Lyminge (modified after John Blair 2018: fig. 34).

Jarrow or Monkwearmouth, associated with Bede. In contrast to the impermanency of the earlier secular élite dwelling, the little monastery was to endure for 200 years, perishing in all likelihood in a ninth-century Viking raid.

Lyminge's outer precinct carries clear evidence of a formalized layout with zones defined by boundaries not dissimilar from royal palace of the East Anglian Wuffingas dynasty at Rendlesham, near Ipswich (Gipeswic) (Minter 2023). The excavator, Gabor Thomas, has made a distinction between an inner zone of domestic habitation, immediately to the south of the boundary of the present churchyard, and an outer sector reserved for agricultural processing and industrial activities. The former appears to have encroached upon a major boundary running from north-east to south-west, traced for a distance of 25 m. This ditch had been purposefully infilled towards the end of its life, with dense concentrations of domestic (and construction) refuse, and it was subsequently cut by rubbish pits. The spatial significance of this boundary is difficult to determine since the area to its north cannot be archaeologically explored (Thomas 2017a; 2023).

Two major activities have come to light in this outer periphery of Lyminge's precinct. First, the management of agricultural surplus, is represented by a large east–west timber building with an associated metalled yard, interpreted as a granary with an exterior threshing floor. Second, ironworking is attested by a manufacturing site identified some 150 metres north-west of the monastic nucleus. This was discovered in trial trenching to investigate a geophysical anomaly confirmed to be an extensive spread of smithing and smelting slag. This deposit was associated with a concentration of pits, some containing fuel ash and evidence of burning, and others fragmented iron objects, predominantly knife blades, that are likely to have been manufactured on the site.

The granary, measuring 19 x 6.5 metres, would have accommodated more than 200 cubic metres of grain, far more cereal than was needed by this community (Thomas 2017b: 361–2, fig. 16. 2). Plainly the minster's community was not consuming anything like this quantity of grain.

Lyminge's rich zooarchaeological assemblages also hold important clues on how daily social practices changed with the spatial reconfiguration. These underline significant transformations in food supply and animal resourcing. The monastic community was consuming marine fish and domestic fowl at a much higher intensity than the prominent household had been as a pre-Christian centre in the sixth century. Prodigious quantities of fish bone provisionally estimated to number in the tens of thousands show the importance of fish to the community. Consumption embraced not only freshwater and coastal fish, but also deep-water marine fish.

The emphasis on the livestock economy is no less striking. There was a shift from the rearing of pigs to that of sheep. In sixth- and seventh-century contexts, pig bones constitute some 45 to 55 per cent of the faunal assemblages (Crabtree 2010; 2018: 68). Many archaeozoologists recognize elevated proportions of pig (30 per cent and higher) as a high-status dietary signature during the early Anglo-Saxon period. The proportion of sheep increases from 19 per cent in the sixth and seventh centuries to between 36 and 54 per cent at the expense of pig, which declined significantly, ranging from 12 to 27 per cent in different contexts. Sheep remains reflect the intensive management of flocks reared for wool, as do the finds of textile manufacturing equipment. Was the emphasis upon a pastoral economy triggered by the Continental demand for wool, in part for sailcloth as well as cloaks, discussed in Chapter 2?

Lyminge's agrarian economy was based upon the minster's land holdings. These occupied the fertile lower slopes of the Nailbourne valley in the immediate environs of the settlement. The discovery of a plough coulter from a seventh-century excavated context (Thomas and Scull 2021: 16; see Thomas 2017b: fig. 16.1.) confirms that imported farming technology – what McKerracher and Hamerow (2022) have termed the mouldboard plough package (see below) – was now being deployed. Lyminge exercised lordship over a territory broadly equivalent to the lathe of Limenwara (an administrative subdivision of Kent) recorded in later sources. This comprised a core embracing the southerly stretch of the valley of the River Nailbourne forming the immediate catchment of the settlement, surrounded by an arc of dependencies. It included chalk downs, Wealden forest and a large tract of marshes running up to a coast perforated with small inlets (Thomas and Scull 2021: 17; fig. 5).

The farming regime at Lyminge appears to belong to a widescale ecclesiastical movement (Blair 2028: 154). Nowhere better illustrates this than the agricultural areas associated with the Fenland monastery of St. Æthelthryth at Ely. Extensive excavations here by the Cambridge Archaeological Unit have uncovered a settlement dating from the late seventh or early eighth centuries comprising (1) the ecclesiastical core, where the monastery and associated structures were located; (2) a waterfront area, to the east of the ecclesiastical area; (3) the West Fen Road enclosures, to the west of the ecclesiastical area (Cessford 2020). The West Fen Road area was laid out about AD 730–50 (over a Romano-British enclosure system that influenced its alignment). Excavations covering approximately 500 x 600 metres exposed evidence of three separate extensive areas of ditched enclosures used primarily for stock management as well as traces of craft activities. This was replanned at least once before reverting to an irregular layout after AD 850. Each of the gridded phases included small timber buildings that conformed to the grid. The location, combined with the relative poverty of material culture, suggests that this was a service settlement on the fringe of the great royal minster at Ely. These enclosures were connected by a network of routeways and droveways and have extensive open areas between them, linked to arable agriculture. The scale of activity combined with the evidence for grid planning indicate that this agricultural landscape was controlled by the contemporary monastic community. 'We know that major minsters were serviced by lower-status *fratres* (analogous to later Cistercian lay-brethren), living a quasimonastic life in settlements linked to the central complex, and the inhabitants of West Fen Road may have been like this' (Blair 2018: 154). The excavator concluded that the enclosures were primarily designed for livestock management, as part of an integrated system of arable and pastoral agriculture where the eighth-century expansion relates primarily to the creation of an arable surplus, followed, tellingly, by the apparent abandonment of parts of the site in the mid-ninth century (Cessford 2020: 60). The scale of operations at Ely, on a par with those discovered at Lyminge, further confirms the economic ambitions of the Anglo-Saxon Church.

These purposes are supported by other data from archaeological projects. New studies of the palaeobotanical and faunal record of the period reveal the granular detail of this fast-changing rural economy (Holmes 2013; 2022; van der Veen 2022). The palaeobotanical and palynological record, for instance, points to a decrease in woodland cover and an extension of arable. Archaeobotanical studies also indicate a planned rotation of crops, the use of an iron coulter to plough heavier soils, the practice of rotation and an emphasis upon storing grain (cf. van der Veen 2022; McKerracher and Hamerow 2022: 18–19). Specifically, there is also evidence of a switch to growing bread wheat. Production of bread wheat could not be maintained or expanded without measures to preserve the necessary soil fertility. Small-scale production during the Early Anglo-Saxon period could have been sustained by intensive cultivation, and using barley, together with limited use of pulses, oats and rye, as buffers. The marked increase in demand for wheat meant that pulses and the supporting cereals came into their own. The conspicuous diversification of crops from the seventh century onwards was probably a response to spreading the risk of crop failure and, with the arrival of the church, also meeting perhaps the demand for bread wheat in church services (van der Veen 2022: 337). This intensification is further supported by the weed data which suggest that the shift to low-input, larger-scale regimes had occurred by AD 800. Pollen evidence and, likewise, an increase in the proportion of male cattle from around 7 per cent during the fifth to seventh centuries to around 23 per cent by about AD 750, also indicate that the eighth century saw an growing emphasis on arable production, at least in some regions (Forster and Charles 2022; Holmes 2022), while the burgeoning emphasis on sheep may at least explain the droveways and ditched enclosures (around dwellings) that are a hallmark of Middle Saxon and later settlements (McKerracher and Hamerow 2022).

With regard to this cerealization process, van der Veen notes that: 'the switch to bread wheat represents a real material difference for those that produced it; it is a demanding and expensive crop that dictates specific soil conditions, different tending and harvesting actions. It also requires distinct, labour- and fuel-intensive processing if a white loaf of bread is wanted, and then represents an artefact with specific social and cultural meanings' (2022: 333). The introduction of new crops changed the working practices at the bottom level of society. Bread, after all, was also a semiotic device. Does it reveal the beginnings of an effective top–down order in Anglo-Saxon society as early as the later seventh century, an invention that occurred as King Ina (and perhaps other kings) was issuing laws to specify taxation at a local level? Or was the invention of bread wheat some index to the bottom level of society looking to engage perhaps in an explicit relationship with the new Christian ideology, one key to which was breaking wheat bread? To be sure, social change was leaving an indelible imprint across England's landscapes as the four emporia were in their early pomp.

The archaeology of English landscapes has provided a context for rethinking the place-name evidence that for many generations has fascinated historians. In a far-reaching analysis of the origins of the Anglo-Saxon built environment – in towns and the countryside – John Blair has employed this combination of sources to first, establish the reorganization of the eighth-century Mercian kingdom, and then, the organization of Northumbria and Wessex. In this forensic approach, Blair has foregrounded the emergence of regional central places, all associated with roads and intersections with rivers. This is the context that he identifies for the widespread existence of minor earthwork enclosures, many of which were minor forts. These emerged over time as incipient markets, he believes, and originate in King

Æthelbald of Mercia's (715–57) exclusion of 'necessary defences of fortresses' from bookland immunities in AD 749. The underlying principle was that kings could reasonably compel landowners to safeguard their localities. Up until the mid-eighth century, it is thought that military leadership over units greater than the select warband (*fyrd*) of élite warriors had been personal and impermanent. Now, it appears, kings sought to maintain more permanent military forces, and perpetuate territorial hegemony based upon new non-kin systems of mobilization and deployment

Blair concluded as follows: 'The organisation and economy of the Mercian age were based not on complex centres, but on central clusters comprising specialised and defined mono-functional foci linked in complementary groups. Many of these foci are identified by the place-name generic -tūn, which seems in this context to have had a more specific meaning than is generally realised' (Blair 2018: 193). He pinpoints these -tūn compound places in the charters to the period AD 760–90, in other words, the period of Metcalf's hypothetical recession. He also contends that these places were chosen for the purpose of control, communication, and defence in Mercia, on its peripheries, and thereafter, too, in the contemporary kingdoms of Wessex and Northumbria. These were quintessential middle grounds where brokerage occurred to exact trade and rents or tribute as well as, importantly, to mobilize military forces. Concurrently, Blair pinpoints the gradual emergence of polyfocal settlements within a number of old Roman towns previously principally colonized by the church – Canterbury and York being two examples (Blair 2018: 258, fig. 94; 257, fig. 93; cf. Canterbury: Corsi 2022: 43–51; York: Mainman 2019). Along with minsters, these new English (polyfocal) centres became the bedrock of periodic regional exchange that expanded steadily through the later eighth and ninth centuries (Astill 2006: 237–8). In terms of their place in society, these were what Frans Theuws and Mirjam Kars have described as transactional centres, using Maastricht as an example. They describe these largely deserted ancient places as points of periodic exchange associated with important religious institutions (Theuws and Kars 2017; see Chapter 5).

By strengthening regional economies, the Mercian kings – especially the long-lived Offa – readily increased their hold over political power by using tribute to raise and sustain military forces and exert control. The model was first implemented by Charles Martel in the late Merovingian realms, and pursued by the early Carolingian, King Pippin III, as I noted above. Was it imitated by neighbouring English kings with whom they shared a new numismatic idiom, as we have seen above? Certainly, the archaeology of eighth-century Wessex indicates that there was an intention to increase regional exchange networks. Michael and Nicholas Costen have identified 'a much older pattern of trading places based not in major royal burhs, but at rural centres, including hill-forts' (2017: 23). The social and economic relationships of the majority of the population were determined, it now appears with plentiful metal-detector evidence, by an older, pre-burh patterns of exchange. It may be no coincidence that at about this time, a likely West Saxon innovation to get a tighter grip on taxation and military service was the implementation of the concept of the hundred. First mentioned in a mid-tenth-century source, commonly known as the 'Hundred Ordinance', surviving in Old English in Cambridge, Corpus Christi College, manuscript 383, and in two Latin versions, the *Quadripartitus* and in the *Consiliatio Cnuti* (Brookes 2023: 53), the text describes the schedule and procedures of the hundred court. Locations were specified for regular assemblies to settle disputes, conduct trade, impose fines and other punishments, and above all mobilize armed military forces. The hundred, then, was an administrative method as well as a geographical entity. As new approaches to military mobilization and deployment were shaped, this unit of administration became a pragmatic method for further consolidating royal power. Administration steadily shifted from comprising a variety of different community forms to one that was embedded in the landscape (Astill 2006: 237–8). Examples of these new productive estate centres, evolving out of earlier villages, have been excavated at Flixborough (Loveluck 2001; 2007), Higham Ferrers, Northamptonshire and at Buckden, Cambridgeshire (Hardy et al. 2007; Clarke and Connor 2024: 77–95). Flixborough, for example, has a nuanced livestock history comprising two different patterns of material culture. First, the late seventh- to eighth-century settlement where, accompanying evidence of hunting, feasting and conspicuous consumption, a high proportion of cattle bones occurred in the faunal assemblage. Then in the ninth century this settlement appears to have changed from a secular to a minor ecclesiastical estate centre (judging from the presence of silver styluses). The faunal remains show an increased proportion of sheep, indicating a shift towards specialized wool production (Crabtree 2010: 129). Materialism, the excavated finds show, mattered to the inhabitants of these places. Such communities, as a result, were no longer tied solely to lineages and regional identities. Existing methods of shire (county) mobilization were now focused on assembly points that a century later were to overlap with new fortresses – the burhs – probably first networked in Wessex under King Alfred in the turbulent decades around AD 900 (Brookes 2023: 53) (see Chapter 4).

Several decades ago, in a critique of the 'idealism' of *Dark Age Economics*, Tom Saunders approached the political economics of Middle Saxon England from an angle which resonates with Blair's analysis of Mercian landscapes and the origins of the West Saxon hundred (Saunders 1991; 2001). Saunders maintained that the Anglo-Saxon emporia were dependent settlements, separated from rural society and therefore not a dynamic force in that society. The wic 'needs to be placed within the context of the rise and fall of the tributary social formation … As long as royal alliances were constructed within the customs of reciprocity and gift-giving, and the social tensions between king and lord were mediated and masked through the exchange of prestige goods, then emporia could be established and maintained' (Saunders 2001: 12). The renegotiation of aristocratic military services during the later eighth and ninth centuries altered this. Grants of land made it possible for the kings to create a more secure basis for their authority. This contributed indirectly to the declining role of the emporia in England, as there was a shift in economic emphasis away from movable wealth to landed wealth (much as Moreland was to propose (2000a; 2000b)).

In sum, the archaeology and place-name evidence confirm a trend towards intensification of agriculture after the late seventh century, which paved the way by the second half of the eighth century for promoting regional foci of exchange, and concurrently an emphasis upon raising the means to mobilize and maintain military forces. The latter led to more political control by England's royal families reflected in the numismatic history.

At this point, the regional distribution of coinage in this experimental period of increasing standardization merits mentioning. West Saxon coins are bafflingly absent. On the other hand, coins minted in London before AD 796 occur in Wessex, and in most other kingdoms other than Northumbria (cf. Naismith 2012a: fig. 8.5). New pennies minted in Canterbury are commonly found in London and most parts of England except Northumbria. Pennies minted at Gipeswic dominate the finds from East Anglia (along with London issues), and occur in London and Kent but only in small numbers in Wessex. East Anglian coins are non-existent in Northumbria. With the introduction of heavier (Offan) pennies in the early 790s, the regional patterns became more embedded. Canterbury, for example, having composed the lion's share of single coin-finds from East Anglia until AD 796, was overtaken by pennies minted in Gipeswic (Ipswich) in the period down to c. AD 830 (Naismith 2012a: 211–12). Naismith records single finds minted in Gipeswic found in East Anglia as follows: c. AD 760–6, at 41 per cent of all coins in the period; c. AD

796–830 this rose to 49 per cent; and in AD 830–65, it was even higher at 63 per cent of all finds. Clearly the circulation of local currency was vibrant, and mirrors that of the prodigious amounts of Ipswich ware pottery produced in the Buttermarket kilns at Gipeswic that occurs on all Middle Saxon sites in the region as well as at Lundenwic and occasionally in ninth-century Eoforwic (cf. Naismith 2012a: 212). Coins minted in Mercia never amounted to more than 9 per cent of single-coin finds in East Anglia, while West Saxon finds range from 3–5 per cent and Northumbrian pennies at 1 per cent. In fact, Gipeswic (Ipswich) itself, for most of the forty years after c. AD 825, displaced London as arguably the most productive mint of southern England after Canterbury (Naismith 2012a: 191; fig. 7.4). Turning to Lundenwic, an estimated output of dies used in AD 765–92 ranged between 20–27 per annum. This rose to between 33–56 in c. AD 792–6, and then in c. AD 805–21 fell to 3–4, and subsequently in the 820s stood at about 7. Naismith (2012a: 190–1; cf. fig. 7.2), however, postulates a resurgence of the London mint under King Berhtwulf

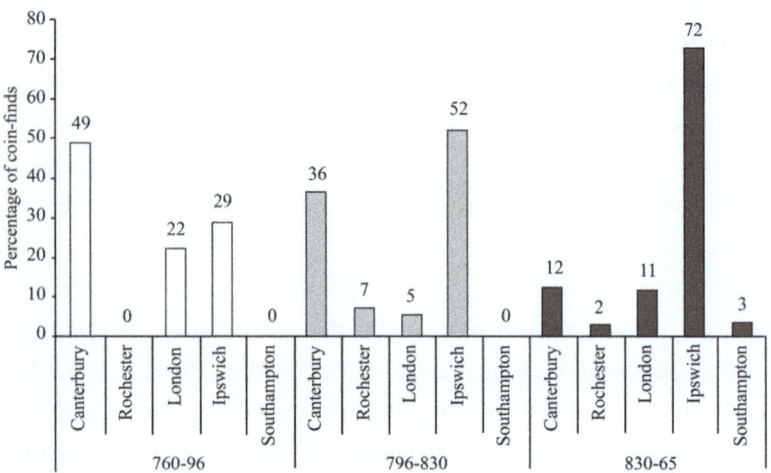

Figure 3.3 Representation of different mints within all finds from East Anglia, c. 760–865 (after Naismith 2012a: fig. 8.2).

of Mercia (839/40–52). Finds of pennies in London show that East Anglian issues amount to 8 per cent of all coins in *c*. AD 760–96; rising to 14 per cent in *c*. AD 796–830; and even higher at 35 per cent in *c*. AD 830–65. Pennies minted in Wessex stand at less than 10 per cent of the assemblage before *c*. AD 830–65 when the figure rises to approximately 20 per cent. Northumbrian coins, it should be noted, are almost absent (Naismith 2012a: 215).

By contrast with this picture of increasing monetization, Southampton is the most poorly represented mint of all in southern England (Naismith 2012a: 216–17; fig. 8.7). Only forty coins survive, twenty of them with known single-find provenances of which Kentish issues make up the majority. Eastern Wessex, on this limited evidence, Naismith concludes, was much more monetized than west Wessex (2012a: 217), unlike the earlier type H sceatta distribution which lay west and north of central Hampshire (Metcalf 2003: 41; fig. 4.1). The comparative rarity of ninth-century West Saxon coins has to be set beside the high-quality Trewhiddle style silver strap-ends that were made in the region, and widely distributed. These distinctive dress accoutrements clearly show that silver bullion existed in some

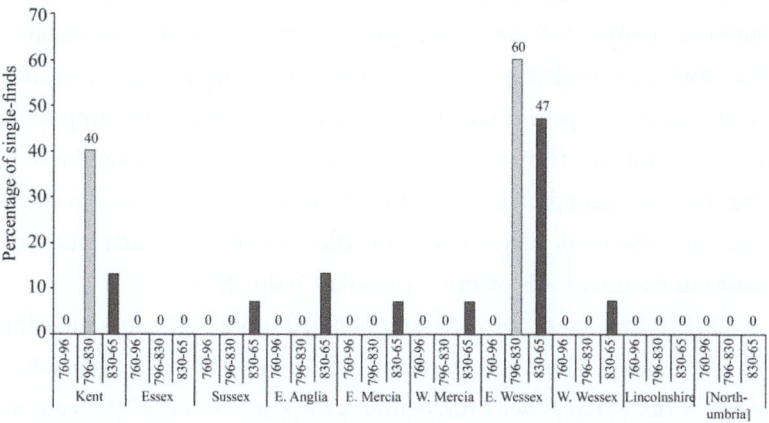

Figure 3.4 Regional representation of finds of pennies minted at Southampton/Winchester, *c*. 760–865 (after Naismith 2012a: fig. 8.7).

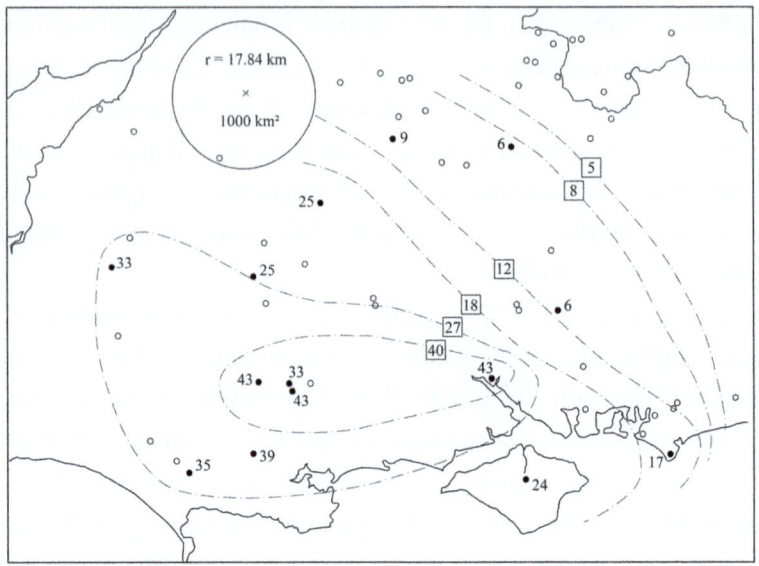

Figure 3.5 Regression analysis of Hamwic type H sceattas (distributed across Wessex) (after Metcalf 2003: fig. 4.1).

quantity in the pre-Alfredian kingdom (Hinton 2005: 113–17). One further archaeological observation about the increasing status of eastern Wessex has been identified by Stuart Brookes following a forensic analysis of landscape, place-name and historical details: the 'soils and landcover in north-west (as perhaps south-west and south-east) Hampshire favoured livestock over arable farming with concomitant effects on the nature of the communities living there. It may be significant that in the north the *regiones* of *Andeferas*, *Basingas*, and *Cleras* were all centred on royal vills for whom the extraction of pastoral resources was priority' (Brookes 2020: 293).

Finally, turning to the kingdom of Northumbria, the loss rates for its issues stand at between 2 per cent and 10 per cent prior to the 840s, when it rises to 57.8 per cent, before settling at around 25 per cent in the 850s and 16 per cent in the 860s. These figures are not dissimilar to southern England until 830s when thereafter the precious metal content in the Northumbrian coinage was reduced to nil. These Northumbrian coins known in this devalued form as stycas were 'the first substantial base-metal coinage in the post-Roman West' (Naismith 2012a: 247). Immediately, the quantity and perhaps the intensity of coin-use in the kingdom increased (Naylor 2006).

Taking all this evidence together, does it throw any new light on the urban histories of the emporia and Naismith's assertion of 'business as usual' (2012b: 331) at these places in the later eighth century? Or does it support Tom Saunders assertion of changing tributary systems in which the emporia had an increasingly ephemeral role as emphasis was placed upon land-owning?

Re-thinking the emporia?

Each of the emporia has a different history in the eighth and ninth centuries, as the coin data tends to confirm. In Gipeswic (Ipswich) the excavations indicate that if there was a mid-eighth-century recession, it is far from evident, and in addition the emporium was flourishing throughout the ninth century. Hamwic has a different history. This much was evident from first systematic phasing of an English emporium involving the seriation of pits from Hamwic made by John F. Cherry (see Cherry and Hodges 1978). This seriation used the five classes of local pottery from twenty pits, certain of which contained coins and imported ceramics. The use of weighed pottery and of a fabric classification that was subsequently re-worked (Timby 1988) may undermine the detailed conclusions but not its general import. The seriation suggested four clusters of pits which might be seen as phases. Phase 1 would appear to lie in the decades around the end of the seventh century; in these pits, organic-tempered pottery occurs most frequently. Phase 2 coincides with the secondary sceattas, BMC 39 and BMC 49. Phase 3 lay around the end of the eighth century, and is dated approximately by pennies of that period as well as the distinctive Tating ware with its tin-foil applied crosses and lozenges (see p.122). The final phase appeared to be modest and post-dated phase 3. The use of multi-dimensional scaling produced further results. The location of the pits along the seriation axis not only showed the best order, but appeared to be accurate to the time scale. It pointed to the abandonment of Hamwic in the first decades of the ninth century (Cherry and Hodges 1978).

Few archaeologists at Southampton have been persuaded by the seriation (note, however, Morton 1992: 27; Riddler and Trzaska-Nartowski 2025). It certainly confirmed that organic-tempered wares belonged to the earliest phases, and shell-tempered wares occurred only in the later phases (cf. Timby 1988: 117–18). Both traditions, separately, appear to characterize the southern English/northern French/Belgian regions. Organic-tempered wares occur early in the sequence at Lundenwic (Blackmore 2001) and in Flanders (cf. Deckers 2017), while shell-tempered wares characterize later phases of Lundenwic (Blackmore 2001) and sites in the Pas-de-Calais (Thuillier 2015: figs 11–12). Beyond this, the seriation suggested strong economic activity throughout the first part of the eighth century, during which time Hamwic minted its own sceattas (series H). Then after a hiatus, a second spike of activity occurred in the later eighth or early ninth centuries, the scale of which merits closer inspection. After this the settlement declined but did not disappear until the late ninth century. Subsequently, Alan Morton and Phil Andrews utilized a revised and slightly different phasing scheme for Hamwic, based on ceramic phasing outlined by Jane Timby (1988: 111–16) and coin evidence, examined by Michael Metcalf with help from Phil Andrews (Morton 1992: 27–8 and 70–3; Andrews 1997: 13–14, 20–1; Metcalf 1988; Andrews and Metcalf 1984). Three principal phases, as opposed to the four found by Cherry, were identified. It was easy to identify the early and late phases, and more difficult to visualize what happened between them. It must be emphasized that much of this work was undertaken when computerized studies were in their infancy.

Now, forty years later, the imported pottery from Hamwic – as well as the many fewer later eighth- to ninth-century coins from rescue excavations – point more clearly to a mid-eighth-century hiatus in both phasing projects, and thereafter a less vibrant town that waned in the earlier ninth century and was a minor port by AD 840, when it was raided by Vikings (see Andrews 1997: 212-13; fig. 99 on the limited mid-ninth-century evidence found at the Six Dials site). As in the case of early Medieval coin-production, studies of later Merovingian and Carolingian pottery have multiplied in the past quarter-century. It is now apparent that later eighth- and ninth-century northern French and Low countries' red-painted wares, as well as Rhenish classic Badorf and Tating wares, while present, are uncommon in Hamwic (see Thuillier and Louis 2015 for an overview of Frankish pottery; also Hodges 2025). The emporium has strikingly few Carolingian imported wares, suggesting, as these were probably accoutrements of traders, that fewer merchants were visiting the port.

Much the same picture derived from coins and ceramics has emerged from Lundenwic. The Frankish imported pottery and archaeological phases point to a downturn in the mid-to later eighth

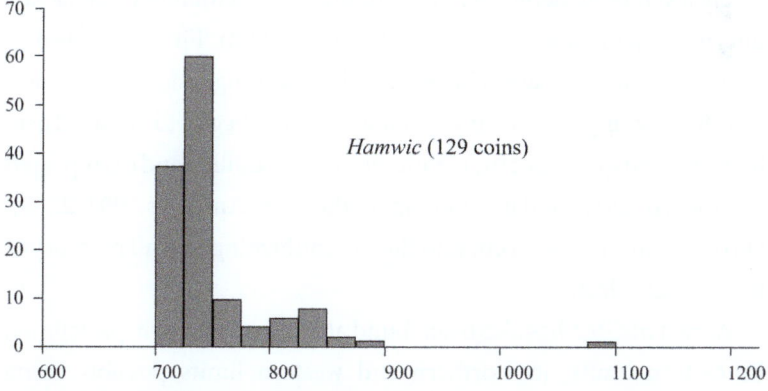

Figure 3.6 Coin finds from Hamwic (after Blackburn 2003: fig 3.3).

century and, a less significant port in the ninth century before it disappeared like Hamwic in the 820s or 830s (see, however, pp.134–5 below, where a settlement lying between Lundenwic and Lundenburg is discussed).

Eoforwic (York) had an altogether different history. The Fishergate sequence shows an abandonment in the mid-eighth century and, surprisingly, as the Northumbrians were issuing their devalued coins in the mid-ninth century, a notable revival. Overall, the picture of continuity in these places overlapping in the later ninth century with their successor towns, apart from Gipeswic, seems highly unlikely now (cf. Hall 2000) (see Chapter 4).

One telling clue to the issue of continuity and change in the emporia during the eighth century is the deep enclosure ditch found at Hamwic. Almost a kilometre long, running along the west side of the town, this V-shaped ditch was 1.5 metres deep and 3 metres across (Andrews 1997: 24). There is only a hint of an inner rampart. First recognized in the Six Dials excavations, it was approximately 35 metres to the west of the main north–south street. The ditch and street were roughly parallel but converged slightly to the north, although a slight bend in the northern end of the ditch may have been intended to avoid the convergence. This enclosure at Hamwic was surely a symbolic definition of the bounds of a settlement that lacked internal tenemental divisions (cf. Squatriti 2002). First conceived in the 680s or thereabouts, it belongs to the founding vision of the place. But this vision plainly changed. First the ditch began to silt up. Then, in the second quarter of the eighth century it was filled and disappeared (on the AD 720x750 date of filling of ditch, see Andrews 1997: 22–3). Subsequently, pits were cut into the fill, confirming that all memory of it was largely lost.

A tract of ditch has also been found at Lundenwic, perhaps defining its eastern limits; its northern and western limits possibly being marked by streams, while the Thames ran along its south side. This

Figure 3.7 The western ditch at Hamwic from above (courtesy of Phil Andrews and Southampton City Museums).

eastern ditch was 3.5 metres wide and 1.5 metres deep and like the Hamwic ditch was abandoned at some point in second or third quarters of the eighth century (Cowie and Blackmore 2012: 114–15). No early ditch has come to light at Gipeswic (Ipswich). One possible explanation for this is that the political genesis of the town, founded only in *c.* AD 715 as the Wuffingas' royal palace at Rendlesham was abandoned, may have differed from the other emporia. By contrast, the emporium at Eoforwic (York), prospered within a ditched area between *c.* AD 700–37 (dated by thirty-four coins) (Mainman 2019: 81–9). After this, the boundary ditch was filled in and, as noted in Chapter 2, the dwellings were dismantled.

The obliteration of the early ditches at Hamwic, Lundenwic and Eoforwic – likely to have been boundary markers – would suggest that the original principles of each emporium altered after the 720s. As the secondary sceatta coinage steadily devalued in silver terms – and then became rare – the political economy, to judge from these details, was taking a different turn. Was this really a recession brought on by a famine of silver bullion or are these indices of the changing political ideology of the age, tacitly referred to by Bede (Wormald 1983: 128; Thacker 1983)? Was the evidently strong pact between the conversion-era English church and the royal families being reconsidered after the early eighth century? Can it be that the authority of the church, having played an important part in the formation of the Anglo-Saxon temple economy after the 660s (Wood 2022), was being disputed by kings set upon controlling exchange to afford their personal armed forces? All this coincides with the emergence of small inland periodic markets in Mercia and then, Northumbria and Wessex, as John Blair has observed (2018: 193). In these circumstances, Hamwic and Lundenwic, would no longer have been monopolistic and separated places but significant settlements in a spectrum of markets. Moreover, as in the competition for markets between Dorestad and Quentovic (Coupland 2002), is it possible that Mercian-controlled Lundenwic steadily drew diminishing numbers of Neustrian traders away from West Saxon-controlled Hamwic? Or was Hamwic being steadily eclipsed by Winchester, the central-place for administering eastern Wessex? Excavations in the old Roman city reveal increasing (pre-Alfredian) occupation after the central decades of the ninth century (Blair 2018: 275).

Gipeswic (Ipswich), by contrast, experienced no such topographical or industrial changes and remained a nodal place throughout this period, notable for its industrial production of Ipswich ware pottery as well as its own coins both of which were principally distributed around East Anglia. Brandon Fathy has identified increasing manufacturing sectors in the town, including blacksmithing at Franciscan Way, coppersmithing at St Stephen's Lane, and two distinct contemporary pottery specialists at Cox's Lane and St Stephen's Lane and potential evidence for an antler/bone carving sector at St Peter's Street and a boat-building sector at Rosemary Lane (Fathy 2023: 292). A possible specialized weaving workshop has also been proposed at St Peter's Street (Fathy 2023: 292). Fathy also proposes that by the ninth century, there was no marketplace in Gipeswic except one for agricultural produce such as grain, timber and livestock. The entire settlement acted as one market, where customers went directly to the crafts workshops to acquire their products (Fathy 2023: 292). Taken at face value, the political economy of East Anglia and its foremost port, a late foundation by comparison with the other English emporia, remained distinct from that of emporia in the neighbouring kingdoms. Certainly, the materialism of East Anglia in the eighth and ninth centuries retained the distinctive ostentatious character of an earlier age. This much can be judged from the prolific number of metal-detector sites found with conspicuous amounts of eighth- to ninth-century coins as well as fine locally made and imported Carolingian metalwork that occur in the region (in contrast to Mercia and Wessex) (Nicolay 2017; Pestell 2017; Pestell and Ulmschneider 2003; Naismith 2012a: 242–3). Finally, we might note in support of this hypothesis that Wickham speculated that these proxies for market relations are a guide to the intensity of aristocratic control in this kingdom on the eve of the Viking conquest (2005: 349).

Discussion

The combination of archaeological evidence throws into doubt the mid-eighth-century recession. This was a period, according to the historian Rosemary Faith, in which land was conceptualized in terms of common-use rights rather than ownership. It was a period of experiment and transition, as I have argued earlier in this chapter, with

Figure 3.8 Selection of Ipswich ware (courtesy of Keith Wade and Suffolk County Council).

increasing peasant and seigneurial investment in cereal agriculture thanks to the mouldboard plough package. Social relationships were embodied in *feorm*, 'this was not taxation, neither was it feudal rent that in kind, cash or labour, transferred surplus to a landlord from land that he in some way owned or controlled and over which his peasant tenants had use-rights only' (2009: 39). Faith describes *feorm* as a reckoning of the commodities necessary for individual meals – bread, beer, meat – and has connotations of hospitality, originally a personal obligation to feed, or feast, a chief. '*Feorm* transferred peasant surplus in order to support the élite of a particular territory – at its largest a kingdom – whose people were peasants who owned or controlled their own land and who in northern Europe were expected to be arms-bearing. The cultural expectation of this system was that the people owed the élite a living or more properly a feeding, and support in battle' (Faith 2009: 31). Strictly speaking, it was not tax or rent in the sense that was to define Frankish feudal relations. This is the social context of the marked changes implemented in English coinage, as well as the background to the individual histories of the emporia.

Clearly, the quantity of silver used in earlier eighth-century coins declined drastically. But was it due to a bullion famine? The first English pennies were mostly silver-rich, and by *c.* AD 792/93 when Offa issued a heavy silver penny, the precious metal was readily available. Now, as Francia appears not to have suffered any similar decline in the silver content in its coinage, it is possible that the metal used by Offa was imported (cf. Kershaw et al. 2024). What now appears less contentious is that the English kings were exercising their royal authority in controlling the minting of coins, and its use in exchange. Parallel to the process of standardization, signaling a king's name on the coin, was an increasing emphasis upon managing production in landscapes, investing in infrastructure and controlling periodic foci of exchange. In these changing circumstances, kings were placing emphasis now not upon gift-giving of imported luxuries but on establishing armed forces and bureaucracy. This marked a shift from tribal societies towards state formation, as many historians have pointed out. In these circumstances, England's four emporia evolved differently. Hamwic and Lundenwic appear to have declined (cf. Astill 2011: 266), essentially now competing for markets in their immediate regions. By contrast, Gipeswic (Ipswich) was sustained, unaffected by these political changes – and operated as a monopolistic transshipment centre dominating local trade in East Anglia. Finally, in the middle decades of the eighth century, Eoforwic (York) was abandoned. Each region's exchange needs, Astill (2011: 266) argues, were now met with a simple, two-level hierarchy of specialized settlements (cf. Moreland 2000b; Palmer 2003). This implies, he deduces, that it is more appropriate to think in terms of a redistributive rather than a market economy. In other words, urbanism was being overtaken by a strategy that was concentrated upon the exploitation of rural societies, similar to the circumstances in early Carolingian Francia (cf. Langlands 2020: 309).

The archaeology of this regionalization is beginning to take shape. Sites such as Barham, Suffolk, 4 miles northwest of Ipswich, and Burrow Hill, close to Sutton Hoo (Woods 2021: 44), would appear to be places where sub-regional exchange (and assemblies) occurred. At Barham, secondary sceattas as well as metalwork and local and imported pottery were inadvertently lost over an area covering 6–7 hectares. Yet, tellingly, limited trial excavations revealed no evidence of either buildings or manufacturing (Hamerow 1998: 198–9). The archaeological footprint is clearer from a remarkable example of this category of site found at Dorney close to the river Thames, west of London. Excavations by Oxford Archaeology on the sites of the Environment Agency's Maidenhead, Windsor and Eton Flood Alleviation Scheme and the Eton College Rowing Course adjacent to the river Thames in Buckinghamshire and Berkshire have provided an unprecedented opportunity to examine a landscape within the middle Thames valley. These sites were located on an important border between Mercia and Wessex with easy access to Lundenwic downstream. Here, in large open-area interventions encompassing hectares, numerous rubbish pits were found resembling those from the emporia, but significantly without any traces of associated buildings. The site(s) appear to be points of periodic exchange involving imported ceramics and Ipswich ware, an assemblage similar to that from Lundenwic, as well as many personal items. Coins, notably, are absent suggesting the occupation occurred after the end of sceatta production when pennies were still uncommon. The personal possessions among the finds assemblage suggest an affluence or status that would not have been exceptional at Hamwic or Lundenwic, but are unusual for a rural site. A number of finds – the bone combs – both in quality and number, the imported pottery (including fragments of a Tating ware chalice like one found at the Viking emporium of Birka, Sweden), an inlaid bucket handle and the vessel glass all attest to the presence of people with disposable wealth.

Another indicator of the presence of private and possibly valuable possessions on the site is the fragmentary remains of a number of locks and padlocks. Two keys, a possible padlock case and possible parts of barb-spring padlock bolt all attest to an interest in securing possessions. The presence of padlocks, however, rather than door-locks and the lack of any structural ironwork such as roves or hinges known from other Middle Saxon settlements suggests they may have been used to secure boxes or chests rather than doors (cf. Sindbæk 2023: 424–5). These Thames-side excavations at Dorney throw light on an emerging category of place for assembly and exchange that was eclipsing the century-old emporia, and at the heart of the Anglo-Saxon political economies in the late eighth and earlier ninth centuries (Foreman, Hiller and Petts 2002: 69).

These changes to England's political economies may have had a knock-on effect outside England: did the English church seek to reinforce its declining status by embarking upon missions to the Continent in the eighth century? Did Quentovic (in northern France) decline as well, as Coupland has proposed (2002)? The first excavations of the emporium are far from conclusive on this point (Cense-Bacquet 2021). Dorestad and Domburg, however, did not decline before the 820s (cf. Theuws 2004; Deckers 2022). Both emporia were connected through their traders to eastern England, and perhaps Gipeswic, but more importantly, their traders as of the 780s found compensatory opportunities in the expanding markets of Jutland and the western Baltic Sea regions (cf. Sindbæk 2022). Ultimately, Dorestad's fate was locked into the changing political ideology of the Frankish realms once it became embraced by the Carolingians in the later eighth century. Frans Theuws summed it up as follows: 'The reasons why Dorestad ultimately perished were the growing discrepancy between the exchange system of the Christian Frankish world.... and the incomplete articulation of the different elements of that system in Dorestad as a central place once it had become fully integrated into that world' (2004: 136). After *c.* AD 820, however, Gipeswic (Ipswich) did not fail, unlike the other three English emporia. Perhaps like Ribe in Denmark, another important destination of Dorestad's merchants, Gipeswic compensated by intensifying its economic footprint in East Anglia. This appears to be supported by the coin-finds from the region. It is also supported by the emergence of polyfocal Middle Saxon settlements beside the river Wensum at *Northwic*, modern Norwich (Adams and Clarke 2022: 5–7; fig. 3; 105–6). In other words, Gipeswic compensated for lost long-distance trade by seeking and perhaps controlling or collaborating with local markets unlike Hamwic and in all probability Lundenwic.

Essentially, as opposed to developing urban-led societies in which mobile merchants and craftsmen played an axiomatic role, as was to be the case in the ninth-century Viking world, the English kingdoms with their close alliance to the political fortunes of the later Merovingian and early Carolingian dynasties opted to invest in rural production and exchange. This said, the evidence does not exist to indicate an eighth-century tendency towards implementing some version of English feudalism (Faith 2009). The successful intensification of England's farms and fields lent these territories a prosperity in which its kings, to judge from their silver proxies in the form of pennies, felt powerful enough to project themselves like earlier Roman and contemporary Carolingian leaders. Parallel to this, by rolling back the compact with the early church, later eighth-century Anglo-Saxon leadership paid only lip-service to the *klosterpolitik* driving the Carolingian revolution. Support for aggrandizing monasteries with new monumental architecture and décor of the kind that came to characterize the Carolingian realm seems not to have occurred. Places like the little minister at Lyminge, for example, were effectively time-warped to the pioneering era of Bishop Wilfrid and his peers. This state of affairs cannot have been lost on the likes of Alcuin, Charlemagne's Northumbrian advisor, and may account for the legates sent to England at this time (Story 2003: 55–92). Coins minted in this period by English archbishops may also in part reflect their intention to lobby for a political status like that enjoyed by their Frankish peers (Naismith 2012a: 67–71). Later eighth-century Anglo-Saxon kings, in other words, charted a path that increased regionalization at the expense of the church and its notion of a temple society (Wood 2022).

4

A Gift from the Vikings?

> *The urban mind in Scandinavia was another product of the Viking Age, a changed perspective on lifestyle and economy that would continue for centuries as another gift to the North.*
>
> Price 2020: 399

The growing prosperity of England based on its productivity was undoubtedly connected to the particular social relations encompassing its kings, the church and farmers. This will not have gone unnoticed at the time. Notably, English kings no longer engaged in power-sharing with the church, thereby resisting the prospect of *klosterpolitik* underpinning the Carolingian economy in the earlier ninth century (cf. Devroey 2020). Then, too, aristocrats and farmers had established tributary relations without recourse to the strict legalistic bonds of feudalism (Faith 2009; cf. Wickham 2005: 344–7). A third order in society, however – those working as artisans and merchants, in Hamwic and Lundenwic, for example – was marginalized. Unlike western Scandinavia, an overt urban culture had yet to materialize. Craftsmen may have had an established place in society but, like Anglo-Saxon merchants, they remain largely undocumented by the archaeological and textual sources. Instead, with the exception of Gipeswic (Ipswich) (see Riddler, Trzaska-Nartowski and Hatton 2023 on the antler and bone-craftsmen in the town), the English kingdoms were increasingly investing in developing rural exchange networks as the numismatic history helps to illustrate. On the face of it, as the emporia waned, England's economy now resembled the immense tracts of Francia as opposed to the growing status of urban communities in the Viking world.

But it is this revitalized trade between the Rhine mouth and western Scandinavia by the later eighth century that has captured most archaeological attention at the expense of the Carolingian investment in redistribution based upon rural central-places. The revitalized North Sea commerce led to the formalization of a distinctive urban culture. Weapons as well as Rhenish wine and commodities were being sent north; in return came Scandinavian specialties such as furs and perhaps slaves to work expanding Frankish estates. The Viking-period emporia may have been separated from their rural hinterlands, but access to the dress accessories, personal accoutrements and weapons made in the emporia meant that their urban culture set the fashion and styles of the time. Before long, the early ninth-century overwintering settlements created by Viking hydrarchs in Francia and Ireland would come to resemble these Scandinavian urban hubs in both topographical details and material culture. One example illustrates the growing difference between the urban cultures in England and western Scandinavia. The distinctive, if idiosyncratic, Tating ware pitchers with apotropaic tin-foil crosses applied as decoration, made in several Frankish workshops, occur in large numbers in the emporia at Dorestad, Ribe and Hedeby as well as Birka and Kaupang. Pieterjan Deckers (2023) in a new assessment of the 159 sherds representing a minimum of eleven vessels found recently in the excavations of a jewellery workshop at Posthustorvet, Ribe, has revealed an obvious yet extraordinary discovery. Each of the eleven or possibly twelve pitchers from the workshop is different. Overtly Frankish Christian visual semiotics were important, Deckers believes. But he proposes these were not for any liturgical purposes, as was long thought. Instead, he postulates, the pots were associated with ritual of drinking Rhenish wine and belonged to the package of Frankish cultural practices (dress, weaponry etc.) favoured in and immediately beyond frontier areas of the Carolingian realm.

Developing this point, Deckers observed: 'The adoption of a visually striking new pitcher type by northern aristocrats, then, more likely occurred via merchant and urban culture in the same way as has been proposed for late-Medieval German stoneware exported (in much larger quantities) by Hansa traders throughout the Baltic' (2023: 79–80). Urban mercantile communities were actively playing a role in setting standards of taste that extended to rural communities in this transformative period. The contrast been the ninth-century Viking lands and England is telling. Tating ware has captured a lot of attention when found in the English emporia. However, sherds of fewer vessels have been found in the massive number of excavations of the four emporia than in one Ribe workshop. Even Gipeswic, the one emporium that operated throughout the ninth century with intermittent Continental connections, has very few sherds of Tating ware (Coutts 1991; Pestell 2017; Wade forthcoming). England, it seems, maintained connections with the Carolingian world, as the common coinage idioms indicate, but remained largely outside its sphere of influence (cf. Naismith 2012a: 175–8).

Eastern England, of course, had an established relationship with the Low Countries and the Rhine-mouth regions of Frisia. As the historian, Stéphane Lebecq put it: 'the result of intermingling populations, the persistence of a common North Sea German and the longevity of the North Sea koiné, more than 60% of the terms of Scandinavian origin . . . relate to maritime life, navigation, fishery resources and their exploitation' (Lebecq 2020: 31). Unsurprisingly, this was to be sustained with the Danish colonizers of eastern England in the late ninth and tenth centuries sharing many common words. Some historians have argued that it was from a base in this region in late AD 865 that the invading Great Danish Army embarked for East Anglia with *Scaldingi*, Vikings and others from the Scheldt delta region (cf. McLeod 2014: 135). Up until the 890s, later factions certainly followed from embarkation points in the region extending down as far as the Pas-de-Calais (the hinterland of the emporium at Quentovic).

The conquest period, c. AD 865–80

The Danish invasion in AD 865–6 bypassed Gipeswic, and overwintered at or near Thetford in Norfolk. This initial force advanced on Northumbria, captured York and established a puppet kingdom. The army then campaigned in Mercia and Wessex. At least two further forces joined the original one in the early 870s, possibly expelled from

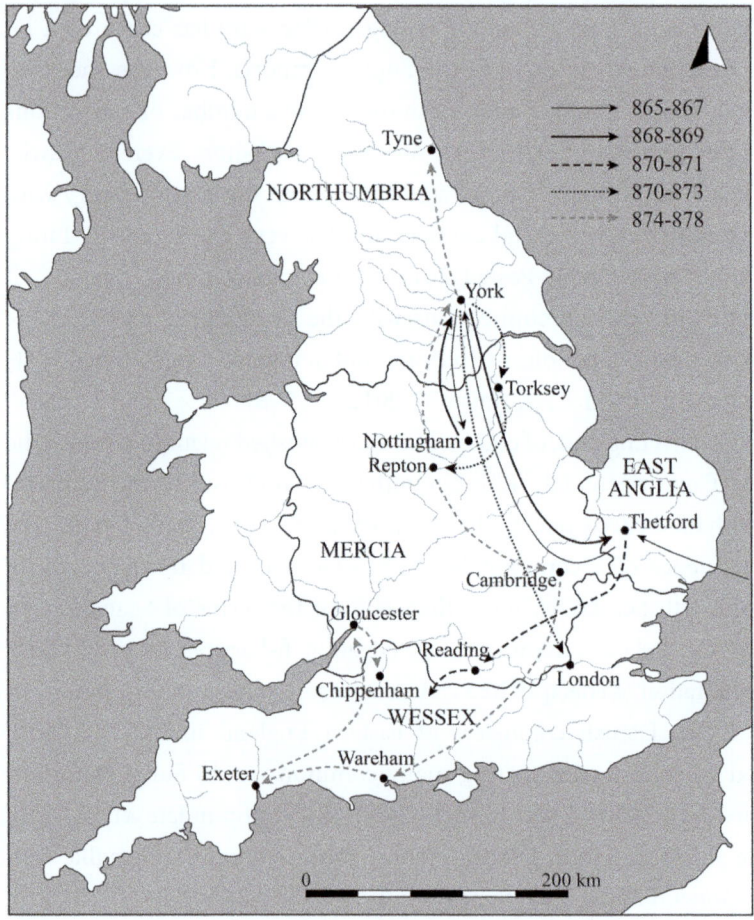

Figure 4.1 A map showing the Viking invasions and the location of Torksey in the later ninth century (after Hadley and Richards 2021: 61).

Frisia after the death of Rorik (a Viking hydrarch who since c. AD 850 had ruled a benefice amounting to Frisia on behalf of the Carolingian court) (McLeod 2014: 168–70). The conflict was effectively ended when King Alfred and the Danish leader, Guthrum, signed a treaty in AD 878. With this the Danes were ceded the old kingdoms of East Anglia, eastern Mercia and Northumbria. Nevertheless, other Viking forces attempted to invade southern England in the next twenty years but were promptly repelled. The historical narrative is largely recorded by West Saxon sources, and effectively charts the unification of England over the following generations as though it was a natural course of events. Yet, the archaeology, as I have shown already, depicts ninth-century Wessex as arguably the least developed English kingdom. The transformation of Wessex at this time owes much to the competition posed by the Danes in the colonial period before AD 900, and especially their imported urban culture.

The origins of the Danish invaders in AD 865 are far from straightforward. King Alfred's biographer, Asser, claimed that the invaders had come from the Danube, but this is almost certainly a confusion on his part (McLeod 2014: 132). The documentary sources point to three possible groups from the Seine valley, northern France and the Scheldt delta region. It is certain, too, that further groups of Danes joined the original army. Shane McLeod proposed, for instance, that the presence of the three kings – Guthrum, Oscytel and Anund – who came in the early 870s may be in Frisia and left after Rorik's brief expulsion from Frisia in AD 867 or his death in about AD 873 (2014: 169). The material evidence offers a much clearer picture of the origins of some, at least, of the invasion force. This evidence includes Carolingian coin-finds, illustrating the use of Frankish moneyers as well as the presence of potters. Both point to a source for the army somewhere in northern France. For example, Guthrum, who was to become King of East Anglia in AD 879, issued a gold penny struck in his new kingdom, found in Norfolk, which had a reverse using a rusty but official die from Chartres, *c.* AD 870–5 (Blackburn 2005: 27; McLeod 2014: 147). Guthrum's earliest pennies are also revealing. A number of the moneyers' names for the coinage were Frankish, and this trend later increased with the St Edmund memorial coinage issued in East Anglia after Guthrum's death. Of the known moneyers on Guthrum's so-called Horizontal coinage, three had Old English names, two had Continental Germanic names, and one had an Old Norse name. By the time of the St Edmund coinage, produced from *c.* AD 890 to *c.* 905, of those that can be read two or three were Old Norse names, eleven Old English, and over sixty, or almost 83 per cent, had Continental Germanic names (Smart 1985: 88; McLeod 2014: 147–8). Moneyers' names do not necessarily reflect their heritage, and some names may have been fashionable for moneyers. Nevertheless, the significant proportion of Continental Germanic moneyers' names is difficult to ignore. The numismatist, Veronica Smart has proposed that the names represent 'a large influx of first-generation immigrants from the Continent' (Smart 1986: 176; McLeod 2014: 148). Smart pointed out that most of the Continental names of the moneyers of the early Scandinavian coinage occur in west Frankish sources, indicating that most of the moneyers came from the region of modern France, with one name probably being Low German. On these grounds, clearly some moneyers in the Danish army had spent significant time in northern Francia before arriving in England. This is supported by a hoard from Laxfield, Suffolk of *c.* AD 878. It included six Carolingian coins; one was from Rouen, but the rest are from further north – from Laon in Picardie, northern France, Quentovic, Nivelles and Saint-Géry, the latter two in modern Belgium (Blackburn 1989: 22; McLeod 2014: 150). These mint sites are consistent with the likely source of the new immigrant potters, much in evidence from this period onwards. As I shall show below, the wheel-thrown pottery introduced to the colonized kingdoms was typologically close to vessels made in northern France and the Low

Countries (but not the Rhineland) and very different from the slow-wheel made Ipswich ware and other Middle Saxon wares made in a limited repertoire. In East Anglia, Keith Wade (forthcoming) has observed, the Ipswich ware industry pottery petered out and was replaced by the Thetford ware industry in the later ninth century. Eight kilns for the production of Thetford ware have now been recorded in Gipeswic. The earliest (Danish period) is the single kiln found at Turret Lane. Another seven kilns belonging to the tenth and eleventh centuries have been found in the north-east corner of Ipswich. The repertoire of vessels would have not been out of place in the kilns found close to Quentovic or in Douai in the Pas-de-Calais (see for example, Louis 2015). The antler combs, however, belonging to the colonial phase resemble those from south Scandinavia and are unlike, for example, those from Frisia (Riddler, Trzaska-Nartowski, and Hatton 2023: 390; cf. Ashby, Coutu, and Sindbæk 2015). In sum, rather like the Carolingian court, the Viking invaders were espousing a variety of contemporary technologies.

The size of the invading force has long been a subject of debate (Hadley and Richards 2016: 24–6). Was the army a few ship-loads of Vikings, or much larger in scale? Almost two centuries later, in 1066, in vessels which still closely resembled Scandinavian plank-built ships, the Viking descendent, William of Normandy reportedly transported some 10,000 men and 2,000 to 3,000 horses across the English Channel, as famously depicted on the Bayeux Tapestry. Two kinds of overwintering sites shed some light on the size of the invasion force. The first type is exemplified by a small D-shaped enclosure found by the River Trent at Repton, occupying only 0.4 hectares, 'once thought to house a small force of three or four ships and a few hundred warriors' (Hadley and Richards 2021: 198; Biddle and Kølbye-Biddle 2001). Was this Repton fort only part of the encampment, or was it designed for a faction of the invading army (Hadley and Richards 2016: 62–3)? By comparison, the remarkable discoveries made at the overwintering camp at Torksey dating to AD 872–3, beside the River Trent, bring the material character of the main invasion force into focus. The enclosure occupies an island and covers 55 hectares. Not all the area was densely occupied, and it may have comprised separate zones for distinct groups. The clear implication is that the Danish army numbered thousands not hundreds (Hadley and Richards 2016: 58). Hadley and Richards describe the evidence from Torksey as 'akin to a town on the move' (2021: 265). A comparable (undocumented) camp has been identified at Aldwark, north of York, and is thought to date to AD 874; it covered about 31 hectares. Hadley and Richards propose that this site beside the River Ouse, again rich in an array of exceptional metal finds, 'is actually the site of the Great Army's winter camp at York' (2021: 218).

The size of these overwintering places is particularly striking when the scale of the three principal Danish emporia of this period is taken into account. Ribe (Denmark) occupied 12 hectares; Kaupang (Norway) covered about 5.4 hectares; and Hedeby (Germany) occupied 24 hectares. Torksey was envisaged as Gipeswic, Lundenwic and Hamwic had been. The camps at Aldwark and Torksey dwarf these emporia. In terms of their scale, these overwintering places are consistent with Kershaw and Røyrvik's calculated estimates that 'the probable number of original [Scandinavian] migrants to be in the region of 20,000–35,000 over the course of the settlement period' (2016: 1679).

The Torksey encampment has been securely identified by a programme of archaeological evaluation, and the plotting of an exceptional concentration of metalwork (see Hadley and Richards 2016: 26–7; 2021). Some seventy metal-detectorists had identified over 1,000 items that caught the attention of the late Mark Blackburn, a numismatist who linked it to the overwintering camp of AD 872–3 described in the *Anglo-Saxon Chronicle*. This led to the systematic archaeological project.

The Torksey camp is located at a strategically important nodal point in the regional transport network, just south of a crossing point over the River Trent, from which the Roman road now known as Till Bridge Lane ran south-east to join Ermine Street just north of Lincoln. According to Domesday Book (1086), the inhabitants of Torksey had the special responsibility of accompanying royal messengers to York 'with their ships and their means of navigation' (Hadley and Richards 2016: 31). Windblown sand covering the islet contains one of the richest assemblages of early Medieval finds from the British Isles, with 1,572 items logged by the national Portable Antiquities Scheme (PAS) by August 2015 (Hadley and Richards 2016: 39, table 1). These included 352 coins (fourteen sceattas; 174 Northumbrian stycas; 124 Arabic dirhems and forty pennies); sixty pieces of hack-silver; twenty-six silver ingots; and twelve pieces of hack-gold. No less important are the 353 lead and copper alloy weights, as well as a balance. In addition, 289

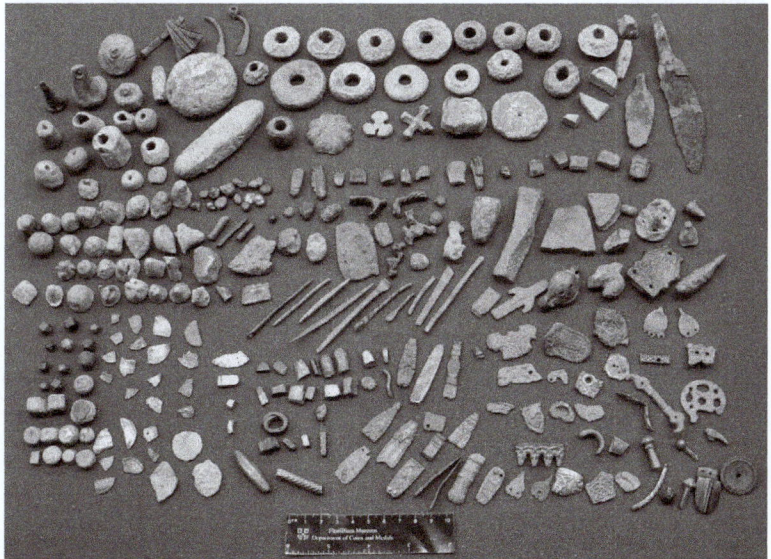

Figure 4.2 A selection of metal-detector finds from Torksey (courtesy of Andy Woods and Dawn Hadley).

metal gaming pieces have been recorded. The coins have a chronological concentration in the 860s and 870s (Hadley and Richards 2016: 43–4; fig. 14). Remarkably, there are 174 Northumbrian copper-alloy stycas, most struck in the 840s during the reign of King Aethelred II (840–8) of Northumbria. which did not circulate widely outside Northumbria and are generally recovered in Lincolnshire only as single finds. The assemblage also includes eleven late stycas of King Osberht (*d.* 867), probably dating to the eve of the Danish conquest of Northumbria. There are also 124 dirhems, the largest concentration on any insular site (Hadley and Richards 2016: 43–5; fig. 15). These had all been cut into smaller fractions, indicating that they had been retained for their silver content rather than their monetary value. Dirhems are notable finds at this time in the Danish emporia, as Christian Kilger has pointed out in the case of Kaupang (2008). The latest dirhems from Torksey have a *terminus post quem* in the late 860s, post-dating the arrival of the Great Danish Army in England, which implies continued contact with Scandinavia during the years of campaigning (Hadley and Richards 2016: 44).

The surprising fact that even gold and silver objects were not recovered at the time indicates the sheer quantity of portable wealth that must have been in the possession of the army. This was principally a bullion economy, as illustrated by the presence of the large number of weights as well as the balance. These may have been made in Scandinavia as they appear to follow the design and weight standards of similar weights from the Viking-period emporia (cf. Kilger 2008). Similarly, finds from the Ouse-side camp at Aldwark has also produced twenty-four cubo-octahedral weights. There is some tentative evidence that the army was minting coins during its campaigns. A strip of lead from Torksey bearing the impression of the die for an imitative gold solidus of the Emperor Louis the Pious (*r.* 814–40) supports the long-held belief that imitative gold solidi were being minted in England, since a number have been found in eastern

England, though not from these actual dies (Hadley and Richards 2016: 50). They seem intended to have served as coins, not pendants, since there is no evidence for suspension loops. A lead impression of a lunette coin of King Burgred of Mercia also suggests the presence of a moneyer. This item has a blundered inscription, as do 23 per cent of the Northumbrian stycas, which may also be an indication that these were Viking imitations (Hadley and Richards 2016: 50).

As in other surface scatters of metal objects from central and eastern England, there are examples of lost silver-gilt jewellery and horse trappings, often clipped or broken. These appear to have been part of the moveable treasure raised as ransom and from raids by the invaders. Rural estate centres like that excavated at Buckden, Cambridgeshire, with its profligate materialism may have been one of the army's victims (Clarke and Connor 2024: 95). This Viking military consumption is little short of astonishing by comparison with the pitiful debris left at Roman marching camps in these parts from the Empire's first-century campaigns. Quite why so many items were lost or discarded is puzzling. Plainly, large-scale deployment of silver in hacked items (coins and jewellery) as well as bullion paved the way for the army's advance as it sustained its own community and negotiated with those being invaded (cf. Kilger 2008: 253). This treasure amounted to the capital at the disposal of the leadership. Individual members of the army were presumably compensated with these items, and many were curiously careless with their stipends. Gold bullion, too, unlike other Viking military theatres, appears to have been extracted, perhaps, from ransom payments (cf. Kershaw 2019: 245).

Metal was used in a variety of processing and production activities judging from the iron and copper-alloy slag. Two hoards merit mentioning: one was of woodworker's tools; the other comprised three plough shares, both hoards indicating the intention to settle and farm (Hadley and Richards 2021: 200). There were also craftsmen in the army. In the excavations undertaken as part of the evaluation project at Torksey, pottery kilns constructed and employed by these craftsmen have been found producing early versions of Anglo-Scandinavian (early tenth-century) Torksey ware. The discarded pottery shows that the camp's potters were pursuing a practised northern French/Low Countries late-Carolingian idiom. Local coil-built Middle Saxon ceramic traditions (in Lincolnshire), with vessels fired in a bonfire, were replaced by new fabrics thrown on a potter's wheel, fired to high temperatures in updraught kilns. The techniques employed were totally unlike those used in the manufacture of Middle Saxon pottery in the region (Hadley, Richards, Craig-Atkins and Perry 2023: 9; Mcleod 2014: 154–5).

As the excavators of this encampment record, 'this industrial revolution had a long-term influence, as the earliest centres of wheel-thrown production spawned 'daughter' industries' (Hadley, Richards, Craig-Atkins and Perry 2023: 29). Almost as soon as the Danes left, the Anglo-Scandinavian town of Torksey was created within the southern part of the footprint of the overwintering camp. In this it resembled the Roman legionary fortresses that became colonies in England. Within the camp, some of the likely immigrants remained and for a century or more continued to make pottery in this Frankish idiom. No less remarkable, it is now becoming evident that animals, dogs and horses, brought from the Baltic, were also present in the overwintering camp (Löffelmann et al. 2023).

The army's abundant treasure was soon to be put to use in a business plan. The archaeology of the Torksey overwintering encampment points to an intention to follow up the invasion with the importation of skilled workers and inward immigration before the Danelaw polities took their geopolitical shape in the following decades (Hadley and Richards 2021: 86–116; 209–18). Paramount on the Great Army's agenda was investment in production, aimed at generating demand focused, however, not in a spectrum of rural settings but in new towns.

Introducing an urban revolution

The Danes targeted the earlier emporium of York as their first objective in AD 867. Was it already their intention at this outset to create a Viking diaspora colony here? Hadley and Richards are doubtful (2021: 218). They suggest that the army had a 'hands-off' relationship with the local population reflected in the installation of a puppet king. This is supported by the decision to create the overwintering camp at nearby Aldwark, as we saw above.

The archaeology of Fishergate by the River Foss shows some revival of Eoforwic before the Vikings arrived. This may have been one outcome of the low denomination stycas that had been widely circulating in Northumbria and surrounding regions on the eve of conquest. The archaeology points to a change of strategy in the later 880s or early 890s, as Lundenburg was founded, as new investment was being made in the diaspora colony at Dublin, and at the Baltic Sea port of Hedeby, and as the rapacious operations of the hydrarchs began to wane (Cooijmans 2020: 210–11). In the following decades, a network was founded in the conquered territories. Apart from York, the pre-eminent town was Gipeswic in East Anglia. In addition, five Danelaw boroughs were established at Derby, Leicester, Lincoln, Nottingham and Stamford. In East Anglia, Dunwich (?), Norwich, Sudbury and Thetford soon emerged as major regional towns to compete with Gipeswic. Many of these places had been foci of earlier Middle Saxon exchange: at Lincoln and Thetford, for example, associated with important minsters; at Norwich, where a possible landing-place existed at Fishergate (cf. Blair 2018: 277; Adams and Clarke 2022: 5–7; fig. 3; 105–6). In sum, the discoveries at Torksey described above, indicate that the revival and in most cases the creation of towns to accommodate a diaspora as in Ireland, and later at Ladoga and Kviv as well as in Normandy, was in the imaginative minds of the invaders.

Town-planning mattered to the conquerors (as it was to in most of the new Viking diaspora settlements). They opted to develop the intramural areas close to York minster inside the old Roman walls. Of the many fine excavations in York, those at Coppergate (the street of the cup-makers) illustrate the colonists' intentions (Hall et al. 2014). A haphazard arrangement of incomplete structures and associated latrines may date to the latest Anglian phase within the walls, or be the earliest evidence of the Danish town seized by the Great Army in AD 867. Following this, property divisions with fence lines were established in the late ninth century, bringing to mind the topographical arrangements at Hedeby, for example, at this time (Kalmring 2024: 163–76). A generation later, in the late 920s and 930s, there was a palpable uptick in production. Structures of post and wattle construction were erected along a street frontage (that in outline still essentially exists). These were replaced in the 970s by plank-built, semi-sunken buildings.

The new topography of workshops at Coppergate has galvanized historical interest. Richard Hall, who directed this ambitious excavation, was struck by the implications of an urban continuity: 'Whoever took the decision to establish the new tenements, they were laid out in plots of equal width . . . It was these new boundaries which remained with a minimum of variation for the next one thousand years . . . even today the outer boundaries of the new . . . development almost directly overlie Viking Age boundaries laid out in 910. This is a remarkable example of pre-Norman town planning . . .' (Hall 1984: 49). Hall suggested that a landowner might have divided a field between new tenants at Coppergate, or else that the system could have been decreed by a city lord (1984: 49). More than thirty years later, the minds behind York's topographic arrangement – the inherent evidence of planning – continues to intrigue historians. John Blair recently observed the following: 'A much-discussed aspect of the Coppergate site is its division into tenement-like strips at right angles to the street. Currently this is unparalleled in tenth-century England, though it must be said that the demarcating fence lines – slighter than the boundary ditches of later Medieval towns or villages – would be invisible in normal excavation conditions. Are 'tenements' – in the strict sense of separate and enclosed house plots – what these really are? The crowdedness of the buildings, and the clear-and-rebuild operation of the 950s, suggest a single proprietor in charge.' (2018: 341). At Lincoln, in excavations at Flaxengate, the built-up frontages from the late ninth or early tenth centuries follow the same formula. A similar sequence – plots for temporary use marked out with fences, permanent buildings erected shortly afterwards – occurred at Kaupang (and Ribe) about a century earlier. Not long after Coppergate was laid out, comparable fenced plots were constructed in Norse Dublin (Blair 2018: 139). In essence, the long tenemental plot appears to have been a genuinely Viking contribution to the built environment of the British Isles (Blair 2018: 281).

Deep deposits of industrial waste like those, for example, in Ribe leave us in no doubt about the explosion of craft activity here and in other parts of the enclosed town (Mainman 2019: 122–3). Imported finds in the town, on the other hand, are few. York's workshops were focused upon exploitation of rural resources and creating demand first in the town then in its hinterland. One exceptional resource, now revealed by isotopic analysis, was the lead ore in the North Pennines, now, judging from the Coppergate finds, exploited effectively by York's new leadership (Kershaw and Merkel 2023).

Unlike Denmark and Ireland, investment in these places was prominent in two contrasting items: coins and pottery. Northumbria's low denomination coinage, stycas, which circulated in large numbers on the eve of the Danish invasion, was now overhauled. Initially, a bullion economy was established, similar to that in, for example, Kaupang accompanying one using silver coins (cf. Kilger 2008; McLeod 2014: 227–8). This appears to have comprised three levels of metal – gold, silver and brass (Pestell 2013: 250). By about AD 895, the bullion was being phased out although hoards with coins and bullion occur as late as the 920s suggesting that the notion of keeping silver as opposed to using coinage in the turmoil of unification lasted beyond the first generation of immigrants (Pestell 2013: 253). Another feature of this transition away from bullion is the end of pecking and bending coins, to assess their silver content (Archibald 1990; Pestell 2013: 244). As of the late ninth century, imitation Frankish deniers replaced the poor-quality Northumbrian brass stycas as Frankish-style media of value. These were followed by a coinage making explicit use of Viking symbolism despite the apparent adoption of Christianity by the Danelaw kings (cf. Coupland 2002: 214; McLeod 2014: 236). Issues of silver pennies depict the raven banner alongside a Christian cross. One coin, minted by the Danish leader of East Anglia, Guthrum, actually includes the mint name Quentovic and probably used official reverse dies produced after the Edict of Pîtres, AD 864. As I have already noted, this was one of several dies that suggest northern French moneyers accompanied the conquering army (McLeod 2014: 147).

Turning to pottery, as Ailsa Mainman noted, York ware was introduced in the late ninth century, replacing poorly made slow-wheel vessels. 'York ware' is an umbrella term for a range of gritty, flat-based, wheel-thrown, kiln-fired and often oxidized vessels that rapidly dominate York's late ninth- to early tenth-century ceramic assemblages. Jars are the most common form, although lamps, pitchers and bowls occur occasionally. There is evidence of experimentation with a new technology which was not always successful. In some cases, the pots were fired to almost stoneware quality, sometimes over-fired, and with a marked variation in surface colouration on individual vessels indicates poor control of airflow during firing. The swift success of these late ninth-century products is striking. By about AD 900, York ware accounts for 70 per cent of the contemporary pottery at the extensive 16–22 Coppergate excavations (Mainman 2020: 68). Pottery imported from the Continent, by contrast, was now rare.

Coin production and potting were just two of a multiplicity of new crafts ranging from leather-working to all kinds of pyrotechnical activities. Unlike the imported crafts, however, textile production appears to have been dominated by established Anglian techniques. The textile crafts that emerge in York in the later ninth century clearly represent a continuation of rural practices. The full chain of textile crafts was still practised as an integrated sequence on one set of premises, with the preparatory stages being accomplished outdoors and the final ones indoors. Significantly, while crafts, such as iron-smithing, silver-working, amber-working and comb-making were concentrated on individual plots, textile manufacturing still maintained a broader background distribution. The most likely explanation for the pattern is that certain families specialized in individual crafts and met the needs of the fast-growing urban population, but textiles were still primarily made to provide for each woman's own household (Walton Rogers 2020: 90).

The new trades included making Scandinavian-style beads with imported Baltic amber. Although known from earlier Anglian levels in York, the amber waste suggests a new level of demand. Schist honestones were also imported, in this case from Norway, while local Yorkshire jet was worked in much greater amounts than previously (Hinton 2005: 137–8).

Establishing a distinctive cultural identity for this diaspora was one of the important purposes of the new urban workshops. People in the region now wore mass-produced dress accessories that melded Scandinavian, Anglo-Saxon and Frankish idioms. Trefoil brooches, originally a Carolingian idiom, occur in Scandinavian styles in some numbers. Of the seventy-four catalogued brooches in England (in 2013), forty-seven (63.5 per cent) occur in Norfolk, and only three in Suffolk (Pestell 2013: 233). No less common, are the pendants known as Thor's hammer, characteristically Danish amulets of the age. Conspicuously, hog-back sarcophagi occur for a period as élite expressions of multi-cultural affinities as the new Anglo-Scandinavian rulers came to terms with an embedded Christian culture. Managing social messaging and inclusion as the West Saxon kings began to threaten the new polities evidently mattered to the Danish leadership.

A dozen other towns blossomed under Danish hegemony, all within fortified enclosures. Each boasted gridded streets and industrialization. Unlike York, Lincoln and Leicester in eastern Mercia issued coins from the early 880s. For a period, a dual use of bullion and coinage was in place. At Stamford in Lincolnshire, where shell-tempered coil-made Middle Saxon wares had once circulated, potters were now making first red-painted and then glazed wares (Hurst 1976). These widely distributed household wares were strikingly similar to those working in the Meuse valley at Huy (Belgium) (Giertz 1996).

The most extensive excavations have been at Ipswich, the erstwhile East Anglian emporium of Gipeswic. Its new lease of life under the Danes has to be viewed in the context of the active initiatives to develop monetary standards in the region (although bullion was still in circulation). The Danish leader, Guthrum, with the Christian name Athelstan, took control of the old kingdom shortly after signing the treaty with Alfred. Guthrum and his followers may have arrived in England from northern Francia (or perhaps southern Frisia), explaining the Scandinavian connection with Frankish moneyers and their familiarity with a monetary economy (McLeod 2014: 228). East Anglia's new ruler soon adopted the idioms of Anglo-Saxon coin, apparently projecting himself as the ruler of an Anglo-Saxon kingdom, and perhaps creating some fictional continuity between Guthrum and his predecessors (McLeod 2014: 229). This new coinage points to an intention to interact with other established monetary economies. This intent is perhaps confirmed by the issuing of imitation coins of King Alfred for a decade from the mid-880s, as Lundenburh was founded (see below). Alfred, however, 'was to reform his coinage soon after Guthrum first issued his, and although Guthrum adopted some of the designs on Alfred's new coinage, he did not copy its heavier weight. This differing weight standard between the kingdoms suggests that their economies were not integrated and that an agreed exchange ratio would have been needed between traders' (McLeod 2014: 230).

Gipeswic, in parallel to the monetary policy of Guthrum, was also subject to investment. A compelling example of the new urban direction is the metalling of all of Gipeswic's roads in c. AD 880 (Fathy 2023: 297). Evidence, too, for the first town defences, dating to the very early tenth century, probably AD 902–17, has now been identified at five excavation sites. Approximately 35 hectares were enclosed by the new defences. The evidence from the School Street site excavations suggests that initially a watchtower was erected looking towards the river and this was then incorporated into the town bank. The curvilinear nature of the defences appears to be a Viking characteristic, rather than the rectangular forms associated with the West Saxon burhs (see below). Two other towns in East Anglia, Sudbury and Thetford, also appear to have acquired curvilinear defences, albeit smaller in area than those at Ipswich. In all cases the early tenth-century ditch was later replaced by larger defences on the same lines but further out. The ditch varied from 2.6 to 6 metres wide and 2 metres deep. After AD 900 there must have been growing concern about the threat posed by the West Saxons under King Edward the Elder. Edward methodically conquered the whole Danelaw with a kingless East Anglia submitting to him without a fight in AD 917. Apart from the new defences, two features of the short-lived Anglo-Scandinavian initiative stand out. First, the townscape took a new topographical form. The major change visible in the archaeological record occurs in building types. A new building type, the sunken-featured building, has been discovered on most of the large Ipswich excavation sites. At St Stephen's Lane, for example, sunken-featured buildings were constructed back from street-frontages to the rear of the sites of earlier Middle Saxon buildings which had clustered along the street fronts. As many of the Middle Saxon buildings had gone out of use, the avoidance of the street frontage implies that it was just less effort to avoid clearing building sites. Second, this period is marked by a major change in material culture. It is associated with thirty coins issued by the Danish rulers and four later Carolingian coins. Another illustration of the prominence of the Scandinavians is apparent from the discovery of thirteen combs of Nordic origin in Gipeswic (Figure 4.3). In addition, other likely items of Scandinavian origin include a pair of cordage toggles, a duck-headed pin and a whale bone clamp. This imported bonework from Ipswich is closest to the array of material from Hedeby, suggesting a southern Scandinavian origin (Riddler, Trzaska-Nartowski, and Hatton 2023: 390). There was also at this time a shift from Ipswich to Thetford ware pottery production, the wheel-thrown pots made to standards imported from either northern France potteries (Wade forthcoming). Imported pottery is scarce until the later tenth century when occasional Rhenish Pingsdorf pitchers and, more commonly, Meuse valley wares occur here (Minter in Wade forthcoming).

The textile industry was overhauled, too. Remains now occur of the two-beam vertical loom as a cloth loom. Walton Rogers interprets the textile industry moving from the rural estates to Ipswich and other towns in the ninth century. After the move, textile workers retained many of the characteristics of a household-run domestic craft (or rather series of crafts), but developed to include the dyeing and manufacture of clothes using finished cloths brought into the town (Walton Rogers 2018: 111; 2020: 100).

The organizational intent behind towns like York and Ipswich cannot be in doubt. The suggestion that these hydrarchs were not capable of such exercises in town-planning, and in York's case it was the archbishop instead who make Jorvik, is implausible in the light of

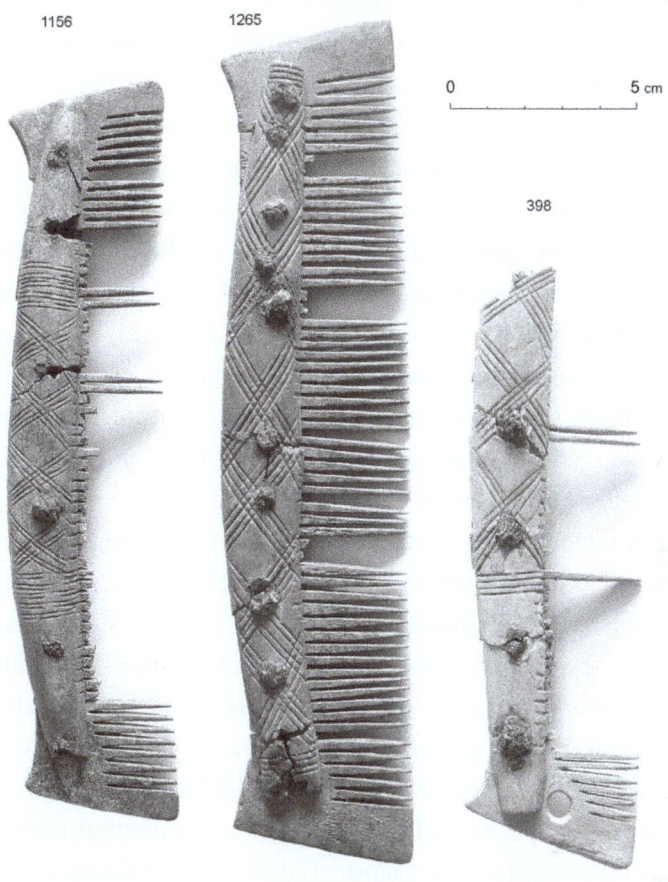

Figure 4.3 Anglo-Scandinavian signature antler combs from Gipeswic with crossing diagonal decoration.

the evidence from Torksey encampment as well as the numismatic history (*pace* Rollason 2003: 223–30; McLeod 2014: 240). The Danish leadership supported or perhaps even encouraged by an established urban entrepreneurial culture in Danish emporia (see Chapter 1), and transformed the agrarian economies of underdeveloped regions once ruled by the kings of Mercian, East Anglia and Northumbria. Initially, a bullion economy was employed to articulate exchange, but this was soon succeeded by coinage, produced in all likelihood, by Frankish moneyers that soon subscribed to established English weight values. Other imported Frankish technologies including pottery and metal production were fundamental to the new direction, while textile production was modified for the new urban communities.

In sum, the Scandinavian diaspora, after a hesitant start between *c.* AD 865–80/90, propelled an industrial revolution that melded together contemporary urban and industrial concepts from Denmark and Francia. By *c.* AD 925, within two generations, as the West Saxons sought to conquer these territories, this revolution was embedded in the Danelaw's towns and regions. Yet as Dawn Hadley has pointed out, there is little in the law of the region that can be claimed as specifically Scandinavian. In northern and eastern England, pre-existing regionalism was reinforced by the political conquests and the arrival of Scandinavian and other immigrants (2000a). Following the unification of England under a single West Saxon king and the codification of the various laws of the country, aspects of the history of the three legal regions of England were called upon in labelling these laws: they became known as the areas of West Saxon, Mercian and Danish law. King Edgar's separate legislation for the region – describing the people as Danes – recognized a political reality that part of the population was Danish in ethnic terms. As Hadley deduces, 'the reason for the use of an ethnonym must derive in part from the recognition that there had recently been a conquest from Scandinavia, partly from the fact that some of the leading magnates in the region were recognizably of Scandinavian origin, and partly from the adoption of Old Norse in legal and administrative contexts' (Hadley 2000a: 300–2). Nevertheless, as John Blair has observed, the disruption of the lives of kings, bishops and minsters had little impact on the vernacular architecture (Blair 2018: 285). Long-term Anglo-Saxon settlement modes established in the sixth century prevailed, as these were articulated to local conditions and materials. Even so, metal-detectorists' jewellery finds from eastern England show an enthusiastic display of Scandinavian identity from the ninth to eleventh centuries (Kershaw 2013), leaving Blair in no doubt that the Viking episode involved mass migration (2018: 306). On these grounds, it appears that the immigrants adapted quickly not just to vernacular traditions, but more importantly integrated into existing Christian communities. This adaptability appears to be one of the hallmarks of the Viking episode. The new leaders could not help but be affected by the traditional concerns of their own territories, and these issues came to influence their political economies as opposed to a simple division between 'Scandinavian' and 'Anglo-Saxon' (Hadley 2000b: 114; McLeod 2014: 226).

This colonial business plan was anchored on new towns in kingdoms where, apart from Gipeswic, the emporia had been reduced to minor ports in networks now embracing periodic ruralized exchange places and polyfocal centres. These networks, with the possible exception of Wessex, had been booming by the mid-ninth century, and may in part explain the bold motives prompting the Danish invasion. Even so, despite the prosperity of much of England and the apparent use of Frankish technical intelligence, the new strategy was not organized in the countryside but was a variant of the booming Scandinavian urban-based economy. Being a radical departure from existing economic norms in England and Francia, this plan must have appeared threatening to the Danes' neighbours in Wessex.

Meeting the threat: Wessex under King Alfred

King Alfred and his court must have been well aware that the settlement of northern and eastern England amounted to a new stage in the century-old conflict with the Vikings. It led to two immediate outcomes: the established kingdoms of East Anglia, Mercia and Northumbria, centuries-old dynastic rivals of the West Saxons, were now essentially consigned to history, and the Danes in their place were creating networks of towns. Alfred was also well aware, as were his peers in Francia, that the Viking threat was still ongoing. Following the treaty with Guthrum in 878, new factions continued to invade England intermittently (McLeod 2014: 112).

King Alfred's response was to invest in London and Winchester, as well as Canterbury, in addition to, over time, creating a new civil defence strategy to safeguard his people against mobile Viking warbands.

One of his earliest major decisions was the revival of London, after AD 886. The emporium at Lundenwic had largely faded away, as the Mercian model of regional centres eclipsed it. The Anglo-Saxon kingdoms at this point were pursuing investment in rural society in lockstep with the Carolingian economic model. This made the decision to replicate Lundenwic at Lundenburh – a town covering about 30 hectares – a visionary initiative that has been attributed unequivocally to royal patronage (Naismith 2019: 121). This happened swiftly as the London mint was established by the late 870s, a year or two after King Alfred's treaty with Guthrum (Blackburn 1998: 122).

London has a curious history in the conflict with the Vikings. It was apparently sacked in AD 842 and again in AD 852 when Lundenwic had virtually disappeared (Naismith 2019: 111–12). Then, the Great Army overwintered either here or close by in AD 871–2, though indubitable archaeological evidence of this has yet to be found (Hadley and Richards 2021: 175). Traces of a possible small camp found in the area of Lundenwic in excavations at Maiden Lane and the Royal Opera House sites may be that associated with the overwintering Vikings close to a mid-ninth-century élite enclave (Cowie and Blackmore 2012: 111; cf. Blair 2018: 270; fig. 102). The diminutive scale of this possible camp resembles the example found at

Repton. Was this a faction of the Great Army who apparently accepted an 'immense tribute' and left, setting their sights on objectives in eastern England (cf. Hinton 2005: 116)? Did the invaders, in other words, deduce that there was greater economic promise to be had at Ipswich and York, and their territories? Nevertheless, both King Alfred and Guthrum surely came to recognize some common potential in this erstwhile emporium. Could this be why London featured as a southern point of the territory ceded to the Danish army in the treaty made between King Alfred and Guthrum in AD 878 (Naismith 2012a: 112–17)? Its re-foundation as an emporium, therefore, may have been not only because it preserved a long-standing status as a crossover between Mercia and Wessex (Naismith 2012a: 118), but also, as the Thetford ware pottery found in at excavations at Bull Wharf shows (see below), a focus for inter-regional trade with East Anglia (now controlled by the Danes). The occurrence of West Saxon coins with silver bullion in early tenth-century hoards in East Anglia illustrates a trading relationship that, for example, did not exist between Wessex and the northern Danish territories (Pestell 2013: 253).

Lundenburh, as its name suggests, was made within the old Roman walls of Londinium, close to St Paul's and in a stroke associated the king and church with commerce. The old site of Lundenwic had been abandoned since the middle decades of the ninth century if not before. Following Lundenwic's decline, Blair proposes that there was a regrouping on its eastern periphery, in the area of Fleet Street, Blackfriars and Temple. Here, there were high-status enclaves, one of which was owned by the Bishop of Worcester, according to a Mercian charter of AD 857 (Blair 2018: 270). Whether these enclaves maintained craftsmen and traders is a matter of speculation, but on the bases of Carolingian items from salvage excavations on the Thames waterfront between Blackfriars Bridge and Southwark Bridge, Blair posits the renewed presence of international traders (see, however, Ziegler 2019, who challenges the implied continuity and employs correspondence analysis to show the many material differences between the *wic* and the burh).

Within Londinium's old walls, following the '*reges ex machina*' model, Alfred over the following decade assembled craftsmen and merchants here. Apart from moneyers, other artisans were probably West Saxon; none appear to have been brought from the Continent, unlike the Danelaw towns. The earliest waterfront activity appears to have been on the western side in the area of Æthelred's hithe (named after the Mercian ealdorman Æthelred *c.* AD 883–911), where a beach market suitable for the shallow-draft vessels may have operated. The use of the suffix 'hithe' in the placename, also used in neighbouring Garlickhithe and Timberhithe, respectively to east and west of Æthelred's hithe, may also be an indicator of the early date of this stretch of waterfront, for it had apparently been replaced by the term 'wharf' by the late eleventh century. Charters of AD 857, 889 and 898–9 are of particular importance as these suggest that trading was underway close to Bull Wharf during the second half of the ninth century, and that at least some commodities were being shipped to London. The charters also indicate that the Bishop of Worcester had commercial interests in London that have been associated with trading salt from brine-pits in his diocese (Ayre and Wray-Brown 2015: 184; Maddicott 2004: 44–5). Excavations at Bull Wharf have revealed the immediate use of the foreshore in the closing years of the ninth century (based principally upon dendrochronology) (Figure 4.4). A limited area has been uncovered below later revetments and reclamation dumps as the foreshore was subsequently remodeled with increases in the size of ships. Remains were found of gangplank trestle walkways leading to the water's edge which had been banked up or revetted. These gangplanks, and the possibly associated low gravel banks at Bull Wharf, are the earliest known early Medieval waterfront structures in the City of London. Two timbers provided tree-ring dates; the first possibly had a bark edge with the final ring

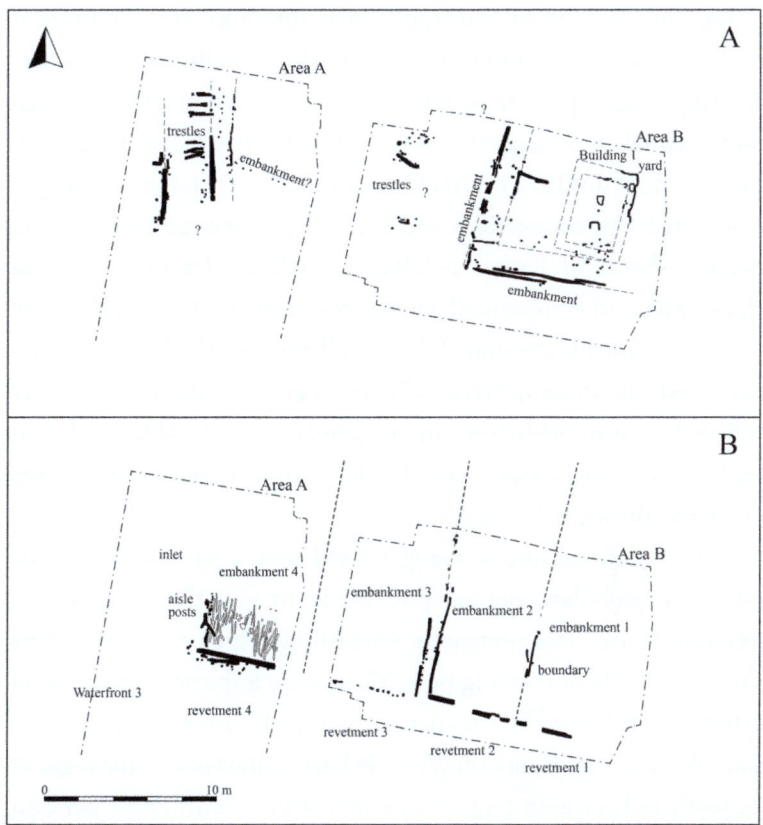

Figure 4.4 Plans of periods 3 (late ninth century) and 4 (late tenth century) found in excavations at the Bull Wharf Thames waterfront (modified after Ayre and Wroe-Brown 2015: illustrations 9 and 13).

dated to AD 890; the second was had provided a *terminus post quem* of AD 887 (Ayre and Wroe-Brown 2015: 133–5). The first clear evidence at Bull Wharf for the division of the embanked riverside into properties dates to the end of the tenth–early eleventh centuries and is probably contemporary with the construction of a waterfront. At this time, the area was divided into at least three, but more probably four, property plots.

The finds associated with the earliest foreshore are important if hardly abundant. The Bull Wharf material is generally similar to other late Anglo-Saxon pottery assemblages from the City of London which have been taken to suggest that there was relatively little trade with the Continent until *c.* AD 970 (Vince 1991: 433–4; cf. Blackmore and Vince 2012; Blackmore, Keily and Stiff 2012). However, the collection includes sherds of Badorf reliefband amphorae (from the central Rhineland) and red-painted tablewares probably from the Meuse valley as well as undecorated Seine valley pots. All these types are associated with the wine trade, which may also be indicated by a silver fir barrel stave, possibly from an imported wine cask, which had been used as a stake in a wattle fence of around AD 900 (Blackmore in Ayre and Wroe-Brown 2015: 184–5).

A more unusual find is a single sherd from a handmade, round-bottomed, globular cooking pot, made in a highly-fired, sandy, greyware fabric. This prefigures Rhenish blue-grey or Paffrath-type ware Kugeltöpfe or cooking pots. These were imported into London *c.* 1040–1150 (Vince and Jenner 1991: 103–4). There are numerous examples of this fabric at Bull Wharf in later contexts dated throughout the tenth and eleventh centuries (a total of 112 sherds or 2.5 per cent of all pottery). Their rarity on City of London sites inland from the waterfront suggests that generally they were not merchandise but items lost or discarded by the crews and merchants on vessels. It may also indicate the presence of small enclaves of Continental traders occupying areas close to the waterfront for short periods and using some of the domestic pottery they had brought with them.

Quantification of all pottery from contexts dated between *c.* AD 900 and 1050 gives an overall total of 6.1 per cent by sherd count and 8.9 per cent by estimated number of vessels for imported Continental pottery, making it the third most common major source at this date, followed by non-local wares from East Anglia and the east Midlands, mostly Thetford-type ware. This demonstrates a steady level of contact with both the Danelaw (East Anglia) and the Continent, increasing towards the end of the tenth century, while remaining constant in terms of sources (Ayre and Wroe-Brown 2015: 181).

The finds also included numerous minor dress and horse accessories as well as two Northumbrian stycas. Apart from the mid-ninth-century coins, the ansate equal arm brooches, disc brooches, a Trewhiddle style strap end, finger rings, hooked tags and harness mounts all date to the later ninth or earlier tenth century as does a (Viking) Borre-style brooch and Scandinavian composite comb, both of which are thought to have been made in western Scandinavia (Ayre and Wroe-Brown 2015: 148–55). The minor metalwork pieces are commonly associated with the North Sea region extending from the Low Countries to western Denmark, and occur in limited numbers in Ipswich (Minter in Wade forthcoming). Quite why so many items were found on this foreshore is puzzling, but they may be associated with traders who periodically resided in this uncomfortable spot for long periods.

One other find was quite extraordinary. A total of sixteen timbers from a Frisian ship were found reused at Bull Wharf. Many of the timbers were still fastened together as they had been in the ship, but all were cut up and somewhat distorted during reuse as part of an early eleventh-century revetment. The constructional details resemble those found in the Utrecht ship and the smaller Waterstraat boat from the same town, and some similarities are also to be found in boat finds from Antwerp (Ayre and Wroe-Brown 2015: 167).

The earliest Bull Wharf evidence provides a small window onto London's Thames foreshore activity soon after the Alfredian foundation. The boats involved – to judge from the finds as well as the reconstruction drawing of the area (Ayre and Wroe-Brown 2015: 186, illustration 36) – were principally river or inshore craft not the larger merchant ships that occur in the Baltic Sea from this time. New jetties at Hedeby dating from late ninth century almost certainly relate to the increasingly diverse forms of shipping in the region (Kalmring 2010: 241–2; fig.

324). Only a century later was the Thames riverside reconfigured, presumably for larger sea-going vessels and an increased volume of trade. The quantities of traded objects point to international commerce beginning with Flanders and the Rhine mouth. Most of the ceramic evidence, however, points to regional trade with East Anglia and the Midlands prior to *c.* AD 970. This regional emphasis is supported by the numismatic evidence. London's coins were widely distributed across England, while almost 40 per cent of the coins found in London derive from all parts of later Saxon England (Metcalf 1998: 21–2). After this, there was an uptick in trade and a corresponding revamping of the foreshore (see Astill 2000: 37–8). By the 1040s a Flemish cleric described it as the *metropoli(s) terrae ... populosissima* (the most populated metropolis in the land) (Naismith 2019: 151–2).

In sum, the new London, with royal, aristocratic, and ecclesiastical properties, occupied a large new defensive space unlike Lundenwic. Lundenburh supplanted a mid-ninth-century élite enclave on the Thames and sprang into life serving a regional market as well as point of perhaps occasional exchange for overseas' traders operating from those Continental regions that had provided the Danes with immigrant craftsmen (cf. Lebecq and Gautier 2010: map 1). In Victoria Zeigler's opinion,

> The evidence for production and consumption in *Lundenburh* stands somewhat in contrast to that identified in *Lundenwic*. Fewer different activities were identified, and there was significantly less evidence for each of those activities, on a per site basis. Only five sites (30%) produced evidence for two or more such activities. The distributions of other categories of material culture in *Lundenburh* also differed from those identified in *Lundenwic*. Vessel glass was not found, and imported pottery was not common at *burh* sites.
>
> 2019

Using correspondence analysis, Ziegler also noted that 'The occupants of *Lundenwic* had a clear preference for surface-laid buildings while those in *Lundenburh* more often built sunken-floored buildings, although surface-laid buildings in *Lundenburh* and the few examples of sunken-floored buildings identified in *Lundenwic*, and do indicate that both traditions were familiar in both settlements'.

By any contemporary standards, Lundenburg's notional peers were new ports like Palermo (Nef 2013), but closer to southern England its late ninth-century model was perhaps Gipeswic and York as well as Hedeby. In reality, however, London's simple foreshore market was makeshift by comparison with the investment in jettied harbour arrangements (for larger merchant shipping) at Hedeby (Kalmring 2010: 241–2; fig. 324) or Palermo's monuments in the later 880s.

Apart from new London, two other West Saxon towns emerged at this time. The West Saxon capital of Winchester, scene of many large excavations over the past fifty years, had been a polyfocal place before Alfred's reign. In urban terms, by comparison with Hamwic, 15 kilometres to the south, it had been underwhelming in terms of topography, production and consumption. Even so, it possessed an important if diminutive minster as well as islands of limited élite settlement. It was, however, at the centre of eastern Wessex, the monetized part of the earlier ninth-century kingdom (Naismith 2012a: 218). Christie (2015) has proposed that from the period AD 840–80 (based on radiocarbon dated evidence) it was accommodating displaced groups from Hamwic. Perhaps pertinent to this revival was the documented Viking attack on Winchester in AD 860/1. According to the *Anglo-Saxon Chronicle*: 'And Æthelbert his [Æthelbald's] brother succeeded to the entire kingdom. And in his day a great raiding ship-army came and broke down Winchester; and Hampshire and Berkshire fought against that raiding-army, and put the raiding-army to flight.' On this evidence, Christie proposes that, like the eighth-century Mercian kings, West Saxon rulers were now starting to muster regional populations and re-stating civil defence duties. Certainly, Winchester changed significantly in the later ninth century, just as York was being reinvented. As at York, the Roman city of Winchester was substantially reorganized (Baker and Brookes 2013: 6). Texts and excavations reveal major royal investment in churches and monasteries, notably the New Minster, under Alfred's son, Edward the Elder. Alfred and his son were also responsible for renewal of the defensive ditches and wall reinforcement; an intra-mural road behind the defences; provision of an ordered network of streets, partly deviating from the underlying Roman design, but with an East-West spine and parallel 'back-lanes', from which were set regularly arranged, parallel North–South roads and alleys, these all defined blocks for housing, workspace and garden plots. Excavations beneath the later Norman castle brought to light eight successive street surfaces, part of a formal master plan in the Alfredian period (with broken flint as a primary surface, with subsequent resurfacings, generally of gravel and chalk). Recent excavations have pinpointed an intensification of occupation and activity in the town's northwestern corner from the mid-tenth century (Christie 2015). At the same time, a proliferation of small private chapels (several discovered in excavations), has suggested the presence of aristocratic holdings not unlike rural manors, occupying insulae within the new gridded settlement (cf. Astill 2006: 246–7). Private fortified castles, however, like those emerging in large numbers all over the Frankish realms, were not to be constructed in English towns or refuges until after the Norman Conquest. Instead, a largely consensual equilibrium established in the later eighth century between kings and the aristocracy that continued to underpin social relations until the eleventh century, thus avoiding the pressure for private defence.

John Blair has made some important observations on Winchester that merit citing to illustrate the centrepiece of this new Alfredian era. It:

> is exceptional .... in providing the only coherent and convincing evidence for a planned street system. Individual metaled streets have been recognized in other 'burghal' places, but only Winchester

manifests a purposefully rectilinear (though not technically grid-planned) framework of streets at right angles to the main axis, with back lanes near the frontages, and intramural streets connecting the far ends. This looks like genuine town planning, although its cultural debt to the earlier technologies of street building recognized in Hamwic (Six Dials) and Lundenwic (Royal Opera House) may have been understated. By the later ninth century, significant levels of occupation had been established within this framework. The clearest radiocarbon evidence yet published is from Staple Gardens, in the northwest quarter of the walled town, and tends to suggest that occupation began there – after the formation of the metaled streets – during circa 840–80. From the outset, the industrial character of this activity is notable, both in smithing and (most strikingly) in cloth dying attested by madder-stained pots

Blair 2018: 275

Charters attest to the proto-urban landscape of large *hagan*, which by the mid-eleventh century had often been subdivided into smaller plots as well as sometimes acquiring commercial premises along

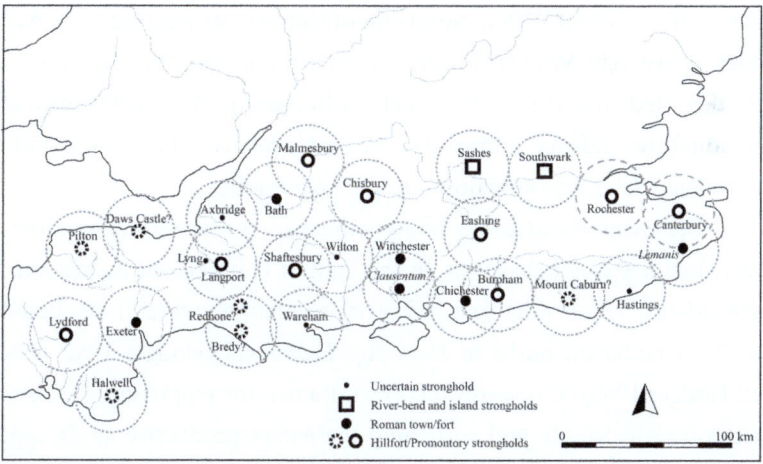

Figure 4.5 A map of the Anglo-Saxon burhs and their hypothetical territories (after Baker and Brookes 2013: fig. 74).

street frontages. This transformation is imprecisely dated, but it was well underway by the later tenth century, when references to specialized craft zones – streets of tanners, butchers, and shield makers – also occur (Blair 2018: 343). During the tenth century, this royal town was monumentalized as a ceremonial capital with basilicas in a West Saxon version of a major Ottonian central-place. Could it have been a West Saxon imitation of Rome (which Alfred had visited as a child), by this time in thrall to a spate of new (later ninth-century) aristocratic buildings (Meneghini and Santangeli Valenziani 2004; Delogu 2022: 357)? This topographical mix could not have been more different to Hamwic's streets of similar craft workshops.

Besides Winchester, Canterbury had a similar makeover. Apart from being the seat of the archbishopric, and one of pre-Viking England's premier mints, like Winchester and York it was slowly transformed into a commercial centre serving Kent. This did not come cheap: 'urban plots with fields and meadow-land around Canterbury could sell for as much as ten times the price of the same area of land in the country' (Brooks 1984: 27). One place overlooked by King Alfred was Southampton. By the mid-ninth century, the status of the Solent Water emporium of Hamwic, as we have seen, had been usurped by Winchester. No longer a major port, the place was to be demoted to a diminutive burh. It became part of a network of regional civil defence, administration and local markets. Foreign trade to Solent Water was now no more than occasional.

Other towns would slowly follow in the shadow of these major centres, as I shall describe below. But, in the light of many recent excavations, the urban take-off ('the first industrial revolution') which I attributed to the Late Saxon burhs in *Dark Age Economics* (Hodges 1982: 165; cf. Hodges 1989) now seems incorrect. Rather, the emphasis in Wessex was on civil defence and sustaining the extant productive landscapes and rural markets (like that at Dorney beside the Thames described in Chapter 3) that had existed since the eighth century (cf. Langlands 2020:

302: 309–10). The Alfredian civil defence strategy comprised three elements: the making of 33 fortifications or burhs in southern England, the creation of a permanent standing army (*fyrd*) in AD 893, and the building of a fleet two years later in AD 896. The most ambitious element was the making of the burhs described in a text known as the Burghal Hidage, dating to the early tenth century and specifies the land (in hides) and men required for the maintenance of each fortress:

> For the maintenance and defence of an acre's breadth of wall sixteen hides are required. If every hide is represented by one man, then every pole [5 metres or 16.5 feet] of wall can be manned by four men. Then for the maintenance of twenty poles of wall eighty hides are required.
> Baker and Brookes 2013: 32–3

Much like the Frankish public works initiated by Charles the Bald after the Edict of Pîtres (AD 864) to confront the Viking raiders, the Burghal Hidage system formed part of an established defensive initiative. Baker and Brookes (2013: 383) have identified five grand strategies, visible in the evidence:

1. Frontier defence (eighth to early ninth century)
2. Defense-in-depth (late ninth century)
3. Linear defence (*c.* late ninth–early tenth centuries)
4. Offensive burhs (early to mid-tenth century)
5. Territorial defence (late tenth century)

The Burghal Hidage, therefore, does not represent the outcome of a single big idea, but the culmination of a series of innovations and restructurings of 100 administrations within the shires. It involved as much organizational oversight to make these new earthwork- and walled-places as to reinvigorate Londinium. As Neil Christie observed:

> The scale of these operations – in terms of planning, logistics, manpower, engineering – appears substantial and is, even to

modern eyes, remarkable, requiring the mustering and exploitation of people not just for war, but for garrisoning, and for the very act of refortifying sites and creating new bases of operations and strongholds. That the kings were successful in formulating this strategy, in engaging manpower for often extended campaigns and in creating a workable and effective defensive system – comprising far more than strongholds alone, but also beacons, dykes, road guards, watchtowers, river defences – as much reflects their determination and leadership as the abilities of the workforces, both male and female, on the ground.

Christie 2015: 66

For Alfred, the tight net of fortified places or refuges across southern England provided defence-in-depth, a militarized frontier zone within which locally mobilized forces could confront or delay an invading army (Baker and Brookes 2013: 387–97). It was designed so that each covered a radius of about twenty miles (Baker and Brookes 2013, fig. 74) (Fig. 4.5). This strategy was augmented by linear defences intended to deny the Vikings access to river and road networks.

The late ninth- and tenth-century places listed in the Burghal Hidage fall into four distinct categories: reused Iron Age hillforts; reused Roman towns with stone walls; regularly planned Anglo-Saxon forts; and Anglo-Saxon forts of irregular or undefined plan. The homogeneity of the hidage (tax/tribute) obligations is in marked contrast to the variety of the places in the list. That variety may be due to the chronology of the forts as well as their topography. An emphasis on the regularity of the West Saxon system has distracted attention from the irregular character of fortresses themselves (Blair 2018: 270–3; cf. Biddle and Hill 1971). Primarily the archaeology indicates that the burhs were intended to meet a civil defence crisis in the face of Viking threat to Wessex (and its people) (Baker and Brookes 2013: 413–14). To achieve this military purpose required aristocratic participation. Aristocrats brought local leadership and provisioning to garrisons. Successive West Saxon kings achieved this involvement by grants of holdings in the burhs to thegns and higher members of the élite (Astill 2006: 246).

The planned grids within Cricklade, Oxford, Wallingford and Wareham hint at a Roman model, but after many excavations in these burhs it is now clear that the beginnings of an urban landscape were slow to take off. Gloucester is a good example of this. The plan of the street grid discovered in excavations at the Mercian burh – a minster with a royal palace nearby – has been likened to that at Winchester (Biddle 1976: 134–5). But Blair has pointed out that there are no signs of 'urban-type' buildings in the burh until c. AD 1000, and the earliest activities – as at comparable Mercian burhs at Hereford and Worcester – are mainly industrial (Blair 2018: 344–5). This slow industrialization compares strikingly with the investment made in fortifying these new places. At Cricklade, 34,000m² of material was used in the ramparts requiring a thousand men for four months, while at Wallingford, an estimated 120,000 man-hours were invested in making the defences (Christie 2015: 62). The interior of Wallingford has been excavated on a large scale to uncover details of the Late Saxon plan and road system. Somewhat surprisingly, these excavations revealed no Late Saxon settlement – and minimal Medieval activity – in the open spaces on the town's western side, the implication being that these were primarily open ground, perhaps for animal pasturing, fairs/markets, and initially for army encampments and refugees. Christie concludes with good reason that Wallingford served primarily as a mustering point, and its size was in anticipation of this civil defence role.

In sum, the archaeological evidence strongly points to urbanization of the burhs as the exception rather than the rule, and when it occurred it was triggered by focusing upon commercial and industrial activities that were already established (Blair 2018: 349–50). This explains why Grenville Astill (2000; 2006) contended that it is necessary to de-couple 'burghal' fortification from actual urban growth. He believes that local exchange systems that had operated before the Viking conquest fragmented and were not replaced. A pronounced reduction occurred in the level of material culture on most rural sites, possibly provoked by the measures to combat the Danish occupation wherein an increased proportion of productive surplus from aristocratic estates was diverted to sustain the military effort (Astill 2019: 48). Only as the threat receded did this centralized – top–down – economy begin to grow, and then grow fast. As Alexander Langlands has pointed out, the (West Saxon) laws of the early tenth century explicitly restrict trade to designated places – principally a burh defined in Frankish terms as a *portus* – an indication that royal authority was attempting to replicate an existing Carolingian model (2020: 309). Developing this observation, Langlands proposes that 'both sheep and cattle farming, and those concerned with their successful management, exerted a pull that influenced key developments in the political control of the late Saxon economy. [King] Edgar's strategies should therefore be viewed as much as responses as they are initiatives in an on-going negotiation. The restrictions on limiting trade to the burhs may have been lifted, and the need for the witnesses to follow the trade, rather than the other way round, may have been conceded, but elsewhere, in the reform of the coinage, we see a tightening up of fiscal arrangements' (2020: 310; cf. Naismith 2014: 82). King Edgar's monetary reform of c. AD 973 was certainly intended to increase centralized controls as well as imbue trust in monetary values. He introduced a uniform design across the kingdom carrying the king's name and bust on the obverse, and a small cross in the centre on the reverse surrounded by an inscription showing the name of the moneyer and mint. The dies were now manufactured centrally, probably at first at Winchester, as part of a new administrative framework. With this reform significant urban growth occurred in many burhs (paralleling that in Lundenburh). By then, though, many of these burhs had become the seats of moneyers, and were soon to be revived as refuges again as a second wave of Danes threatened England. The renewed Viking attacks in the early eleventh century led to the recommissioning of hill forts such as South Cadbury and Old Sarum (Biddle 1976: 140–1; Astill 2006: 242). The apparent wealth of England was inherently attractive to a new generation of eleventh-century Danish kings, Sven Forkbeard and Cnut, as well as the Norman, William. Moveable wealth from these places was deployed as Danegeld to pay off the new Danish invaders. One projected statistic estimate is that 12 million or more silver coins were circulation by the eleventh century, principally to sustain an army (Hudson 2016: 37–8).[1]

One further point emerges from the archaeological evidence, now much enriched by the discoveries made at the Danish overwintering camp at Torksey. Imported Frankish pottery techniques and repertoires were essentially not adopted in Wessex. Production, too, appears to have based in the countryside until the late tenth or eleventh centuries at earliest, when kilns were established in new towns such as Chichester and Exeter (Astill 2006: 248). This resistance to Frankish technical ideas in contrast to the Danelaw is curious. After all, the West Saxon court had a strong relationship with the Counts of Flanders through marriage (cf. Grierson 1941; see Chapter 5). One exception was glazed Winchester fine ware. This was a late and (in industrial terms) small-scale imitation of glazed Meuse valley wares by comparison with the major (glazed-ware) potteries started under Danish control at Stamford and York (Biddle and Barclay 1974). Instead, wheel-thrown wares were produced in an indigenous West Saxon idiom. Is pottery a proxy for other industries wherein West Saxon craftsmen pursued established practices as opposed to imported ones as much as anything to signal social inclusion? This appears to be the case for the finest metalwork of the Alfredian age and afterwards. Wessex had long since

---

[1] Metcalf (1998: 27) calculated the Danegeld payment made in AD 1018 amounted to 25 million silver coins.

boasted exceptional silversmiths, pursuing a distinctive style using niello as background to a wide range of contorted animals, birds, plants, leaves, knots and occasional humans, taking its name from a coin hoard at Trewhiddle (Cornwall). Strap-ends in this style occur in large numbers and were widely distributed around pre-Danelaw England. Goldwork in this style was also technically good (Hinton 2005: 113–17). The Trewhiddle style was succeeded by the Winchester style, a Carolingian-inspired acanthus-leaf ornament. Whether it was made in Winchester is a moot point, but the capital lent its name to the finest of a number of large, tongue-shaped, cast openwork strap-ends discovered in a mid-tenth-century grave in the minster cemetery. These display pairs of birds and animals on either side of a plant stem, presumably a Tree of Life, taking its narrative from manuscript decoration. Enamel-working, on the other hand, introduced to Wessex at this time, is the first known use in England of the technique of fusing the colours into cells, not setting pieces of glass in as inlays, such as garnets (Hinton 2005: 133–4).

Apart from outstanding works of art (the Alfred Jewel, the Fuller, Pentney and Strickland Brooches), alongside the steady monumentalization of Winchester, the West Saxon lineage introduced regalia in royal inauguration ceremonies. Taking a leaf out of Carolingian regal practices, the West Saxons now conspicuously displayed their ascendent political authority. Alfred's son, Edward the Elder (r. 899–924) may have been the first English king to be crowned, rather than anointed. His son Athelstan (r. 924–39) made a significant change by being shown wearing a crown, a band with upright spikes, but he did not dispense with tradition altogether as at the back of the crown were diadem ties (Hinton 2005: 132).

In sum, King Alfred invested in imposing his political status, and conveying through the creation of a capital and new port, his commitment to political and economic stability. Essential to the political ideology was a comprehensive programme of civil defence.

By contrast, West Saxon investment in urbanization was modest by the standards being set in the Danish territories after *c.* AD 890, and it is far from clear whether investment in technological change can be chalked up as one of Alfred's achievements. Nevertheless, Alfred's investment in reviving London, Winchester and perhaps Canterbury with managed minting of silver coinage shows a shift towards a political economy that was markedly different to that he had inherited.

Discussion

King Alfred's skill was to establish around his person a mythology of righteous resistance. Sir Frank Stenton attributed to him a Churchillian status: 'He had created at least a rudimentary organization for the protection of his people, and had made the greatest of English towns an outpost against the national enemy. On any estimate, he was the most effective ruler who had appeared in western Europe since the death of Charlemagne' (1971: 269). This was so effective that in many respects, not unlike Charlemagne's lasting place in history, this reputation persists until today (Baker and Brookes 2013: 8). In signing his charters as *rex Angul-Saxonum* rather than *rex Saxonum*, he established his claims to much more than West Saxon inheritance. He used the crisis to unite his (Christian) people, and effectively foreshadowed the elimination of Mercia as a kingdom (in about AD 918) as well as the unification of England. Perhaps his greatest legacy, as Sarah Foot concluded, was to shape 'an English imagination' (Foot 1996: 34). Certainly, the imaginary community evident in the West Saxon material culture remained distinct from the Anglo-Scandinavian world of utilitarian Frankish-style pottery and dress and funerary accessories that evoked a Viking origin until well after the unification.

Alfred's resistance centred upon re-setting his political economy to afford a civil defence strategy against the Vikings. His commitment to London's mint, then to the re-making of London as a port, were major initiatives. Its promise as an economic hub lay as much in trading with southern England, as interacting with established regional traders from East Anglia (albeit under Anglo-Scandinavian hegemony). Nevertheless, tellingly, the revival of London was achieved using indigenous artisans rather than importing skills. A half-century had passed since the waning of Hamwic and Lundenwic in which a rural redistributive strategy with only a gradual emphasis upon monetization had replaced the pre-eminence of the emporia as networked exchange hubs. As we have seen, only the kingdom of East Anglia had maintained an earlier urban hub at Gipeswic which, judging from the distribution of its distinctive Ipswich ware, served smaller markets and centres throughout the kingdom. In Northumbria, the revival of Eoforwic on the eve of the Viking invasion as well as the issuing of a low denomination coinage, stycas, suggests the kingdom may have been attempting to emulate the East Anglian economic model. Lastly, the Viking decision to accept a ransom payment and withdraw from London in AD 871–2 suggests, given their subsequent strategy, that they may not have considered London to be economically promising.

The discoveries made at the large overwintering camp at Torskey dated to AD 872–3, and Aldwark, close to York, show that the Great Danish Army amounted to a town on the move. At first, the invaders ruled through puppet officials, but changed course as of the 880s. The foundation of York as well as the later ninth-century history of minting using Frankish moneyers point to a Danish urban-based economic plan articulated by values initially calculated using silver bullion then coinage. Explicit changes were made to the material culture of the newly conquered territories, creating an Anglo-Scandinavian idiom for the diaspora. Yet the immigrants appear to have been integrated into the pre-existing rural landscape.

The explosion of urban and industrial activity in the Danish territories was exceptional by any standards. A network of towns minting coins and producing wheel-thrown pottery were yet to be founded in Denmark. In Ireland, the Norse created enclaves in which coinage was not in circulation for a further century, and wheel-thrown pottery did not exist. Normandy, once in the hands of Duke Rollo in the tenth century, may have pursued this Anglo-Scandinavian programme, but the archaeological evidence is presently insufficient. We cannot doubt that these urban diasporas made an impression on King Alfred and his court. Yet the West Saxons prioritized civil defence paired with an emphasis on monumentalization and regal display. From the 920s there was a steady growth in the number of mints established in burhs, reflecting royal determination to control coinage, and oversee and protect moneyers and their bullion (Allen 2014). The loss of coins in this period was considerably less than that of sceattas in the eighth century, which would suggest a reduced level of regional trading during most of the tenth century (Astill 2006: 244; fig. 11. 2). 'The tenth century, then, appears to be the lost century for the burhs of Wessex', Grenville Astill posits (2006: 245). Astill's sequence suggests that for several generations the burhs and their occupants were unsure of their status because the relationship with their region had not been settled. It is not yet clear how significant these civil defence foci were as administrative, religious or economic centres before King Edgar's coin reform in the 970s. The eleventh century was a critical time when the potential for the emergence of an urban identity was being realized. But, Astill asks, was this identity still dependent in the old West Saxon realm on continued royal supervision or intervention (2006: 251)?

By contrast, this was not the case in the Anglo-Scandinavian territories. There is plentiful evidence for town growth in the north where urban identities were well established. This differential development may be explained by a greater economic vitality in the north thanks to the diaspora's entrepreneurial ethos which was not experienced in the south until the later tenth century (Blair 2018:

342–4; Astill 2000; 2006). This topsy-turvy archaeological narrative masks many nuances which are still being investigated as more metal detector evidence complements forensic studies of landscapes and their agricultural products. Most of all, care needs to be taken in interpreting the West Saxon story principally emanating from the court at Winchester. In essence, one principal difference between the two regions can be summed up by the presence of an artisanal and mercantile ethos in the overwintering camp at Torksey. The Great Danish Army invaded with intent to make versions of Hedeby, Kaupang and Ribe, and to colonize underdeveloped English central places with artisans and traders, schooled in Carolingian best practices.

The sum of the archaeology could not be clearer: under the often-violent spell of the Viking conquest, England shifted to becoming a matrix of new kingdoms then, as of the later tenth-century unified kingdom, where the political economy was anchored upon a combination of towns and strategically-placed refuges. Alert to this difference, this may account for King Alfred's curiosity about the Arctic trader, Ohthere (Bately and Englert 2007). The Nordic visitor described his life to King Alfred who recounts the encounter in his Old English version of *Orosius*. Above all, it illustrates a boldness and worldview that ran in parallel to the infamy of the sea-kings. Without recourse to monsters or marvels, this was a sober and restrained account, never over-stretching credulity (Bately 2007: 34). It is not difficult to imagine how the West Saxon king and his councillors were captivated equally by the daring seamanship and business acumen of this Norwegian. Ohthere, after all, was a representative of an entrepreneurial culture that in the 890s was being actively promoted by Alfred's nemeses in the old kingdoms of East Anglia, Mercia, and Northumbria. Was the English king curious to understand the cultural background from which his Viking adversaries came? Was he equally enraptured by the Viking's belief in *hamingja*, luck-spirit, that got him home from his long voyages (Price 2020: 61; 503)? Did he want to understand the parameters of the Viking diaspora economies which now mattered to his administration (given his commitment to the reinvention of London as a port)? Symbolically, the Norwegian's presence at court and Alfred's account about him illustrates the beginnings of a new age in the 890s, one that was also to have ramifications beyond England.

5

Re-reading Pirenne (Again)

Historians and archaeologists will dissect [Henri Pirenne's] ... work in relation to the ideological expectations of their own day and will replace still-imperfect approaches with alternative interpretive strategies and analytic techniques. However discouraging it may be to recognize the cyclical nature of this scholarship, this cycle of reinterpretation should not prevent medievalists from exposing the way in which the contemporary perspective we have, in this specific moment in history, has colored our understanding of the medieval past. New findings and methodologies should inspire scholars to find more nuanced ways in which to conceive of the transformation of the Roman world.

Effros 2017: 208

By the tenth century, England was pursuing two different urban models: the Anglo-Scandinavian colonial model and the West Saxon model that grafted at least three substantial towns onto a spectrum of rural settlements including refuges with their roots in the later eighth century. The colonists had imposed Danish urban practice on the earlier English regional economies of managed rural redistribution at estate centres, in essence a version of a Carolingian economic strategy. The Carolingians, as Frans Verhaeghe pointed out, 'had only a limited or perhaps even parasitic interest in the urban phenomenon' (2005: 284). Their rural economies – including craft production and distribution – continued instead to be anchored on estate centres like the royal fisc excavated at Vetricella, Tuscany (Bianchi 2022: 189–201; cf. Peytremann 2023). This clear distinction in the tenth century between the English urban story and the genesis of later Carolingian and Ottonian towns makes the case of the County of Flanders and Pirenne's interest in it all the more intriguing. But then, the County of Flanders, unlike other Carolingian regions, had strong connections with both the Vikings and, after AD 890, the West Saxons. It is these relationships, in the light of the English urban story, which beckons us to re-read and critique Pirenne.

Pirenne was born in the industrial east of Belgium, but spent forty years as a professor in Ghent, close to the North Sea (Lyon 1974; Keymeulen and Tollebeek 2011). His scholarship was devoted to the origins of his homelands, but his heart was rooted firmly in the coastal towns of Flanders. Inevitably this shaped his reading of history. Unsurprisingly, he had a romantic view that mariners and people on the move rather than farmers were the founders of European Medieval civilization. A decade before *Medieval Cities*, he wrote: 'Of the condition of the *negociatores* who served as the instruments of these exchanges, we know almost nothing. Many of them were unquestionably merchants of occasion, men without a country, ready to seize on any means of existence that came their way. Pursuers of adventure were frequent among these roving creatures, half traders, half pirates ... Clearly no one will try to find in this strong and fortunate bandit an ancestor of the capitalists of the future ...' (1914: 498). These adventurers were strong and fortunate bandits who seized the many opportunities which commercial life offered by using their wits to get a living (Pirenne 1936: 46–8; 2014: 139). Medieval civilization, in his telling, grew out of the places where merchants were present and shaped the burgher communities of the western cities of eleventh- and twelfth-century Francia. In Pirenne's words: 'The birth of cities marked the beginning of a new era in the internal history of Western Europe. Until then, society had recognized only two active orders: the clergy and the nobility. In taking its place beside them, the middle class rounded the social order out or, rather, gave the finishing touch thereto. Thenceforth its composition was not to change; it had all its constituent elements, and the modifications which it was to undergo in the course of centuries were, strictly speaking, nothing more than different combinations in the alloy' (2014: 138). Pirenne's thinking was in line with those of sociologist, Max Weber's conclusions about the western city. Writing at this time, in Weber's view the Medieval city was simultaneously a defensive organization, a market, the independent generator of law and justice, and the possessor of rights to self-government. It was an emotional community, based upon a mutual contract (Weber 1966; Boone 2012: 339). Nevertheless, as Søren Sindbæk has astutely pointed out, these observations from the 1920s belong to hindsight, an imagined picture of the primitive origins of twelfth-century communes in the Low Countries. Pirenne, Sindbæk proposed, was reverse-engineering on the expressed assumption that 'the steady progress of economic activity from the end of the tenth century would result in [...] aggregations of like character but much more important and more stable' (2020: 134, n.24).

It is to storied mariners and pirates, then, that Pirenne attributes the origins of Christendom's post-Roman urban revival. As we saw in Chapter 1, his reading of the beginnings of Flemish towns like Ghent has been challenged by many historians, notably his fellow Belgian historian, Adriaan Verhulst (1989; 1999). Verhulst has argued, *contra* Pirenne, that these places emerged first as regional centres before engaging in long-distance trade in staples (Verhulst 1999). Verhulst's conclusion, as it happens, is consistent with the emerging history of the Danish towns in England as well as, for example, the earlier periods of Anglo-Saxon Lundenburh. As such, given the marriage connections between the courts of later ninth-century Wessex and the County of Flanders, and given the status of places like Ghent in European Medieval history thanks to Pirenne and Verhulst, it is pertinent to make a brief excursus into the beginnings of Flemish towns and their particular culture.

The rise of Flemish towns

Two essential details have emerged from the post-Pirenne studies of the Flemish towns. First, they were forerunners of town-building elsewhere within the post-Carolingian realms, and notably approximate models for the eleventh to twelfth-century North Italian communes (cf. Wickham 2023: 671). In a key passage on the formation of the Italian city states and the revival of commerce in the tenth-eleventh-century Mediterranean, Wickham opines:

> The main particularity of the Flemish case is that take-off there was linked, strikingly and interestingly, to a very long-distance luxury and semiluxury exchange projection across the Rhine river basin, the North Sea, and, soon, even the Baltic. The reason is that Flanders had become, by the late eleventh century, almost unparalleled in the intensity of its productive activity in the whole of northern Europe, and therefore the elites of a very wide range of neighbouring regions wished to buy its goods.
>
> 2023: 671

Second, the origins of these Flemish towns have been associated with the documented passage of the Vikings through this region in the fifty-year period between AD 840–890 as well as, in particular, the strong connections between King Alfred and Count Baldwin II of Flanders who married Alfred's daughter, Aelfthryth (Grierson 1941: 83–87; Verhulst 1999: 151). The likely crossover with the making of towns in the Danelaw territories and in Wessex is striking. This common history is reinforced now by recent archaeological research which sheds further light on urban origins in this County. Beginning with the post-war excavations in Antwerp at Mattenstraat near the waterfront led by Adelbert Van de Walle (1961), as in England this has now been richly enhanced by many salvage excavations and new studies (for example, Tys 2010; 2018; Tys, Deckers and Wouters 2015; Deckers 2022).

Flanders lay on the southern limits of Frisia. It had been a liminal territory of cultural brokers since the seventh century (see Tys 2017: 41–2). This may explain why Walcharen, the island on which the seventh- to ninth-century emporium of Domburg was located, was for a time in the hands of a Viking sea-king, Harald (Cooijmans 2020: 175; Deckers 2022). This would soon become the domain of the 'Scheldt-Vikings' (*Scaldingi*). Harald was operating as a poacher turned gamekeeper: the Carolingians aimed to incorporate foreign aggressors into a domestic system of government. This may account for King Louis the German's decision in the 850s to award the territory to the north, Frisia, as a benefice to a Danish sea-king, Rorik. Rorik's new benefice included the great emporium at Dorestad where he was charged with handling taxes and resisting piratical attacks by the Danes (Cooijmans 2020: 173; Coupland 1998). Rorik held onto the benefice into the 870s, his status having been confirmed by Charles the Bald. As Dorestad declined as an emporium, and Domburg on Walcharen with it, the old Frisian heartland was steadily reinvigorated under the jurisdiction of Viking leaders, familiar with Frankish practices yet steeped in the political ideology of Denmark and its wider Baltic Sea sphere. By AD 885, though, the Dorestad benefice was returned to Frankish control as the hydrarchs withdrew from the region (Cooijmans 2020: 218).

This history of liminality and seaborne connectivity cannot have been lost on the indigenous Frankish aristocrats of Frisia and Flanders. It set the scene for the emergence of the County of Flanders towards the end of the Viking presence in the region (cf. Verhulst 1999: 66–7). Not unlike the new Viking colonies, the County is a remarkable historical case study where a successful warlord established governance in a relatively short period. The warlord, however, drew upon a particular Carolingian history that would give shape to its post-Viking story. Ecclesiastical and aristocratic estates existed here, but free landholders held as much sway in determining production and the distribution of wealth. Places such as Ghent, Dries Tys proposes, began as assembly points organized by free landholders that attracted élite attention (Tys 2017: 41–2). Tys finds similarities in these liminal circumstances with those that led to the foundation of Dorestad and probably Domburg (see Chapter 2). This was to change when the earliest counts, Baldwin II and Arnulf I, established their authority in the landscape by investing in monumentality, private fortifications as well as halls and churches. But we should rather see this new imposition of authority as a largely consensual arrangement as opposed to a top-down oversight over much of Flanders. Integral to the new political economy was a civil defensive strategy that has been likened to the system of Alfredian burhs created by Baldwin's father-in-law (Tys 2017: 37–8; 2018: 176). It also happened to coincide with the re-emergence of London after *c.* AD 886, where limited late ninth- to early tenth-century archaeological evidence of Flemish traders has been discovered (see Chapter 4).

The new Flemish fortifications were erected as early as the late ninth century, as the last Viking factions were leaving the Pas-de-Calais to invade England. In several places in the Low Countries, between the mid-ninth century and the mid-tenth century, various types of fortifications appeared, indices of a general sense of social instability. The smaller royal fortifications are associated with the policy of Charles the Bald following the Edict of Pîtres, such as Petegem and Bruges (mid- to third quarter of the ninth century), while larger fortifications were related to significant settlements, such as the circular fortress at Domburg (Deckers 2022), and garrison forts such as Oost-Souburg (dating to the early tenth century: Deckers 2022). However, rather than being the result of a single initiative, these fortifications were responses to a growing climate of social tension (Tys 2017: 37). Amongst the larger fortifications, for example, was the D-shaped fort at Ghent (Medieval *Gandavum*), situated at the confluence of the Rivers Lys and Schelde, controlling traffic on the river between northern West-Francia and the estuary of the Schelde and Maas. Ghent's story, as Verhulst and now Tys have shown, is representative of an early urban history that has also been traced at other Flemish towns, notably Arras, Bruges, Cambrai, Douai, St Omer, Veurne and Ypres (Verhulst 1999: 68–113).

Ghent's first comital fortification seems to have been a D-shaped ditch and earthwork dating from the late ninth century. A consensus exists amongst archaeologists and historians that the polyfocal origins of the town were fostered around the hill known as Blandinum with St Peter's Abbey, the site of Ganda (at the confluence of Lys and Scheldt) and St Bavo's Abbey (Tys 2017: 35–6). The fortifications protected an area of approximately 7 hectares near the earlier landing-place (and assembly point) dating from the sixth and seventh centuries. By the middle of the tenth century, several streets had been developed westward of the D-shape fortification, connecting the *portus* with the main road towards Bruges (another comital fortification). Around the mid-tenth century, the town was enlarged when a second princely fortification was constructed between the road to Bruges and the (expanding) semi-circular *portus*. This historical sequence was imitated at several other coastal ports along this perforated coastline (Tys, Deckers and Wouters 2016).

Through a network of fortifications like that at Ghent, the Counts of Flanders came to exercise direct military and political control over Flanders' maritime region and its society of sheep farmers involved in regional and international trade networks from at least the seventh century onwards. The fortifications evolved as regional hubs, with markets, tolls and levies imposed on traded goods. Critically, exemptions from these existed for the inhabiting merchants from the tenth century onwards. The counts' power was supported by the incomes from their estates, mainly in coastal Flanders, whose revenues were brought to storehouses inside the forts like Ghent, where they were either processed by craftsmen or transshipped.

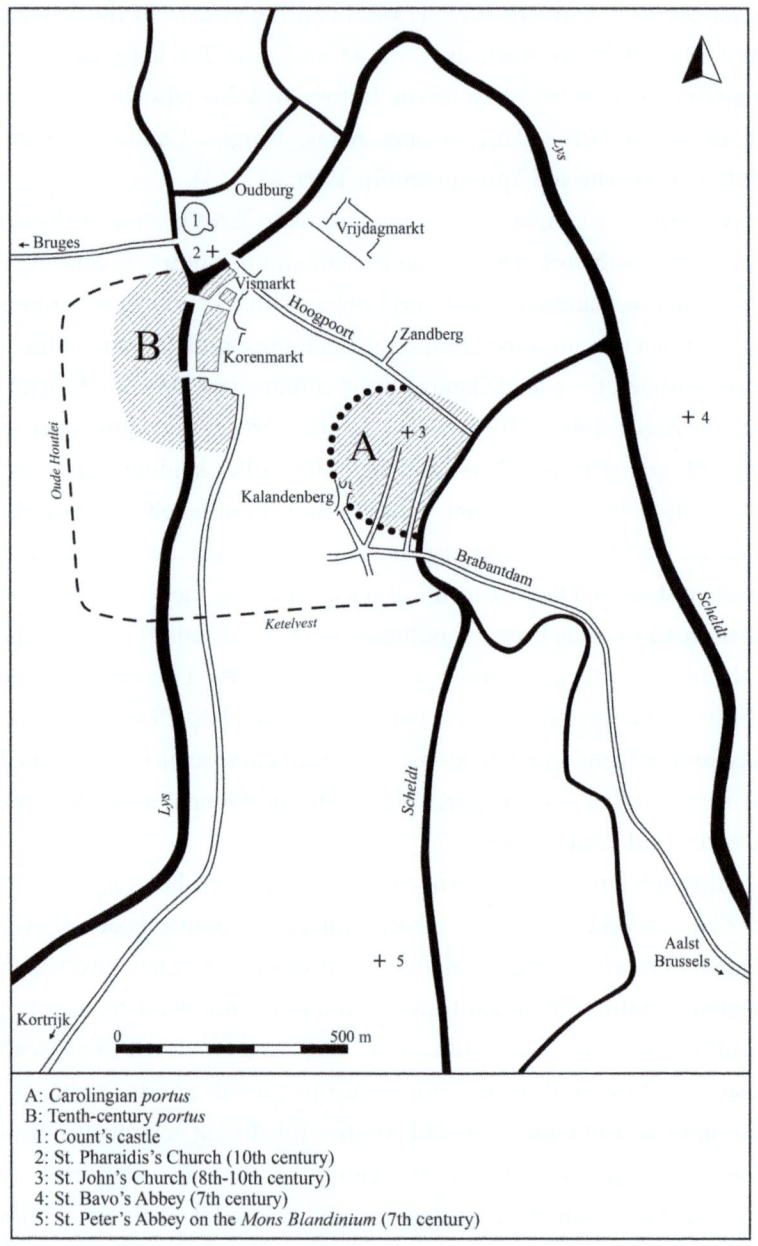

Figure 5.1 Map showing the location of the late ninth- to early tenth-century D-shaped fortress at Ghent (modified after Verhulst 1989: 25, map 4).

The strategy of implementing power in the landscape through the foundation of multifunctional fortifications like Ghent marked a decisive step in the creation of a successful feudal princedom, the County of Flanders. In the course of the tenth century the Counts of Flanders used the full potential of the maritime landscape of Flanders to secure their authority. Essentially, this freed them from the constraints of the old Carolingian political structures (Tys 2010; 2018). Dries Tys likens this to a policy of disobedience (Tys 2017: 37). In doing so, the Counts recognized the importance of an established idea of a central place that had survived from earlier times. These were the places where freemen, administrators, traders, landowners and others gathered for deliberation, justice, trade, social relations and more. It is precisely this ancient concept of the assembly that the Counts of Flanders seized upon and reformed, in the new context of building their own centrally governed principality. This set of social relations was to emerge as a central ingredient of the state-building of the tenth and eleventh centuries with the flourishing of the trading towns. The social alchemy of this urbanization process was not unique.

Like the contemporary West Saxon burghal strategy, investment in infrastructure was accompanied by the development of governmental institutions and the accumulation of wealth and power, which were deployed as political and symbolic capital. Unlike Wessex, however, these Flemish aristocrats invested in developing regional trade, and thus indirectly in the emancipation of the *mercatores*, albeit for their own advantage. In this respect the history of the Flemish towns paralleled not the West Saxon burhs but the new Danelaw towns. Like the Anglo-Scandinavian territories in England, lords encouraged the assembly of traders and craftspeople around their own central places. The Counts of Flanders aimed to benefit from encouraging the emerging early Medieval commerce and artisanal specialization in order to accumulate the means and wealth to invest in governance and power. Underlying this, Tys identifies a remarkable spatial relationship between the count's other centres of political power located at Ypres, Veurne and Bruges, where in each case markets were developed based upon the commodities stored in local estates (Tys 2017: 38; cf. Verhulst 1999: 68–118). Thus, by consciously or unconsciously melding together West Saxon and Danelaw urban concepts, the Counts succeeded in binding recently established Viking-Age dynamics to their own political advantage (cf. Tys 2018: 177).

The archaeological evidence challenges the narrow attribution of the Flemish fortifications as indices of resistance to the Viking attacks. Clearly, the circumstances were more complex, as in Wessex and in the Anglo-Scandinavian territories in England. Of course, the threat of Danish warbands played a role in the making of a network of defences. But as we have seen, the centuries-long connections between merchants and farmers in this coastal region (best seen at the sixth- to eighth-century Rhine-mouth village of Oegstgeest, see Chapter 2) with western Scandinavia, followed by the mid- to later ninth-century Viking benefices held between the Scheldt and northern Frisia must have played a part in shaping the local histories of these new towns. Merchants were not new social actors in this world of transactions and exchange. Market and commodity exchange were not alien to later ninth-century Flemish society, pursuing the century-old Carolingian reforms to revitalize rural production. In other words, the Counts of Flanders belonged to an established lineage of cultural brokers. Did the Counts find role models in the (Danish) rulerships of Harald and Rorik, discerning strategies not just for defence but also for the development of urban communities in which artisans and traders possessed a recognized status that evaded the texts of the time? Were they unintentionally exploiting 'spillover' ideas in the closely-tied networks connecting the Low Countries and England to Denmark at this time? This is an abstract issue that Verhulst instinctively recognized, requiring further research with regard to tracing the links between the Flemish landscape, economy and society in the ninth and tenth centuries. Without doubt, though, Pirenne's thesis about Flemish urban origins oversimplified the historical sequence to highlight the role of mariners and craftsmen, and understated the importance of the regional economy (Verhulst 1989; 1999: 150–1). As much as Pirenne knew about the 'half traders, half pirates' that founded the Viking towns of western Russia (2014: 29–30), he might have been startled that the marauding warbands of the ninth century played at least an abstract part in the rise of tenth-century Flemish towns like Ghent.

Introducing an urban spirit to England?

This brings us back to some central issues about urban origins in England, now clearer than ever a century after Pirenne's *Medieval Cities* thanks to archaeological research. To understand the making of towns in England (and indeed in Flanders), it helps to borrow from the models of later Iron Age (ie. late prehistoric) Scandinavia. Here, as I showed in Chapter 1, thanks principally to the high-definition excavations (employing the Third Scientific Revolution techniques) in Ribe, the evolution of a Viking-Age urban culture can be traced through the eighth and ninth centuries. This was based upon a number of criteria as non-kin-based communities assumed cultural characteristics that were as important to the Viking Age as the infamous sea-kings. As Johann Callmer persuasively argued, craftsmen by necessity working together played an important part in shaping the emporia as nodal markets. In these exceptional places, skilled individuals brokered their own customs and played a major social part in the Viking Age. In a sense, Pirenne recognized this as he identified the far-reaching tenth-century trade connections between Flanders by way of western Russia to the Caliphate (cf. 2014: 61–5). But, as we focus upon English urban history, by analogy with Scandinavia, it is the polyfocal central-places associated with political rituals to oversee first, landing-places, then on occasion permanent towns, the emporia, in the late seventh century that heralds the first phase of English urban development. As we saw in Chapter 2, even this signal stage was more complex in political terms than was once envisaged. On the bases of the new evidence for the investment in and exploitation of agricultural production, in parallel with the short-lived political apogee of the English church in the late seventh century, it appears that certain of the emporia were managed expressions of what Ian Wood has described as a temple economy (2022) and a compact between the church and secular leaders. As emporia appeared successively across different tribal kingdoms, their consumption and productive patterns had an impact upon associated landscapes and communities. This experimental episode, though, to quote Joachim Henning once more, was in some respects a false dawn in England unlike, for instance, Scandinavia, as we saw in Chapter 3 (Henning 2007: 31).

In England, the next phase proved to be more enduring although more complex in terms of organization and management. A step-change occurred in the development of early Medieval exchange reflected in the changing role of the aristocracy in relation to the royal families, and in particular their ability to create wealth in regional economies (Astill 2011: 272). With increasingly centralized political leadership, and their need for military support from the aristocracy and their dependents to sustain it, the political economies were adapted accordingly. Broadly, the economic strategy – *minus* the emphasis upon *klosterpolitik* (with its emphasis upon a compact between the church and political élite) – was loosely based upon the Frankish model of rural production leading to redistributive exchange through dispersed rural market-places often associated with Christian cults (cf. Astill 2011: 259; Langlands 2020: 309). On the evidence of the middle Thames periodic site excavated at Dorney, such places had a superficial urban character without permanent buildings. If Dorney is a reliable guide, traders and others met to exchange imported and locally manufactured items brought in locked chests.

Similar places existed in many parts of the Carolingian commonwealth. In a study of just such a centre associated with a cult at Maastricht, Frans Theuws and Mirjam Kars have described these Carolingian places as transactional. Excavations of the cemeteries associated with the abbey-church of St Servatius at Maastricht lead Theuws and Kars to appraise a model that the revival and/or emergence of 'towns' in the Low Countries were probably integrated into river-based exchange networks, rural transformation and the development of religious institutions. Early Medieval centres, they argue, are not only spatial but they also play a part in the 'whole transactional order'. Theuws acknowledges, of course, that not only did Maastricht change through time between the Merovingian and Ottonian eras, but so did its norms and values. Only by dissecting the ordering of elements (houses, churches, open areas, cemeteries, streets etc) through time is it possible to grasp how past space was used, transformed and served a transactional purpose. Towns like Maastricht (and many similar throughout the later Carolingian realms) functioned only as markets during festivals associated with the cult (Theuws and Kars 2017; cf. Pirenne 2014: 25; 27). They were also similar in their ecological and cultural context to many of the minster and royal sites that arose as points of redistribution and exchange throughout the principal kingdoms of pre-Viking England (Astill 2006: 237–8; Blair 2018; Moreland 2000b; Palmer 2003).

These Carolingian non-urbanized – transactional – places were very different to the Anglo-Scandinavian model town introduced to northern and eastern England after *c.* AD 890. The Anglo-Scandinavian towns were created as an explicitly monetized variant of the redistributive economies based upon minsters and other Middle Saxon exchange foci. The Danish model espoused a political strategy in which urban communities had the social flexibility to develop unlike the earlier Anglo-Saxon emporia. Judging from the remarkable discoveries of the Great Army's overwintering camp at Torksey (Lincolnshire), as well as the earliest phases of York, the conquerors came with a diaspora mentality. Judith Jesch (2015: 70), quoting the sociologist, Robin Cohen (2008: 161–2), proposes that the Viking diaspora exhibited several or most of the following nine features:

1. Dispersal from an original homeland, often traumatically.
2. Alternatively, the expansion from a homeland in search of work, in pursuit of trade or to further colonial ambitions.
3. A collective memory and myth about the homeland.
4. An idealization of the supposed ancestral home.
5. A return movement or at least a continuing conversation.
6. A strong ethnic group consciousness sustained over a long time.
7. A troubled relationship with host societies.
8. A sense of co-responsibility with co-ethnic members in other countries.
9. The possibility of a distinctive creative, enriching life in tolerant host countries.

These features open up new ways of thinking about the Vikings, their mental template and, of course, their impact as colonialists. Put simply, as Neil Price concluded, 'underneath these currents of raiding aggression ran the constant undertow of trade and more peaceful interaction' (2020: 364). Fundamental to this was a Viking spirit that, as has been discovered in the Scandinavian emporia, was engaged in a highly articulated network of North Sea and Baltic Sea connections (cf. Kalmring 2024). Viking norms of the later ninth century were inventive and worldly, as well as steeped in the evolving values of a silver economy. Central to the making of these places was the evolution of legal systems that were a cornerstone of organized economic activity, including a fiscal system, systematic economic specialization and the possibilities of deferred payments such as credit (cf. Ögren et al. 2022:

173). The major point here is that to the generations of Anglo-Saxons who had engaged in small-scale regional trade, this cosmopolitan urban ethos wedded to a continuing conversation with the wider Viking Eurasian network must have appeared entrepreneurial and risky.

The appearance of semi-autonomous, hierarchically-organized social groups, differentially engaged in production, exchange, military and religious activities broadly characterize the Danish experiment in places like York and the Danelaw towns, just as in time they would in the Flemish ports and eventually in Wessex (after *c.* AD 970) after the kingdom had invested in a rigorous programme of civil defence. Unlike the diffused redistribution model in Francia (and pre-Viking England) largely based upon rural central-places (cf. Devroey 2020), the imported Danish model championed urbanism to make the shift from a centralized tributary economy towards a stratified political system.

We cannot imagine that this was a mystery to the principal actors of the age. In Wessex and Flanders, order, legitimacy and wealth were the key criteria for sustaining a new centralized leadership. From these grew concepts of collective action and group identity, features that were very apparent both in the factions fighting for the sea-kings and those opposing them. Tellingly, it is these social and economic features that King Alfred appears to be observing in his commentary to Boethius's *Consolation of Philosophy* (Baker and Brooks 2013: 9).

Such social changes, as consensual arrangements of power were harnessed by new leadership, did not happen in an isolated bubble. It may be no coincidence that the resumption of urban life in England and Flanders occurred with the end of the era of the hydrarchs (Cooijmans 2020: 210–11). As Christian Cooijmans concludes: 'following its early rise and success, the tenth-century decline and downfall of hydrarchy reveals its overall development to have been parabolic in nature' (2020: 211). The invasions of England and Francia by sea-kings, in Cooijmans' reading of them, was tied to the mid-ninth-century economic crisis in the Baltic Sea region. This was plainly over by the 880s, as the harbour development at Hedeby from AD 886 onwards shows (Kalmring 2010: 241–2; fig. 324). Trade across the vast breadth of the Baltic Sea and beyond was to be revived on an even greater scale. In addition, Sven Kalmring has associated the development of the enhanced harbour facilities at Hedeby, an axiomatic port for western Baltic Sea trade, with the presence of the first dedicated Viking-era cargo vessels (cf. 2010: 352, note 154; fig. 269). Christensen (2007: 114) calculates that the Gokstad ship which dates from this time could have transported about 10 tons of cargo. Even if Ohthere, the Norwegian visitor to King Alfred's court, in the 890s had a smaller vessel than Gokstad, it could have still accommodated 5 to 6 tons of down, furs, walrus- and seal-hide ropes and walrus tusks. Was no more than a ripple-effect of this revival resonating around the North Sea, where long-distance trade had languished in scale since the 820s? This ripple was translated by Pirenne as a cornerstone of the making of places like his home university-town of Ghent. Karl Polanyi was to enlarge Pirenne's reading of the evidence (1963), establishing the place of long-distance trade as a driver in early states. His allusion to 'roving traders' almost certainly was an acknowledgement to *Medieval Cities*, where Pirenne's phrase is repeatedly employed (1925: 114). Now, though, the archaeological evidence cautions us against exaggerating the scale and significance of long-distance commerce in this period as an economic driver. On the contrary, it shows that the impact of Ohthere's peers on the English and Flemish economies was minimal. Yet, is it a coincidence that Lundenburh's Thameside shore (close to Bull Wharf) was planned in about AD 886 as carefully as the earliest emporia had been?

What, nevertheless, is becoming clear is that Adriaan Verhulst's criticism of Pirenne about North Sea trade sustaining the earliest

Figure 5.2 Reconstruction of Hedeby (Germany) in the tenth century (courtesy of Flemming Bau).

Flemish towns is amply supported by recent archaeological evidence showing an emphasis upon regional investment (1999: 152; see Tys 2017). As in the Anglo-Scandinavian regions, and in Wessex including London, long-distance commerce as opposed to regional trade only took off again around the North Sea in the last quarter of the tenth century. By this time, international exchange was grounded in well-developed networks of regional markets (cf. Astill 2000: 37–8; Astill 2011; 2019). Moreover, *pace* Pirenne, imported pottery assemblages from places like Gipeswic and Lundenburg as well as Ghent show far greater emphasis upon cross-Channel trade between northern France and the Low Countries. Evidence for long-distance trade to northern Frisia, Hamburg and western Scandinavia shows that it plainly revived after the 880s but not yet on the scale it had enjoyed in the earlier ninth century. Rhenish-made Pingsdorf wares, for example, occur in Ribe and Hedeby, but are dwarfed in quantity by Baltic Sea imported pottery at these places (cf. Keller 2023: 59–60; Janssen 1987: 19–21; 22–4). In sum, the Baltic Sea epicentre of trade may have sent mercantile ripples towards the lower North Sea, but these were ephemeral.

What the archaeology now emphasizes is the importance of agent-oriented socioeconomics in the creation of the four (or more) emporia for the particular political direction of the English kingdoms, and then, no less significantly, the effective marginalization of three of the places (the exception being Gipeswic in East Anglia) as kings centralized their control over their regions. The emporia were functions of a compact between kings and the church on the occasion of the intensification of rural landscapes and investment to meet Frankish and Frisian demand. Intensified agricultural production, in effect a Secondary Products Revolution (as Sherratt described it for the Neolithic period), was the driver of this temple society. In these circumstances, the archaeology casts doubt on the creation of the kind of English urban culture and collective practices that, by contrast, were to become the hallmark of emporia in Scandinavia. Even a century after the Viking conquest it is difficult to isolate obvious signs of an urban identity among the larger towns in southern England (formerly Wessex). While this contrast is telling, the Viking gift to the English in the later ninth century cannot be dismissed. The Danes imported an urban culture based upon established values that set it (and perhaps, in parallel, Flanders) apart from an alignment with the Carolingian revolution based upon rural redistribution controlled by feudal lordships.

Finally, is it farfetched to conclude that this Viking gift ultimately paved the way for the fusion of both economic strategies – the Frankish rural redistributive and the Danish urban policies – leading in the twelfth century to what Henri Pirenne defined as Medieval civilization? Pirenne may have been mistaken in reaching the conclusions that have formed his century-old thesis, but in compelling us to examine the impact of long-term shifts, and the corresponding changes in incentives and opportunities, he has forced archaeologists and historians to carefully examine maritime engagement alongside rural investment. Of course, with the benefit of the past fifty years of professional archaeology, it is more than obvious that further archaeological evidence is certain to develop and even transform this century-old historical debate. In particular, there is now a need to document and interrogate the archaeology of the craftsmen and their procurement strategies in the English emporia, as well as the part played by the otherwise enigmatic English traders, and then to track their practices in English towns after *c*. AD 890. In sum, much has still to be learnt about the origins of an English urban identity in the early Middle Ages and what, if anything, its contribution was to Europe.

The debate about the origins and genesis of English towns is far from finished.

Bibliography

Adams, D. and G. Clarke 2022. *Aspects of 7th–11th-century Norwich, Bar Hill, Cambridgeshire*, East Anglian Archaeology no 179.

Addyman, P. V. 1973. Saxon Southampton: a town and international port of the eighth to the tenth century, in H. Jankuhn, W. Schlesinger and H. Steuer (eds), *Vor- und Frühformen der europäischen Stadt im Mittelalter*, vol 1, Göttingen, Abhandlungen der Akademie der Wissenschaften, Philologisch-Historische Klasse, 218–28.

Addyman, P. V., and D. H. Hill. 1968. Saxon Southampton: a review of the evidence, Part 1, *Proceedings of the Hampshire Field Club & Archaeological Society* XXV, 61–93.

Addyman, P. V., and D. H. Hill. 1969. Saxon Southampton: a review of the evidence, Part 2, *Proceedings of the Hampshire Field Club & Archaeological Society* XXVI, 61–96.

Allen, M. 2014. The Mints of Anglo-Saxon and Anglo-Scandinavian England, 871–1066, in G. R. Owen-Crocker and S. D. Thompson (eds), *Towns and Topography (Essays in Memory of David H. Hill)*, Oxford, Oxbow Books, 68–73.

Andrews, P. (ed.). 1988. *Southampton Finds, Volume 1: The Coins and Pottery from Hamwic*, Stroud, Alan Sutton.

Andrews, P. 1997. *Excavations at Hamwic, Volume 2: excavations at Six Dials*, York, CBA Research Report 109.

Andrews, P., and D. M. Metcalf. 1984. A coinage for King Cynewulf of Wessex?, in D. Hill and D. M. Metcalf (eds), *Sceattas in England and on the Continent*, British Archaeological Reports, British Series 128, Oxford (British Archaeological Reports), 175–9.

Archibald, M. 1990. Pecking and Bending: The Evidence of British Finds, in K. Jonsson and B. Malmer (eds), *Proceedings of the Sigtuna Symposium on Viking Age Coinage, 1–4 June 1989 CNS Nova Series* 6, London, Spink and Son, 11–24.

Ashby, S. P. 2014. Technologies of Appearance: Hair Behaviour in Early Medieval Europe, *Archaeological Journal* 171, 151–84.

Ashby, S. P., N. B. Coutu and S. M. Sindbæk. 2015. Urban Networks and Arctic Outlands: Craft Specialists and Reindeer Antler in Viking Towns, *European Journal of Archaeology* 18, 679–704.

Ashby, S. P. and S. M. Sindbæk (eds). 2020. *Crafts and Social Networks in Viking Towns*, Oxford, Oxbow Books,

Astill, G. 2000. General Survey 600–1300, in D. M. Palliser (ed.), *The Cambridge Urban History of Britain, Vol. 1*, Cambridge, Cambridge University Press, 27–50.

Astill, G. 2006. Community, Identity and the Later Anglo-Saxon Town: The Case of Southern England, in W. Davies, G. Halsall and A. Reynolds (eds), *People and Space in the Middle Ages 300–1300*, Turnhout, Brepols, 233–54.

Astill, G. 2011. Exchange, coinage and the economy of Early Medieval England, in J. Escalona and A. Reynolds (eds), *Scale and Scale Change in the Early Middle Ages*, Turnhout, Brepols, 253–72.

Astill, G. 2019. Understanding the identities and workings of local societies in Early Medieval England, AD 800–1100, in J. Escalona, O. Vésteinsson, and S. Brookes (eds), *Polity and Neighbourhood in Early Medieval Europe*, Turnhout, Brepols, 39–56.

Augé, M. 1995. *Non-Places: Introduction to an Anthropology of Supermodernity*, London, Verso.

Ayre, J., and R. Wroe-Brown, 2015. The Post-Roman Foreshore and the Origins of the Late Anglo-Saxon Waterfront and Dock of Æthelred's Hithe: Excavations at Bull Wharf, City of London, *Archaeological Journal* 172, 121–94.

Bagnall, R. S. and Bransbourg, G. 2019.The Constantian Monetary Revolution. *ISAW Papers*, 14. http://dlib.nyu.edu/awdl/isaw/isaw-papers/14/

Baker, J., and S. Brookes. 2013. *Beyond the Burghal Hidage: Anglo-Saxon Civil Defence in the Viking Age*, Leiden, Brill.

Barrett, R. 1993. *The Making of Europe: Conquest, Colonization and Culture Change, 950–1350*, Princeton, Princeton University Press.

Bately, J. 2007. Ohthere and Wulstan in the Old English, in J. Bately, J. and A. Englert (eds), *Ohthere's Voyages*, Roskilde, The Viking Ship Museum, 18–59.

Bately, J., and A. Englert (eds). 2007. *Ohthere's Voyages*, Roskilde, The Viking Ship Museum.

Bavuso, I. 2017. *The Sixth and Earlier Seventh Centuries: Preconditions of the Rise of the Emporia*, Oxford, unpublished D.Phil. thesis.

Bell, C. 1997. *Ritual: Perspectives and Dimensions*, Oxford, Oxford University Press.

Bianchi, G. 2022. *Archeologia dei beni pubblici. Alle origini della crescita economica in una reggione mediterranea (secc. IX–XI)*, Florence, Insegna del Giglio.

Biddle, M. 1976. The Towns, in D. M. Wilson (ed.), *The Archaeology of Anglo-Saxon England*, London, Methuen, 99–150.

Biddle, M. 1984. London on the strand, *Popular Archaeology* 6, 23–7.

Biddle, M., and B. Kølbye-Biddle. 2001. Repton and the 'Great Heathen Army', 873–4, in J. Graham-Campbell et al. (eds), *Vikings and the Danelaw: Select Papers from the Proceedings of the Thirteenth Viking Congress*, Oxford, Oxbow Books, 45–96.

Biddle, M., and K. Barclay. 1974. Winchester ware, in V. I. Evison, H. Hodges, and J. G. Hurst (eds) *Medieval Pottery from Excavations: Studies Presented to Gerald Clough Dunning*, London, John Baker, 137–65.

Biddle, M., and D. Hill. 1971. Late Saxon planned towns, *Antiquaries Journal* 51, 70–85.

Birbeck, V. 2005. *The Origins of Mid-Saxon Southampton: Excavations at the Friends Provident St Mary's Stadium 1998–2000*, Salisbury, Wessex Archaeology Ltd.

Blackburn, M. 1989. The Ashdon (Essex) Hoard and the Currency of the Southern Danelaw in the Late Ninth Century, *British Numismatic Journal* 59, 13–38.

Blackburn, M. 1998. The London mint in the reign of Alfred, in M. A. S. Blackburn and D. N. Dumville (eds), *Kings, Currency and Alliances*, Woodbridge, Boydell Press, 105–23.

Blackburn, M. 2003. Productive Sites and the Pattern of Coin Loss in England, 600–1180, in T. Pestell and K. lmschneider (eds), *Markets in Early Medieval Europe: Trading and Productive Sites, 650–850*, Macclesfield, Windgather, 20–36.

Blackburn, M. 2005. Currency under the Vikings: Part 1, Guthrum and the Earliest Danelaw Coinages. Presidential Address 2004, *British Numismatic Journal* 75, 18–43.

Blackmore, L. 2001. Pottery: Trade and Tradition, in D. Hill and R. Cowie (eds), *Wics: The Early Mediaeval Trading Centres of Northern Europe*, Sheffield, Sheffield Academic Press, 22–42.

Blackmore, L., and A. Vince. 2012. The pottery, in R. Cowie and L. Blackmore, *Lundenwic: Excavations in Middle Saxon London, 1987–2000*, London, MOLA, 177–9.

Blackmore, L., J. Keily and M. Stiff. 2012. Continental wares, in R. Cowie and L. Blackmore, *Lundenwic: Excavations in Middle Saxon London, 1987–2000*, London, MOLA, 249–56.

Blair, J. 2018. *Building Anglo-Saxon England*, Princeton, Princeton University Press.

Blanton, R., and G. M. Feinman. 2024. New views on price-making markets and the capitalist impulse: beyond Polanyi, *Frontiers in Human Dynamics*, DOI: 10.3389/fhumd.2024.1339903.

Boone, M. 2012. Cities in late medieval Europe: the promise and the curse of modernity, *Urban History* 39, 329–49.

Bourdillon, J. 1980. Town life and animal husbandry in the Southampton area as suggested by the excavated bones, *Proceedings of the Hampshire Field Club Archaeological Society* 36, 181–91.

Bourdillon, J. 1988. Countryside and town: the animal resources of Saxon Southampton, in D. Hooke (ed.), *Anglo-Saxon Settlements*, Oxford, Blackwell, 177–95.

Brisbane, M., and R. Hodges. 2018. An emporium for all eras: David Hinton and four institutional phases in the rise of Hamwic, Anglo-Saxon Southampton, in B. Jervis (ed.), *The Middle Ages Revisited*, Oxford, Archaeopress, 21–32.

Brookes, S. 2020. On the Territorial Organisation of Early Medieval Hampshire, in A. Langlands and R. Lavelle (eds), *The Land of the English Kin: Studies in Wessex and Anglo-Saxon England in Honour of Professor Barbara Yorke*, Leiden, Brill, 276–93.

Brookes, S. 2023. Assembly practices in tenth-century England: continuities and innovations in military mobilization, in I. S. Salazar and C. Tente (eds), *The Tenth Century in Western Europe: Change and Continuity*, Oxford, Archaeopress, 53–63.

Brooks, N. P. 1984. *The Early History of the Church of Canterbury*, Leicester, Leicester University Press.

Brown, P. 2012. *Through the Eye of the Needle: Wealth, the fall of Rome and the Making of Christianity in the West, 350–55 AD*, Princeton, Princeton University Press.

Brown, R., S. Teague, S., L. Loe, L., B. Sudds and E. Popescu. 2020. *Excavations at Stoke Quay, Ipswich: Southern Gipeswic and the parish of St Augustine*, Bury St Edmunds, East Anglian Archaeology.

Brownlee, E 2021. Connectivity and funerary change in early medieval Europe, *Antiquity* 95, 142–59.

Callmer, J. 2002. North-European trading centres and the Early Medieval craftsmen: Craftsmen at Åhus, north-eastern Scania, Sweden c. AD 750–850+, in B. Hårdh and L. Larsson (eds), *Central Places in the Migration and Merovingian Periods*, Lund, Uppåkra-studier, vol. 6, 125–57.

Callmer, J. 2007. Urbanisation in Northern and Eastern Europe, ca. AD 700–1100, in J. Henning (ed.), *Post-Roman towns, trade and settlement in Europe and Byzantium. Vol. 1. The heirs of the Roman West*, Berlin, Walter De Gruyter, 233–70.

Callmer, J. 2020. Craft: some pragmatic notes on the study of craft production and craftspeople in early medieval northern Europe, in S. P. Ashby, and S. Sindbæk (eds), *Crafts and Social Networks in Viking Towns*, Oxford, Oxbow Books, 32–49.

Campbell, E. 2007. *Continental and Mediterranean Imports to Atlantic Britain and Ireland, AD 400–800*, London, Council for British Archaeology.

Cense-Bacquet, D. 2021. L'habitat alto-médiéval du Chemin de Visemarais à La Calotterie (Pas-de-Calais): approches de l'occupation d'un quartier du *portus* de Quentovic, *Archéologie médiévale* 51, 7–53.

Cessford, C. 2020. Middle Anglo-Saxon Downham Road, Ely: extending the West Fen Road site, *Archaeological Journal* 177, 31–62.

Cherry, J. F., and R. Hodges. 1978. The chronology of Hamwih: Saxon Southampton reconsidered, *Antiquaries Journal* LVIII, 199–209.

Christensen, A E. 2007. Othere's vessel, in J. Bately and A. Englert (eds), *Ohthere's voyages*, Roskilde, The Viking Ship Museum, 112–17.

Christie, N. 2015. Creating defended communities in Late Saxon Wessex, in N. Christie and H. Herold (eds), *Fortified Settlements in Medieval Europe*, Oxford, Oxbow Books, 52–68.

Clarke, G. and Connor, A. 2024. *A Middle Bronze Age Cremation Cemetery and an Anglo-Saxon Estate Centre at Stirtloe Lane and Luck's Lane, Buckden, Cambridgeshire*, Oxford, Oxford Archaeology unpublished report.

Clarke-Neish, K. M. 2021. *The (Re-)Making of the Southern North Sea World*, unpublished PhD thesis, University of Durham.

Cohen, R. 2008. *Global Diasporas: An Introduction*, London, Routledge.

Corsi, C. 2022. *The route of the Franks: The journey of archbishop Sigeric at the twilight of the First Millennium AD*, Oxford, Archaeopress.

Cooijmans, C. 2020. *Monarchs and Hydrarchs: The conceptual developments of Viking activity across the Frankish realm (c. 750–940)*, Abingdon, Routledge.

Costen, M., and N. Costen. 2016. Trade and Exchange in Anglo-Saxon Wessex *c.* AD 600–780, *Medieval Archaeology* 60, 1–26.

Coupland, S. 1998. From poachers to gamekeepers: Scandinavian warlords and Carolingian kings, *Early Medieval Europe* 7, 85–114.

Coupland, S. 2002. Trading places: Quentovic and Dorestad reassessed, *Early Medieval Europe* 11, 209–32.

Coutts, C. 1991. *Pottery and the Emporia: Imported pottery in Middle Saxon England with particular reference to Ipswich*, unpublished PhD thesis, University of Sheffield.

Cowie, R., and L. Blackmore. 2012. *Lundenwic: Excavations in Middle Saxon London, 1987–2000*, London, MOLA.

Crabtree, P. J. 2010. Agricultural innovation and socio-economic change in early medieval Europe: evidence from Britain and France, *World Archaeology* 42, 122–36.

Crabtree, P. J. 2018. *Early Medieval Britain: The rebirth of towns in the West*, Cambridge, Cambridge University Press.

Crabtree, P. J. 2021. *Provisioning Ipswich: Animal Remains from the Saxon and Medieval Town*, Bury St Edmunds, E. Anglian Archaeology.

Croix, S., M. Neiss and S. Sindbæk. 2019. The réseau opératoire of urbanization: craft collaborations and organization in an early medieval workshop in Ribe, Denmark, *Cambridge Archaeological Journal* 29, 345–64.

Crumlin-Pedersen, O. 2010. *Archaeology and the sea in Scandinavia and Britain: A personal account*, Roskilde, Viking Ship Museum.

de Bruin, J., C. Bakels and F. Theuws. 2021. *Oegstgeest: A riverine settlement in the early medieval world system*, Bonn, Habelt-Verlag.

Deckers, P. 2010. An illusory emporium? Small trading places around the southern North Sea, in A. Willemsen and H. Kik (eds), *Dorestad in an international framework*, Turnhout, Brepols, 159–68.

Deckers, P. 2012, 'Productive' sites in the Polders? 'Griffin brooches' and other early Medieval metalwork from the Belgian coastal plain, *Medieval and Modern Matters* 3, 21–43.

Deckers P. 2017. Cultural Convergence in a Maritime Context, in J. Hines N. and IJssennagger-van der Pluijm Nelleke (eds), *Frisians of the Early Middle Age*s, Woodbridge, Boydell and Brewer, 173–92.

Deckers, P. 2022. The Long History of Early Medieval Urbanism on the Island of Walcheren (Netherlands) Towards a Biography of Urban Continuity, *Journal of Urban Archaeology* 5, 191–210.

Deckers, P. 2023. Tating ware, in S. M. Sindbaek (ed.), *Northern Emporium. Vol. 2: The networks of Viking-age Ribe*, Aarhus, Aarhus University Press, 69–82.

Delogu, P. 2022. *Roma all'inizio del Medioevo*, Rome, Carocci.

Devroey, J.-P. 2003. *Economie rurale et société dans l'Europe franque (VIe–IXe siècles)*, Paris, Éditions Belin.

Devroey, J.-P. 2020. Monastic Economics in the Carolingian Age, in A. I. Beach and I. Cochelin (eds), *The Cambridge History of Medieval Monasticism in the Latin West*, Cambridge, Cambridge University Press, 466–84.

Doyle, I. W. 2021. The early medieval imported ceramics from Lisnacaheragh and Lisnamanroe, in W. O'Brien and N. Hogan, *Garranes: An Early Medieval Royal Site in South-West Ireland*, Oxford, Archaeopress, 249–63.

Dhondt, J. 1962. Les problèmes de Quentovic, in *Studi in onore di Amintore Fanfani (Antichità e alto medioevo)*, Mila, Giuffré, vol. I, 181–248.

Dhondt, J. 1966. Henri Pirenne: historien des institutions urbaines, *Annali della Fondazione italiana per la storia amministrativa* 3, 81–129.

Duggan, M. 2018. *Western Europe and Britain: Links to Late Antiquity. Ceramic exchange and contacts on the Atlantic Seaboard in the 5th to 7th centuries AD*, Oxford, British Archaeological Reports.

Eagles, B. 2015. 'Small shires' and *regiones* in Hampshire and the formation of the shires of eastern Wessex', in H. Hamerow (ed.), *Anglo-Saxon Studies in Archaeology and History*, 19, Oxford, Oxbow Books, 122–52.

Effros, B. 2017. The enduring attraction of the Pirenne thesis, *Speculum* 92, 184–208.

Ellmers, D. 1972. *Frühmittelalterliche Handelsschiffart in Mittel-und Nordeuropa*, Neumünster, Wachholtz.

Escalona, J., O. Vésteinsson and S. Brookes. 2019. Polities, Neighbourhoods and Things In-between, in J. Escalona, O. Vésteinsson, and S. Brookes (eds), *Polity and Neighbourhood in Early Medieval Europe*, Turnhout, Brepols, 11–38.

Faith, R. 1997. *The English Peasantry and the Growth of Lordship*, London, Leicester University Press.

Faith, R. 2009. Forces and relations of production in early medieval England, *Journal of Agrarian Change* 9, 23–41.

Fathy, B. 2023. *A New Materialist Approach to Understanding Post-Roman Urban Emergence: A Study of Ipswich, AD 600–900*, Unpublished University of Leicester doctoral thesis.

Fleming, R. 2021. *The Material Fall of Roman Britain, 300–525 CE*, Philadelphia, University of Pennsylvania Press.

Foot, S. 1996. The making of *Angelcynn*: English identity before the Norman Conquest, *Transactions of the Royal Historical Society* 6, 25–49.

Foreman, S., J. Hiller and D. Petts 2002. *Gathering the people, settling the land*, Oxford, Oxbow Books.

Foster, E., and M. Charles. 2022. Agricultural Land Use in Central, East and South-East England: Arable or Pasture? in M. McKerracher and H. Hamerow (eds), *New Perspectives on the Medieval 'Agricultural Revolution': Crop, Stock and Furrow*, Liverpool, Liverpool University Press, 61–86.

Fouracre, P. 2000. *The Age of Charles Martel*, Harlow, Longmans.

Fritze W. 1971. Zur Entstehungsgeschichte des Bistums Utrecht. Franken und Friesen 690–734, *Rheinische Vierteljahrsblätter* 35, 107–51.

Gannon, A. 2003. *The iconography of early Anglo-Saxon coinage: Sixth to eighth centuries*, Oxford, Oxford University Press.

Gannon, A., 2013. *Sylloge of coins of the British Isles 63. British Museum. Anglo-Saxon coins 1. Early Anglo-Saxon gold and Anglo-Saxon and *continental silver coinage of the North Sea Area, c. 600–760*, London, British Museum.

Gardiner, M., R. Cross, N. Macpherson-Grant, I. Riddler, L. Blackmore and D. Chick. 2001. Continental Trade and Non-Urban Ports in Mid-Anglo-Saxon England: Excavations at *Sandtun*, West Hythe, Kent, *Archaeological Journal* 158, 161–290.

Garner, M. 2025. Boundaries and Burials: investigating the extent of Hamwic and the development and phasing of its cemeteries, in M. Maltby and D. James (eds), *Producers, Traders and Consumers in Urban Societies in southern Britain and Europe*, Oxford, Archaeopress, *forthcoming*.

Gerrard, C. 2003. *Medieval Archaeology: Understanding Traditions and Contemporary Approaches*, London, Routledge.

Giertz, W. 1996. Middle Meuse ceramics of Huy-type: a preliminary analysis, *Medieval Ceramics* 20, 33–64.

Godelier, M. 2002. Some Things You Give, Some Things You Sell, but Some Things You Must Keep for Yourselves: What Mauss Did Not Say about Sacred Objects, in E. Wyschogrod, J.-J. Goux and E. Boynton (eds), *The Enigma of the Gift and Sacrifice*, New York, Fordham University Press, 19–37.

Goody, J. 1987. *The Interface between the Written and the Oral*, Cambridge, Cambridge University Press.

Granovetter, M. 1973. Weak ties and strong ties, *American Journal of Sociology* 78, 1360–80.

Grierson, P. 1941. The Relations between England and Flanders before the Norman Conquest, *Transactions of the Royal Historical Society* 23, 71–112.

Grierson, P., and M. Blackburn. 1986. *Medieval European coinage with a catalogue of the coins in the Fitzwilliam museum, Cambridge. I The early middle ages (5th–10th centuries)*, Cambridge, Cambridge University Press.

Guesnerie, R. 1996. *L'économie de marché. Un exposé pour comprendre; un essai pour réfléchir*, Paris, Flammarion.

Hadley, D. 2000a. *The Northern Danelaw: its social structure, c. 800–1100*, Leicester, Leicester University Press.

Hadley, D. 2000b. 'Hamlet and the Princes of Denmark': Lordship in the Danelaw, c. 860–954, in D. M. Hadley and J. D. Richards (eds), *Cultures in Contact: Scandinavian Settlement in England in the Ninth and Tenth Centuries*, Turnhout, Brepols, 107–32.

Hadley, D., and J. Richards. 2021. *The Viking Great Army and the Making of England*, London, Thames and Hudson.

Hadley, D., J. Richards, E. Craig-Atkins and G. Perry. 2023. Torksey after the Vikings: urban origins in England, *The Antiquaries Journal* 103, 102–34.

Hahn, H. P. 2018. Introduction. Markets as places: Actors, structures and ideologies, in H. P. Hahn and G. Schmitz (eds), *Market as place and space of economic exchange: Perspectives from archaeology and anthropology*, Oxford, Oxbow Books, 1–18.

Hall, R. A. 1994. *The Viking Dig*, London, Bodley Head.

Hall, R.A. 2000. The decline of the wic? in T. R. Slater (ed.), *Towns in Decline AD 100–1600*, Aldershot, Ashgate, 120–36.

Hall, R. A., D. T. Evans, K. Hunter-Mann and A. J. Mainman. 2014. *Anglo Scandinavian occupation at 16–22 Coppergate: defining a landscape*, York, Council for British Archeology.

Hamerow, H. 2007. Agrarian production and the emporia of mid Saxon England, ca. AD 650–850, in J. Henning (ed.), *Post-Roman towns, trade and settlement in Europe and Byzantium. Vol. 1. The heirs of the Roman West*, Berlin, Walter de Gruyter, 219–32.

Hamerow, H. 2020. *Early medieval settlements: the archaeology of rural communities in Northwest Europe 400–900*, Oxford, Oxford University Press.

Hamerow, H. 2022. The 'FeedSax' Project: Rural Settlements and Farming in Early Medieval England, in M. McKerracher and H. Hamerow (eds), *New Perspectives on the Medieval 'Agricultural Revolution': Crop, Stock and Furrow*, Liverpool, Liverpool University Press, 3–24.

Hamilton-Dyer, S. 2005. Animal bones, in V. Birbeck, *The Origins of Mid-Saxon Southampton: Excavations at the Friends Provident St Mary's Stadium 1998–2000*, Salisbury, Wessex Archaeology Ltd, 140–54.

Hardy, A., Charles, B. and Williams, R. 2007. *Death and Taxes: The Archaeology of a Middle Saxon Estate Centre at Higham Ferrers, Northamptonshire*, Oxford, Oxford Archaeology Monograph Series.

Harrington, S., and M. Welch. 2014. *The early Anglo-Saxon Kingdoms of Southern Britain AD 450–650: Beneath the Tribal Hidage*, Oxford, Oxford University Press.

Helms, M. 1993. *Craft and the Kingly Ideal*, Austin, University of Texas Press.

Helms, M. W. 2004. Tangible materiality and cosmological others in the development of sedentism, in E. De Marrais, C. Gosden and C. Renfrew (eds), *Rethinking materiality: The engagement of the mind with the material world*, Cambridge, Cambridge University Press, 117–22.

Henning, J. 2007. Early European towns: The development of the economy in the Frankish realm between dynamism and deceleration AD 500–1100, in J. Henning (ed.), *Post-Roman Towns: Trade and Settlement in Europe and Byzantium, vol. 1: The Heirs of the Roman West*, Berlin, Walter de Gruyter, 3–40.

Hilberg, V. 2022. *Haithabu 983=1066. Der Untergang eines dänischen Handelszentrums in der späten Wikingerzeit*, Munich, Verlag Dr. Friedrich Pfeil.

Hill, D. 1969. The Burghal Hidage: The establishment of the text, *Medieval Archaeology* 13, 84–92.

Hill, D., and R. Cowie (eds). 2001. *Wics: The Early Medieval Trading Centres of Northern Europe*, Sheffield, Sheffield Academic Press.

Hill, David, D. Barrett, K. Maude, J. Warburton and M. Worthington. 1990. Quentovic defined, *Antiquity* 64, 51–8.

Hinton, D. A. 2005. *Gold and Gilt, Pots and Pins*, Oxford, Oxford University Press.

Hodges, L. 2025. *The Anglo-Saxon Cemetery at Foundry Field, Burnham Market, Norfolk*, Bonn, Peter Lang Verlag.

Hodges, R. 1981. *The Hamwih Pottery: the local and imported wares from 30 years' excavations at Middle Saxon Southampton and their European context*, London, Council for British Archaeology.

Hodges, R. 1982. *Dark Age Economics: The Origins of towns and Trade 600–1000*, London, Duckworth.

Hodges, R. 1989. *The Anglo-Saxon Achievement*, London, Duckworth.

Hodges, R. 2012. *Dark Age Economics: A new audit*, London, Bloomsbury Academic.

Hodges, R. 2022. Becoming Europe: re-tracing the origin of Medieval Cities from Comacchio and Oegstgeest, *Journal of Urban Archaeology* 6, 87–110.

Hodges, R. 2025. Hamwic Deconstructed: Imported Pottery and Issues of Middle Saxon Urban Discontinuity, in M. Maltby and D. James (eds),

Producers, Traders and Consumers in Urban Societies in southern Britain and Europe, Oxford, Archaeopress, 1–12.

Hodges, R., and D. Whitehouse. 1983. *Mohammed, Charlemagne and the Origins of Europe*, London, Duckworth.

Holmes, M. 2013. Entrepreneurs and traditional farmers: the effects of an emerging market in Middle Saxon England, in M. D. Groot, M. Lentjes and J. Zeiler (eds), *Barely Surviving or More than Enough? The environmental archaeology of subsistence, specialisation and surplus food production*, Leiden, Sidestone Press, 247–78.

Holmes, M. 2022. Innovation, Technology and Social Change: The Adoption of the Mouldboard Plough and Its Impact on Human–Animal Relationships, in M. McKerracher and H. Hamerow (eds), *New Perspectives on the Medieval 'Agricultural Revolution': Crop, Stock and Furrow*, Liverpool, Liverpool University Press, 87–110.

Holwerda, J. H. 2029. *Dorestad en onze Vroegste Middeleeuwen (Dorestad and our Earliest Middle Ages)*, Leiden, A.W. Sijthoff's Uitgeversmij N.V.

Hoskins, W. G. 1954. *The Making of the English Landscape*, London, Hodder and Stoughton.

Hudson, J. 2016. England and *The Making of Europe*: Conquest, Colonization and Culture Change, in J. Hudson and Crumplin (eds), *England and The Making of Europe: Conquest, Colonization and Cultural Change*, Leiden, Brill, 33–52.

Hurst, J. G. 1976. The Pottery, in D. M. Wilson (ed.), *The archaeology of Anglo-Saxon England*, London, Metheun, 283–48.

Hurst, J. G., and S. E. West. 1957. An account of middle Saxon Ipswich ware, *Proceedings of the Cambridge Antiquarian Society* 1, 29–42.

IJssennagger, N. 2013. Between Frankish and Viking: Frisia and Frisians in the Viking Age, *Viking and Medieval Scandinavia* 9, 69–98.

Jankuhn, H. 1937. *Haithabu. Eine germanische Stadt der Frühzeit*, Neumünster, Wachholtz.

Janssen, W. 1987. *Die Importkeramik aus Haithabu. Die Ausgrabungen in Haithabu 9*, Neumünster, Wachholtz.

Jervis, B. 2011. A patchwork of people, pots and places: Material engagements and the construction of 'the social' in Hamwic (Anglo-Saxon Southampton), *Journal of Social Archaeology* 11, 239–65.

Jesch, J. 2015. *The Viking Diaspora*, Abingdon, Routledge.
Jones. A.H. 1953. Inflation under the Roman Empire, *The Economic History Review* 5, 293–318.
Kalmring, S. 2010. *Der Hafen von Haithabu*, Neumünster, Wacholtz.
Kalmring, S. 2020. Birka's Fall and Hedeby's Transformation, *Journal of Urban Archaeology* 2, 31–50.
Kalmring, S. 2024. *Towns and Trade in Viking-Age Scandinavia*, Cambridge, Cambridge University Press.
Keller, C. 2023. Rhenish and other imported pottery, in S. Sindbæk (ed.), *Northern Emporium. Vol 2: The networks of Viking-age Ribe*, Højbjerg, Jutland Archaeological Society, 53–68.
Kershaw, J. 2013. *Viking Identities: Scandinavian Jewellery in England*, Oxford, Oxford University Press.
Kershaw, J. 2019. Gold as a means of exchange in Scandinavian England c. AD 850–1050), in J. Kershaw, and G. Williams (eds), *Silver, Butter, Cloth: Monetary and social economies in the Viking Age*, Oxford, Oxford University Press, 227–50.
Kershaw, J., and S. Merkel. 2023. International Trade in Outland Resources: the Mining and Export of Lead in Early Medieval England in Light of New Isotope Data From York, *Medieval Archaeology* 67 (2), 249–82.
Kershaw, J., and E. C. Røyrvik. 2016. The 'People of the British Isles Project' and Viking settlement in England, *Antiquity* 90 (354), 1670–80.
Kershaw, J., Merkel, S.W., Imporzano, P. D. and Naismith, R. 2024. Byzantine plate and Frankish mines: the provenance of silver in north-west European coinage during the Long Eighth Century (c. 660–820), *Antiquity* 98, 502–17.
Keymeulen, S., and J. Tollebeek. 2011. *Henri Pirenne historian: A life in pictures*, Leuven, Lipsius Leuven.
Kilger, C. 2008. Wholeness and holiness: counting, weighing and valuing silver in the early Viking period, in D. Skre (ed.), *Means of Exchange: Kaupang Excavation Project Publication Series, vol. 2,* Aarhus, Aarhus University Press, 253–325.
Kristiansen, K. 2014. Towards a new paradigm? The third science revolution and its possible consequences in archaeology, *Current Swedish Archaeology* 22, 11–34.

Langlands, A. 2020. *Ceapmenn* and *Portmenn*: Trade, Exchange and the Landscape of Early Medieval Wessex, in A. Langlands and R. Lavelle (eds), *The Land of the English Kin: Studies in Wessex and Anglo-Saxon England in Honour of Professor Barbara Yorke*, Leiden, Brill, 295–311.

Lebecq, S. (2000). The role of the monasteries in the systems of production and exchange of the Frankish world between the seventh and the beginning of the ninth centuries, in I. L. Hansen and C. Wickham (eds), *The Long Eighth Century: Production, Distribution and Demand*, Leiden, Brill, 121–48.

Lebecq, S. 2020. En milieu littoral, sur l'eau et outre-mer. Regards sur les communautés et solidarités maritimes dans le bassin des mers du Nord du viie au xie siècle, in A. Gautier et L. Malbos (eds), *Communautés maritimes et insulaires du premier Moyen Âge*, Turnhout, Brepols, 23–36.

Lebecq, S., and A. Gautier. 2010. Routeways between England and the Continent in the Tenth Century, in D. Rollason, C. Leyser and H. Williams (eds), *England and the Continent in the Tenth Century*, Turnhout, Brepols, 17–34.

Lebecq, S., B. Béthouart and L. Verslype (eds). 2010. *Quentovic. Environnement, Archéologie, Histoire*, Lille, Université Charles de Gaulle.

Le Mayo, J. 2003. The fate of Ports in the Lower Seine Valley at the end of the Ninth Century, in T. Pestell and K. Ulmschneider (Eds), *Markets in Early Medieval Europe: Trading and 'Productive' Sites, 650–850*, Bollington, Windgather Press, 234–48.

Löffelmann T., C. Snoeck C., J. D. Richards, L. J. Johnson, P. Claeys and J. Montgomery. 2023. Sr analyses from only known Scandinavian cremation cemetery in Britain illuminate early Viking journey with horse and dog across the North Sea, *PLoS ONE* 18 (2): e0280589. https://doi.org/10.1371/journal.pone.0280589

Louis, É. 2015. Ateliers céramiques du Douaisis au Haut Moyen Age (VIe–XIIe siècles). Un bilan, in F. Thuillier, and É. Louis (eds), *Tourner Autour du Pot. Les ateliers de potiers médiévaux du Ve au XIIe siècle dans l'espace européen*, Caen, Publications du Craham, Presses Universitaires de Caen, 51–81.

Loveluck, C. 2001. Wealth, waste and conspicuous consumption: Flixborough and its importance for Middle and Late Saxon rural settlement, in H. Hamerow and A. McGregor (eds), *Image and Power in the Archaeology of Early Medieval Britain*, Oxford, Oxbow Books, 78–130.

Loveluck, C. 2007. *Rural Settlement, Lifestyles and Social Change: Anglo-Saxon Flixborough in its Wider Context*, Oxford, Oxbow Books.

Loveluck, C., and D. Tys. 2006. Coastal societies, exchange and identity along the Channel and southern North Sea shores of Europe, AD 600–1000, *Journal of Maritime Archaeology* 1, 140–69.

Loyn, H. 1971. Towns in late Anglo-Saxon England, in P. Clemoes and K. Hughes (eds), *England before the Conquest: Studies in primary sources presented to Dorothy Whitelock*, Cambridge, Cambridge University Press, 115–28.

Lyon, B. 1974. *Henri Pirenne: a Biography and Intellectual Study*, Ghent, E. Story-Scientia.

MacLean, S. 2020. The Edict of Pîtres, Carolingian defense against the Vikings, and the origins of the Medieval Castle, *Transactions of the Royal Historical Society* 30, 29–50.

Maddicott, J. R. 2004. London and Droitwich, c. 650–750: trade, industry and the rise of Mercia, *Anglo-Saxon England* 34, 7–55.

Mainman, A. 2019. *Anglian York*, Pickering, Blackthorn Press.

Mainman, A. 2020. The emergence of professional pottery production: York, a case study, in S. P. Ashby, and S. Sindbæk (eds), *Crafts and Social Networks in Viking Towns*, Oxford, Oxbow Books, 59–82.

Malcolm, G., and D. Bowsher. 2003. *Middle Saxon London: Excavations at the Royal Opera House 1989–99*, MoLAS Monograph 15, London, Museum of London Archaeology Service.

Mawer, A. 1923. The redemption of the five boroughs, *English Historical Review* XXXVIII, 551–7.

McBride, A., 2020. *The Role of Anglo-Saxon Great Hall Complexes in Kingdom Formation, in Comparison and in Context AD 500–750*, Oxford, Archaeopress.

McCormick, M. 2001. *Origins of the Medieval Economy*, Cambridge, Cambridge University Press.

McCormick, M. 2007. Where do trading towns come from? Early medieval Venice and the northern emporia, in J. Henning (ed.), *Post-Roman towns, trade and settlement in Europe and Byzantium. Vol. 1: The heirs of the Roman West*, Berlin, Walter de Gruyter, 41–68.

McKerracher, M., and H. Hamerow (eds). 2022. *New Perspectives on the Medieval 'Agricultural Revolution': Crop, Stock and Furrow*, Liverpool, Liverpool University Press.

McLeod, S. 2014. *The Beginning of Scandinavian Settlement in England: The Viking 'Great Army' and Early Settlers c. 865–900*, Turnhout, Brepols.

Meneghini, R., and R. Santangeli Valenzani. 2004. *Roma nell' altomedioevo*, Rome, Carocci.

Metcalf, D. M. 1988. The Coins, in P. Andrews, *The Coins and Pottery from Hamwic*, Southampton Finds Volume One, Southampton, Southampton City Museums, 17–59.

Metcalf, D. M. 1998. *An Atlas of Anglo-Saxon and Norman Coin Finds, c. 973–1086*, London, Royal Numismatic Society.

Metcalf, D. M. 2000. Determining the mint attribution of East Anglian sceattas through regression analysis, *British Numismatic Journal* 70, 1–11

Metcalf, M. 2003. Variations in the composition of the currency at different places in England, in T. Pestell and K. Ulmschneider (eds), *Markets in Early Medieval Europe: Trading and 'Productive' Sites, 650–850*, Bollington, Windgather Press, 37–47.

Metcalf, D. M. 2009. Betwixt sceattas and Offa's pence: mint attributions and the chronology of a recession, *British Numismatic Journal* 79, 1–33.

Metcalf, D. M. 2014. Thrymas and sceattas and the balance of payments, in R. Naismith, M. Allen and E. Screen (eds), *Early medieval monetary history: Studies in memory of Mark Blackburn*, Farnham, Ashgate, 243–56.

Middleton, N. 2005. Early Medieval port customs, tolls and controls of foreign trade, *Early Medieval Europe* 13, 313–58.

Minter, F. 2023. *Rendlesham Revealed: The heart of a kingdom*, Bury St Edmunds, Suffolk County Council Archaeological Service.

Moffett, C. 2017. Slate discs at Tintagel castle: evidence for post-Roman mead production, *Antiquaries Journal* 97, 119–44.

Moreland, J. 2000a. Concepts of the early medieval economy, in I. L. Hansen and C. Wickham (eds), *The Long Eighth Century*, Leiden, Brill, 1–34.

Moreland, J. 2000b. The significance of production in eighth-century England, in I. L. Hansen and C. Wickham (eds), *The Long Eighth Century*, Leiden, Brill, 69–104.

Morton, A. D. 1992. *Excavations at Hamwic Volume 1: excavations 1946–83 excluding Six Dials and Melbourne Street*, York, Council for British Archaeology.

Morton, A. 1999. Hamwic in Its Context, in M. Anderton (ed.), *Anglo-Saxon Trading Centres: beyond the Emporia*, Glasgow, Cruithne Press, 48–62.

Naismith, R. 2012a. *Money and Power in Anglo-Saxon England*, Cambridge, Cambridge University Press.

Naismith, R. 2012b. Kings, crisis and coinage reforms in the mid-eighth century, *Early Medieval Europe* 20, 291–332.

Naismith, R. 2014. Prelude to reform: tenth-century coinage in perspective, R. Naismith, M. Allen and E. Screen (eds), *Early Medieval Monetary History: Studies in Memory of Mark Blackburn*, Farnham, Ashgate, 39–83.

Naismith 2019. *Citadel of the Saxons: The rise of early London*, London, Bloomsbury Academic.

Nef, A. 2013. Islamic Palermo and the *Dār Al-Islām*: politics, society and the economy (from the mid-ninth to the mid-eleventh century), in A. Nef (ed.), *A Companion to Medieval Palermo: The History of a Mediterranean City from 600 to 1500*, Leiden, Brill, 39–59.

Nowakowski, J. A. 2018. Working in the shadows of the giants: Charles Thomas, Courtenay Arthur Ralegh Radford (and King Arthur) – past and current archaeological fieldwork at Tintagel, Cornwall, in A. M. Jones and H. Quinnell (eds), *An Intellectual Adventurer in Archaeology: Reflections on the work of Charles Thomas*, Oxford, Archaeopress, 83–100.

Nelson, J. L. 2003. England and the Continent in the ninth century: II, the Vikings and others, *Transactions of the Royal Historical Society*, sixth series 13, 1–28.

Nicolay, J. 2017. Power and Identity in the Southern North Sea Area: The Migration and Merovingian Periods, in J. Hines and N. Ijssennagger (eds), *Frisians and their North Sea Neighbours*, Woodbridge, Boydell Press, 75–92.

Ögren A., C. Hedenstierna-Jonson, J. Ljungkvist, B. Raffield and N. Price. 2022. New institutional economics in Viking studies: Visualising immaterial culture, *Archaeological Dialogues* 29, 172–87.

Oosthuizen, S. 2016. Recognizing and Moving on from a Failed Paradigm: The Case of Agricultural Landscapes in Anglo-Saxon England c. AD 400–800, *Journal of Archaeological Research* 24, 179–227.

Palmer, B. 2003. The hinterlands of three southern English emporia: some common themes, in T. Pestell and K. Ulmschneider (eds), *Markets in Early Medieval Europe: Trading and 'Productive' Sites*, Bollington, Windgather Press, 48–60.

Palmer, J. T. 2009. *Anglo-Saxons in the Frankish world, 690–900*, Brepols, Turnhout.

Parkhouse, J. 1976. The Dorestad quernstones, *Berichten van de Rijksdienst voor het Oudheidkundig Bodemonderzoek Jaargang* 26, 181–6.

Pestell, T. 2013. Imports or immigrants? Reassessing Scandinavian metalwork in Late Anglo-Saxon East Anglia, in D. Bates and R. E. Liddiard (eds), *East Anglia and the North Sea World in the Middle Ages*, Woodbridge, Boydell and Brewer, 230–55.

Pestell, T. 2017. The Kingdom of East Anglia, Frisia and Continental connections, c. AD 600–900, in J. Hines and N. Ijssennagger (eds), *Frisians and their North Sea Neighbours*, Boydell Press, 193–222.

Pestell, T., and K. Ulmschneider (eds). 2003. *Markets in Early Medieval Europe: Trading and 'Productive' Sites, 650–850*, Bollington, Windgather Press.

Peytremann, É. 2023. The contributions of the settlement to the understanding of the rural societies of Northern Gaul in the 10th century, in I. S. Salazar and C. Tente (eds), *The 10th Century in Western Europe: Change and Continuity*, Oxford, Archaeopress, 23–37.

Pirenne, H. 1914. The Stages in the Social History of Capitalism, *The American Historical Review* 19, 494–515.

Pirenne, H. 1936. *Economic and Social History of Medieval Europe* (trans. I. E. Clegg), London, Kegan Paul.

Pirenne, H. 2014 [1925]. *Medieval Cities: Their Origins and the Revival of Trade*, Princeton, Princeton University Press.

Pirenne, H. 1939. *Mohammed and Charlemagne*, London, G. Allen and Unwin.

Polanyi, K. 1957. The economy as instituted process, in K. Polanyi, C. Arensberg and H. Pearson (eds), *Trade and Market in Early Empires*, Glencoe, IL, Free Press, 243–69.

Polanyi, K. 1963. Ports of trade in early societies, *The Journal of Economic History* 23, 30–45.

Price, N. 2020. *Children of Ash and Elm: A history of the Vikings*, New York, Basic Books.

Radford, C. A. R. 1957. The Saxon house: a review and some parallels, *Medieval Archaeology* 1, 27–38.

Randsborg, K. 1990. Beyond the Roman Empire: Archaeological Discoveries in Gudme on Funen, Denmark, *Oxford Journal of Archaeology* 9, 355–66.

Rieth, E. Carrierre-Desbois, C. and Serna, V. 2001. *L'épave de Port Berteau II (Charente-Maritime): Un Caboteur Fluvio-Maritime du Haut Moyen Age et Son Contexte Nautique*, Paris, Maison des Sciences de L'Homme.

Révillion, S., L. Verslype, P. Barbet, G. Fosse, I. Poirier and J.-C. Routier. 2010. Quentovic: Réalités et Perspectives Archéologiques, in S. Lebecq, B. Béthouart and L. Verslype (eds), *Quentovic: Environnement, Archéologie, Histoire*, Lille, Université de Charles de Gaulle, 509–21.

Reynolds, S. 1994. *Fiefs and Vassals: The Medieval Evidence Reinterpreted*, Oxford, Oxford University Press, 1994.

Riddler, I. and Trzaska-Nartowski, N. 2025. Phasing Hamwic, in M. Maltby and D. James (eds), *Producers, Traders and Consumers in Urban Societies in Southern Britain and Europe*, Oxford, Archaeopress.

Riddler, R., N. Trzaska-Nartowski and S. Hatton 2023. *An Early Medieval Craft: Antler and Bone Working from Ipswich Excavations 1974–1994*, Bury St. Edmunds, East Anglian Archaeology Report No. 181.

Rippon, S., C. Smart and B. Pears. 2015. *The Fields of Britannia: Continuity and Change in the Late Roman and Early Medieval Landscape*, Oxford, Oxford University Press.

Rogerson, A. 2003. Six Middle Anglo-Saxon Sites in West Norfolk, in T. Pestell and K. Ulmschneider (eds), *Markets in Early Medieval Europe: Trading and 'Productive' Sites, 650–850*, Macclesfield, Windgather Press, 110–21.

Rollason, D. 2003. *Northumbria, 500–1100: Creation and Destruction of a Kingdom*, Cambridge, Cambridge University Press.

Samson, R. 1999. Illusory Emporia and Mad Economic Theories, in M. Anderton (ed.), *Anglo-Saxon Trading Centres: Beyond the Emporia*, Glasgow, Cruithne Press, 76–90.

Saul, M. 2018. Markets in West Africa: Karl Polanyi, or what sort of social formation, in H. P. Hahn and G. Schmitz (eds), *Market as place and space of economic exchange: Perspectives from archaeology and anthropology*, Oxford, Oxbow Books, 127–51.

Saunders, T. 1991. Markets and individuals: the idealism of Richard Hodges, *Scottish Archaeological Review* 8, 140–6.
Saunders, T. 2001. Early medieval emporia and the tributary function, in D. Hill and R. Cowie (eds), *Wics: The Early Medieval Trading Centres of Northern Europe*, Sheffield, Sheffield Academic Press, 7–13.
Scarfe, N. 1972. *The Suffolk Landscape*, London, Hodder and Stoughton.
Scull, C. 1997. Urban centres in pre-Viking England, in J. Hines (ed.), *The Anglo-Saxons from the Migration Period to the Eighth Century*, Woodbridge, Boydell and Brewer, 269–310.
Scull, C. 2009 *Early Medieval (Late 5th–Early 8th Centuries AD) Cemeteries at Boss Hall and Buttermarket, Ipswich, Suffolk*, London, Soc. Medieval Archaeol. Monograph.
Scull, C. and Naylor, J. 2016. Sceattas in Anglo-Saxon Graves, *Medieval Archaeology* 60, 205–41
Sherratt, A. 1981. Plough and pastoralism: aspects of the secondary products revolution, in G. L. Isaac and N. Hammond (eds), *Pattern of the past: studies in honour of David Clarke*, Cambridge, Cambridge University Press, 155–99.
Sindbæk, S. M. 2020. Communities on the Edge: Retracing the Northern Emporia, in A. Gautier and L. Malbos (eds), *Communautés maritimes et insulaires du premier Moyen Âge*, Turnhout, Brepols, 127–42.
Sindbæk, S. M. (ed.). 2022. *Northern Emporium. Vol. 1: The making of Viking-age Ribe, Ribe Studier 3,* Jutland Archaeological Society, Højbjerg.
Sindbæk, S. M. (ed.). 2023. *Northern Emporium. Vol. 2: The networks of Viking-age Ribe, Ribe Studier 3,* Jutland Archaeological Society, Højbjerg.
Skre, D. 2007. Towns and markets, kings and central places in south-western Scandinavia, in D. Skre (ed.), *Kaupang in Skiringssal. Kaupang Excavation Project,* Aarhus University Press, Aarhus, 445–69.
Skre, D. 2008. Post-substantivist towns and trade AD 600–1000, in D. Skre (ed.), *Means of Exchange: Dealing with silver in the Viking Age*, Aarhus, Aarhus University Press, 327–41.
Skre, D. 2015. Post-substantivist production and trade: specialized sites for trade and craft production in Scandinavia AD c.700–1000, in J. H. Barrett and S. J. Gibbon (eds), *Maritime societies of the Viking and Medieval world*, Leeds, Maney Publishing, 156–70.

Skre, D. 2017, Monetary Practice in Early Medieval Scandinavia (5th–10th centuries), *Medieval Archaeology* 61, 277–99.

Skre, D. (ed.). 2020. *Rulership in 1st to 14th century Scandinavia*, Berlin, Walter de Guyter.

Smart, V. 1985. The Moneyers of St Edmund, *Hikuin* 11, 83–90.

Smart, V. 1986. Scandinavians, Celts, and Germans in Anglo-Saxon England: The Evidence of Moneyers' Names, in M. A. S. Blackburn (ed.), *Anglo-Saxon Monetary History: Essays in Memory of R. H. M. Dolley*, Leicester, Leicester University Press, 172–84.

Soulat, J. 2010. La présence Saxonne et Anglo-Saxonne sur le littoral de la Manche, in S. Lebecq, B. Béthouart and L. Verslype (eds), *Quentovic: Environnement, Archéologie, Histoire*, Lille, Université de Charles de Gaulle, 147–63.

Squatriti, P. 2002. Digging ditches in early medieval Europe, *Past and Present* 176, 11–65.

Søvsø, M. 2020. *Ribe 700–1050: From emporium to civitas in southern Scandinavia*, Højbjerg, Jutland Archaeological Society.

Stenton, F. M. 1971. *Anglo-Saxon England*, 3rd edn, Oxford, Oxford University Press.

Stephenson, C. 1933. *Borough and Town: a study of urban origins in England*, Cambridge, MA, Harvard University Press.

Story, J. 2003. *Carolingian Connections: Anglo-Saxon England and Carolingian Francia, c.750–870*, Aldershot, Ashgate.

Tait, J. 1933. Review of C. Stephenson, *Borough and Town: a study of urban origins in England*, Cambridge, MA, Harvard University Press, 1933, *English History Review* 48, 642–8.

Tait, J. 1936. *The Medieval English Borough*, Manchester, Manchester University Press.

Talbot, C. H. 1954. *The Anglo-Saxon Missionaries in Germany, Being the Lives of SS. Willibrord, Boniface, Leoba and Lebuin together with the Hodoepericon of St Willibald and a selection from the correspondence of St Boniface*, New York, Sheed and Ward.

Thacker, A. 1983. Bede's Ideal of Reform, in P. Wormald (ed.), *Ideal and Reality in Frankish and Anglo-Saxon Society*, Oxford, Blackwell, 130–53.

Theuws, F. 2004. Exchange, religion, identity and central places in the early Middle Ages, *Archaeological Dialogues* 4, 121–38.

Theuws, F. 2008. Settlement excavations and the process of 'manorialization' in northern Austrasia, in S. Gasparri (ed.), *774: ipotesi su una Transizione*, Turnhout, Brepols, 199–220.

Theuws, F. 2019. Reversed directions: Re-thinking sceattas in the Netherlands and England, *Zeitschrift für Archäologie des Mittelalters* 46, 27–84.

Theuws, F., and M. Kars (eds) 2017. *The Saint-Servatius complex in Masstricht: The Vrijthof excavations (1969–1970). Roman infrastructure – Merovingian cemetery – Carolingian cemetery – early town development*, Bonn, Habelt.

Thomas, G. 2017a. Monasteries and places of power in pre-Viking England, in G. Thomas and A. Knox (eds), *Early Medieval Monasticism in the North Sea Zone* (Anglo-Saxon Studies in Archaeology and History, 20), Oxford, Oxbow Books, 97–116.

Thomas, G. 2017b. Downland, Marsh, and Weald: Monastic foundation and rural intensification in Anglo-Saxon Kent, in R. Flechner and M. Ni Mhaonaigh (eds), *The Introduction of Christianity into the Early Medieval Insular World, Vol. 1*, Turnhout, Brepols, 349–76.

Thomas, G. 2023. *In the shadow of saints: the long durée of Lyminge, Kent, as a sacred Christian Landscape*, London, Society of Antiquaries.

Thuillier, F. 2015. L'atelier de Carolingien de la Rue de Cassel à Racquinghem (Pas-de-Calais), in F. Thuillier, and É. Louis (eds), *Tourner Autour du Pot: Les ateliers de potiers médiévaux du Ve au XIIe siècle dans l'espace européen*, Caen: Publications du Craham, Presses Universitaires de Caen, 123–37.

Thuillier, F., and É. Louis (eds). 2015. *Tourner Autour du Pot: Les ateliers de potiers médiévaux du Ve au XIIe siècle dans l'espace européen*, Caen: Publications du Craham, Presses Universitaires de Caen.

Timby, J. 1988. The Middle Saxon pottery, in P. Andrews (ed.), *Southampton Finds Volume 1: the coins and pottery from Hamwic*, Stroud, Alan Sutton, 73–124.

Tys, D. 2010. The Scheldt estuary as a framework for early medieval settlement development, in A. Willemsen and H. Kik (eds), *Dorestad in an International Framework: New Research into Centres of Trade and Coinage in Carolingian Times*, Turnhout, Brepols, 169–76.

Tys, D. 2017. Macht, nederzetting en landschap in vroegmiddeleeuws Gent, in K. De Groote and A. Ervynck (eds), *Gentse Geschiedenissen ofte Nieuwe Historiën uit de oudheid der stad en illustere plaatsen omtrent Gent,* Gent, Stad Gent, 35–44.

Tys, D. 2018. Cult, assembly and trade: the dynamics of a 'central place,' between the 7th and 11th centuries, in M. Kars, R. van Oosten, M. A. Roxburgh and A. Verhoeven (eds), *Rural Riches and Royal Rags? Studies on medieval and modern archaeology, presented to Frans Theuws,* Zwolle, Society for Medieval Archaeology, 171–8.

Tys, D., P. Dekkers and B. Wouters. 2016. Circular, D-Shaped and Other Fortifications in 9th- and 10th-Century Flanders and Zeeland as Markers of the Territorialisation of Power(s), in N. Christie and H. Herold (eds), *Fortified Settlements in Medieval Europe,* Oxford, Oxbow Books, 173–89.

Van Carnap-Bornheim, C., V. Hilberg, S. Kalmring and J. Schulze. 2010. Hedeby, the settlement and harbour: old data and recent research, in J. Sheehan and D. O' Corráin (eds), *The Viking Age: Ireland and the West: Papers from the proceedings of the fifteenth Viking Congress, Cork 18–27 August 2005,* Dublin, Four Courts Press, 511–24.

van Der Veen, M. 2022. All Change on the Land? Wheat and the Roman to Early Medieval Transition in England, *Medieval Archaeology* 66, 304–42.

van, Es, W. A. 1990. Dorestad centred, in J. C. Besteman, J. M. Bos and H. A. Heidinga (eds), *Medieval Archaeology in the Netherlands,* Assen, Van Gorcum, 151–82.

van Es, W. A., and V. Verwers. 1980. *Excavations at Dorestad 1: The Harbour: Hoogstraat 1,* Amersfoort, Nederlandse Oudheden 9.

van Es, W., and W. Verwers. 2015. *Excavations at Dorestad 4: The Settlement on the River Bank Area,* Nederlandse Oudheden 18. Amersfoort, Rijksdienst voor Cultureel Erfgoed.

Van de Walle, A. L. J. 1961. Excavations in the ancient centre of Antwerp, *Medieval Archaeology* 5, 123–36.

Vannieuwenhuyze, B. and R. Rutte (eds) 2023. *The Rise of Cities Revisited: Reflections on Adriaan Verhulst's Vision of Urban Genesis and Developments in the Medieval Low Countries,* Turnhout, Brepols.

Verhaeghe, F. 2005. Urban Developments in the Age of Charlemagne, in J. Story (ed.), *Charlemagne: Empire and Society*, Manchester, Manchester University Press, 259–87.

Verhulst, A. 1989. The Origins of Towns in the Low Countries and the Pirenne Thesis, *Past and Present* 122, 1–35.

Verhulst, A. 1999. *The rise of cities in North-West Europe*, Cambridge, Cambridge University Press.

Verhulst, A. 2002. *The Carolingian Economy*, Cambridge, Cambridge University Press.

Vince, A. 1984. The Aldwych: Saxon London rediscovered, *Current Archaeology* 8, 310–12.

Vince A. G. 1991. *Aspects of Saxon and Norman London: II Finds and Environmental Evidence, London Middlesex Archaeology Society*, London, Museum of London.

Vince, A. G., and A. Jenner. 1991. The Saxon and early medieval pottery of London, in A. Vince (ed.), *Aspects of Saxon and Norman London: II Finds and Environmental Evidence, London Middlesex Archaeological Society*, London, Museum of London, 19–119.

Wade, K. forthcoming. *Gipeswic: The Anglo-Saxon Town of Ipswich*, Bury St Edmunds, East Anglian Archaeology.

Walton Rogers, P. 2018. From farm to town: the changing pattern of textile production in Anglo-Saxon England, *Dynamics and Organisation of Textile Production in past societies in Europe and the Mediterranean*, Fasciculi Archaeologiae Historicae, Fasciculus XXXI, 103–14.

Walton Rogers, P. 2020. Textile networks in Viking-Age towns of Britain and Ireland, in S. P. Ashby and S. M. Sindbæk (eds), *Crafts and Social Networks in Viking Towns*, Oxford, Oxbow Books, 83–122.

Weber, M. 1966 [1921]. *The City*, New York, Free Press, originally published as *Die Stadt, Archiv für Sozialwissenschaft und Sozialpolitik 47*, 621–772.

Weber, M. 1978. *Economy and Society: An outline of Interpretive Sociology*, Berkeley, CA.

West, S. E. 1963. Excavations at Cox Lane (1958) and at the town defences, Shire Hall Yard, Ipswich (1959), *Proceedings of the Suffolk Institute of Archaeology* XXIX, 233–303.

Wheeler, R. E. M. 1934. The topography of Saxon London, *Antiquity* 8, 290–303.

Wheeler, R. E. M. 1935. *London and the Saxons*, London, London Museum.

Whitelock, D. 1955. *English historical documents I, c. 500–1042*, London, Eyre & Spottiswoode.

Wickham, C. 1991. Systactic structures: social theory for historians, *Past and Present* 152, 188–203.

Wickham, C. 2005. *Framing the Middle Ages*, Oxford, Oxford University Press.

Wickham, C. 2023. *The Donkey and the Ship*, Oxford, Oxford University Press.

Williamson, T. 2013. *Environment, Society and Landscape in Early Medieval England*, Woodbridge, Boydell and Brewer.

Willemsen, A., and H. Kik (eds). 2010. *Dorestad in an International Framework: New research on centres of trade and coinage in Carolingian times*, Turnhout, Brepols.

Wood, I. 1983. *The Merovingian North Sea*, Alingsås, Viktoria Bokförlag.

Wood, I. 2001. *The Missionary Life: Saints and the Evangelization of Europe 400–1050*, Routledge, New York.

Woods, A. R. 2021. The production and use of coinage in East Anglia 500–800, *British Numismatic Journal* 91, 13–59.

Wood, I. 2022. *The Christian Economy in the West: Towards a Temple Society*, Binghamton, Punctum Books.

Wormald, P. 1983. Bede, the Bretwaldas and the origins of the *Gens Anglorum*, in P. Wormald (ed.), *Ideal and Reality in Frankish and Anglo-Saxon Society*, Oxford, Blackwell, 99–129.

Yorke, B. 2018. Competition for the Solent and 7th Century Politics, in B. Jervis (ed.), *The Middle Ages Revisited: Studies in the Archaeology and History of Medieval Southern England Presented to Professor David A. Hinton*, Oxford, Archaeopress, 35–44.

Ziegler, V. 2019. From Wic to burh: a new approach to the question of the development of Early Medieval London, *Archaeological Journal* 176, 336–68.

Index

Addyman, P. V. xvi, 12, 53
Aelfthryt, daughter of King Alfred 162
Æthelbald, King of Mercia 92
Aethelred II, King 122
Alcuin 70, 73, 110
Aldfrith, King 72
Aldwark 120, 122, 125, 154
Alfred Jewel 152
Alfred, King 29, 31, 69, 94, 98, 104, 117, 130, 131, 135, 136, 137, 138, 141, 143, 144, 146, 147, 148, 151, 152, 153, 155, 156, 157, 162, 164, 173, 174
amber 40, 129
Anglo-Saxon Chronicle 31, 120
Antwerp 7, 9, 141, 162
Aquitaine 38, 42, 82
army xv, 24, 29, 31, 35, 40, 115, 116, 117, 118, 119, 120, 122, 123, 124, 125, 126, 128, 136, 137, 143, 147 (*fyrd*), 148, 149, 151, 154, 156, 172
Arnulf I, Count of Flanders 164
Asser 117
Astill, Grenville 77, 78, 107, 155

Badorf ware 101, 140
Baldwin II, Count of Flanders 162, 164
Baltic Sea 5, 24, 39, 40, 109, 115, 124, 125, 129, 141, 162, 163, 172, 174, 175, 176
Beonna, King xvi, 80, 81, 82
Berhtwulf, King 96
Biddle, Martin 12, 13, 53
Birka 24, 108, 114
Blair, John 18, 61, 65, 70, 91, 92, 94, 104, 126, 134, 135, 137, 144, 145, 149

Boniface 47
Borough and Town: A Study of Urban Origins in England (by Carl Stephenson) 10
brooches 57
   ansate equal arm, disc and Borre-style 141
   Fuller, Pentney and Strickland 152
   trefoil 129
Brown, Peter 74, n.1
Bruges 9, 164, 165, 168
Buckden, Cambridgeshire 94, 123,
bullion 31, 33, 81, 82, 97, 104, 107, 122, 123, 127, 128, 130, 133, 137, 154, 155
Burghal Hidage 12, 31, 147, 148
Burgred, King of Mercia 123
burh xvi, 10, 15, 59, 93, 94, 131, 138, 142, 145, 146, 147, 148, 149, 150, 155, 164, 167
Burham Overy (Norfolk) 43
Bull Wharf, London 137–41, 174

Callmer, Johan 21, 22, 23, 27, 29, 74, 169
Canterbury 11, 44, 82, 85, 92, 95, 96, 136, 146, 153
cereal/cerealization 64, 87, 90, 91, 106
Charlemagne xiii, 3, 10, 24, 48, 70, 73, 82, 83, 110, 153
Charles Martel 93
Charles the Bald 147, 163
Christie, Neil 143, 147, 149
Coenwulf, King of Mercia 70, 82
combs 27, 28, 72, 108, 119, 129, 132, 133, 141
Consolations of Boethius 173
Cooijmans, Christian 173, 174
Coppergate, York 12, 126, 127, 129

Cricklade 149
cubo-octahedral weights 122

Danegeld 151
Danelaw 31, 124, 125, 128, 131, 134, 140, 141, 151, 152, 163, 167, 168, 173
Dark Age Economics 13, 14, 15, 18, 20, 21, 22, 43, 44, 94, 146
denier 82, 83, 128
Dhondt, Jan 6
dirhem 121, 122
Domburg 39, 44, 50, 52, 109, 163, 164
Dorestad 9, 14, 22, 39, 41, 44, 47, 50, 51, 52, 58, 61, 77, 83, 104, 109, 110, 114, 163, 164
Dorney, Buckinghamshire 17, 108, 109, 146, 170
Douai 119, 165
Dover 53
Dublin xv, 125, 127
Dumnonia 37, 38, 43
Dunwich 125

E-ware 38
Eadberht, King of Northumbria 78, 81
Eadberht II, King of Kent 82
Eadwald, King of East Anglia 82
Edgar, King 134
    monetary reform 150, 155
Edict of Pîtres 128, 147, 164
Edward the Elder, King 131, 144, 152
Ely, monastery of St. Æthelthryth 89
Eoforwic (York) 44, 53, 68, 70–3, 74, 96, 102, 103, 104, 107, 125, 154

Five Boroughs (Derby, Leicester, Lincoln, Nottingham and Stamford) 10, 125
Flanders, Counts of/County of 7, 8, 9, 32, 100, 142, 151, 160, 162, 163, 164, 165, 167, 168, 169
Flixborough, Lincolnshire 94
Foot, Sarah 153

Francia 60, 78, 80, 81, 83, 85, 107, 114, 118, 128, 134, 135, 136, 160, 165, 173
Frankish Annals 9
Frere, Sheppard 11
Frisia/Frisian/Frisians 9, 39, 41, 43, 45, 46, 47, 48, 51, 52, 70, 75, 80, 85, 115, 117, 119, 130, 141, 163, 168, 175, 176

Gewisse 60
Ghent xv, 2, 6, 9, 160, 161, 164, 165, 166, 167, 169, 174,
Gipeswic (Ipswich) xv, 44, 52, 53–8, 61, 72, 73, 74, 79, 82, 86, 95, 96, 99, 102, 103, 104, 105, 107, 109, 110, 113, 115, 116, 119, 120, 125, 130, 131, 132, 133, 135, 143, 154, 175, 176
Gloucester xvi, 13, 149
Godfred, King of Denmark 24
Gokstad ship 174
Granovetter, Mark 23
Great Danish Army 15, 29, 31, 122, 154, 156
Gudme 66
Guthrum, King 117, 118, 128, 130, 131, 136, 137

hack-gold 121
hack-silver 121, 123
Hamwic (also Hamwih) (Southampton) xiii, xvi, 12, 13, 14, 17, 44, 53, 58–70, 72, 73, 74, 79, 98, 99, 100, 101, 102, 103, 104, 107, 108, 110, 113, 120, 143, 145, 146, 154
Harald, King 163, 168
Heaberht, King of Kent 82
Hedeby (also Haithabu) 132, 141, 143, 156, 174, 175
Henning, Joachim 75, 170,
Higham Ferrers, Northamptonshire 94
Hill, D. H. xvi, 12, 18, 53
Hinton, David xvi, 60

Index

hoards 118, 123, 128, 137, 152
honestone 129
Hoskins, W. G. 18
Hurst, J. G. xv, xvi, 11
hydrarchs xv, 114, 117, 125, 132, 163, 173

Ina, King of Wessex 48, 60, 85
ingots (*see also* bullion *and* silver) 121
Ipswich ware xvi, 11, 56, 69, 96, 104, 106, 108, 119, 154

jewellery 41, 43, 58, 60, 114, 123, 135
Jorvik (*see also* York) 12, 132

Kaupang 19, 44, 66, 114, 120, 122, 127, 156
Kershaw, Jane 120
Kilger, Christian 122, 123
klosterpolitik 110, 113, 170
Kviv xv, 125

landscape xiv, xv, 18, 31, 40, 77, 83, 89, 91, 94, 98, 107, 108, 145, 146, 149, 154, 156, 164, 167, 169, 170, 176
laws 3, 134, 150
  of Kings Hlothhere and Eadric 44, 67, 70
  of King Ina 48, 85, 91
Lebecq, Stéphane 46
Lincoln 13, 121, 125, 127, 130
Lincolnshire (Middle Saxon) ware 72, 124, 130
Louis the German, King 163
Louis the Pious, Emperor 122
Loveluck, Christopher 21, 42
Lundeborg 66
Lundenburg (London) 67, 102, 125, 137–43, 175
Lundenwic (London) 18, 44, 47, 53, 60, 67–70, 73, 74, 96, 100, 101, 102, 104, 107, 108, 110, 113, 120, 136, 137, 142, 143, 145, 154
Lyminge 85–8, 89, 90, 110

Maastricht 92, 171
Madelinus 51
Mainman, Ailsa 72, 128
Medieval Cities (by Henri Pirenne) xiii, xv, 1, 2, 3, 8, 10, 32, 160, 169, 174
Melle 82
Merovingian North Sea 39, 48
Metcalf, D. M. 79, 80, 82, 92, 100, 151, n.1
Mercia, Kingdom of xvi, 31, 70, 82, 91, 92, 93, 94, 96, 97, 104, 105, 108, 116, 117, 123, 130, 133, 134, 136, 137, 138, 143, 149, 153, 156
Meuse valley 9, 39, 43, 55, 57, 62, 130, 132, 140, 151
Mohammed and Charlemagne (by Henri Pirenne) xiii, 3, 10
moneyer 31, 81, 82, 117, 118, 123, 128, 130, 134, 138, 150, 151, 154, 155
Moreland, John xv, 15, 17, 21, 95
mouldboard plough package 19, 88, 106

Naismith, Rory 70, 81, 82, 95, 97, 99
niello 152
Northern Emporium Project 25
Northumbria, Kingdom of 31, 70, 72, 80, 85, 91, 92, 95, 96, 97, 98, 99, 102, 104, 110, 116, 117, 121, 122, 123, 125, 127, 128, 132, 133, 136, 141, 154, 156
Norwich/*Northwic* 11, 13, 110, 125

Oegstgeest 22, 39, 40, 41, 42, 43, 44, 168
Offa, King 48, 82, 83, 93, 95, 107
Ohthere 28, 156, 174
Oost-Souburg 164
organic tempered wares 59, 99, 100
Osberht, King 122
Ottonian 8, 12, 146, 159, 171
Oxford 11, 149

Paffrath-type ware 140
Palermo 143
Petegem 164
Pippin II 51
Pippin III 81, 82, 83, 93
Pirenne, Henri xiii, xiv, xv, 1, 2, 3,
    4, 5, 6, 7, 8, 9, 10, 11, 18, 32,
    42, 169–1, 162, 169, 174,
    175, 176
Polanyi, Karl 14, 15, 16, 174
Portable Antiquities Scheme xvi, 15,
    50, 78, 81, 121
Port Berteau II wreck 47
portus 10, 150, 165
Price, Neil xiv, 172

Quentovic (also Vismarest) 9, 18, 39,
    52, 57, 60, 62, 104, 109, 115,
    118, 119, 128
quernstones 72
    Niedermendig 57

Radbod 51
Rendlesham 55, 58, 86, 103
reform, monetary
    Alfred 131
    Carolingian 82, 83, 168
    eighth-century 81
    tenth-century 12, 150, 155
Reric (at Groß Strömkendorf) 24
Rhine, river/Rhineland 22, 36, 39, 40,
    41, 42, 43, 55, 69, 72, 73, 80,
    114, 115, 119, 140, 142, 162,
    168
Ribe xv, 19, 20, 25, 26, 27, 28, 30, 44,
    61, 83, 110, 114, 115, 120, 127,
    156, 169, 175
Rollo, Duke 155
Rome 49, 146
Rorik, King 51, 117, 163, 168
Rouen 8, 52, 62, 118

sail/sailcloth 46–9, 74, 88
Sandtun 43
Saunders, Tom 94, 99

sceatta xvi, 26, 41, 46, 48, 49, 50, 52,
    55, 58, 62, 72, 80, 81, 97, 98,
    99, 100, 104, 108, 121, 155
Scheldt, river 36, 50, 55, 69, 72, 115,
    117, 163, 165, 168
Scull, Christopher 49, 55
seax 60
Secondary Products Revolution 84,
    176
Seine valley 39, 57, 62, 73, 117, 140
ship 46, 47, 49, 74, 119, 121, 138, 141,
    142, 143, 174
silver 25, 31, 41, 48, 49, 56, 58, 62, 72,
    78, 79, 80, 81, 82, 94, 97, 104,
    107, 110, 121, 122, 123, 127,
    128, 129, 137, 140, 151, 152,
    153, 154, 172
Sindbæk Søren xv, 9, 20, 23, 25, 26,
    29, 161
Skre, Dagfinn 19, 29, 66
Stamford 125, 130, 151
St Albans 35
Stenton, Frank 153
Stephenson, Carl xiii, 8, 10, 18
strap end 97, 141, 152
styca 99, 121, 122, 123, 126, 127, 128,
    141, 154
Sudbury 125
Sutton Hoo ship burial 46, 49, 55

Tait, James 10, 11, 13,
Tating ware 63, 100, 101, 108, 114,
    115
The Medieval English Borough (by
    James Tait) 11
Thetford 13, 116, 125, 131
Thetford ware 56, 119, 132, 137, 140
Theuws, Frans xv, 22, 42, 48, 49, 75,
    77, 92, 109, 171
Third Science Revolution 15, 19, 25,
    169
Tintagel 36, 37, 38, 44
Torksey/Torksey ware xvi, 19, 116,
    120, 121, 122, 124, 125, 133,
    151, 156, 172

town planning 126, 132, 145
Trewhiddle (Cornwall) hoard/style 97, 141, 152
Tys, Dries xv, 21, 22, 42, 43, 164, 165, 167, 168

Utrecht 51
Utrecht ship 141

Van de Walle, Adelbert 7, 162
Verhaeghe, Frans 7
Verhulst, Adriaan 6, 7, 161, 165, 168, 174
Vetricella (Tuscany) 159
Violante, Cinzio 6

Wade, Keith xv, xvi, 53, 55, 58, 73, 119
Walcharen, island 50, 163
Wallingford 149
Waterstraat boat 141
Weber, Max 22, 32, 161
Wessex, Kingdom of 31, 60, 62, 63, 79, 91, 92, 93, 94, 95, 97, 98, 104, 105, 108, 116, 117, 135, 137, 143, 146, 148, 151, 152, 155, 161, 162, 167, 168, 173, 175, 176

West, S. E. 11
Wheeler, Mortimer 11
Wickham, Chris 6, 7, 78, 105, 162
Wilfrid, Bishop 110
Willibrord 51
Winchester 12, 13, 31, 44, 97, 104, 136, 143, 144, 146, 149, 150, 152, 153, 156
Winchester Minster 12, 143, 144, 152
Winchester Research Unit 12
Winchester style 152
Winchester ware 151
wine trade 37, 49, 57, 74, 114, 140
 in barrels 41, 51, 58
Wood, Ian 39, 74, n.1
wool 43, 47, 48, 65, 84, 88, 94
Wroxeter 35, 36, 38

York (*see also* Jorvik) 12, 13, 43, 44, 53, 68, 70, 71, 92, 102, 103, 107, 116, 120, 121, 125, 126–30, 132, 137, 143, 144, 146, 151, 154, 172, 173
York ware 128

Ziegler, Victoria 70, 137, 142